Looking for Orthon

Also by COLIN BENNETT

The Infantryman's Fear of Open Country
The Entertainment Bomb

Looking for Orthon

*The story of George Adamski,
the first flying saucer contactee,
and how he changed the world*

COLIN BENNETT

Foreword by John Michell

PARAVIEW PRESS

NEW YORK

LOOKING FOR ORTHON:

The story of George Adamski, the first flying saucer contactee
and how he changed the world

All photos courtesy of the Fortean Picture Library
Book design by smythtype
ISBN: 1-931044-32-5
Library of Congress Catalog Card Number: 2001096220

To my beloved wife, Philomena

Contents

Foreword

In a thousand year's time, if there are still people studying history, someone is sure to ask, what is the most important thing that happened in the twentieth century? What will be the answer to that, I wonder? Almost certainly it will be quite different from anything we would think of today. In that case, an unlikely guess is more likely to come true than a likely one. So Colin Bennett is on the right track in suggesting something that few would suggest—that the defining moment of the twentieth century will prove to be 12:30 pm on Thursday, November 20, 1952, when George Adamski met Orthon, a long-haired youth from Venus. It happened in the Californian desert in the presence of witnesses. From that moment the cat was out of the bag, the space people were among us and nothing has ever been the same since.

That is a provocative thesis. But evidence has been building up over the near-fifty years, from 1953 and the publication of Adamski's worldwide best seller, *Flying Saucers Have Landed,* which he co-wrote with Desmond Leslie. Since then images of the UFO and the space alien have continued to haunt us. The effects of this on popular culture are to be seen everywhere and, as Bennett points out, UFOs and space imagery has long outlasted the various fads and fashions that have since arisen. In the modern imagination the UFO is a constant, not just a spacecraft but a reminder that the world is not as rational as our educators pretend.

The prophetic Carl Jung was quick to see what was happening. In 1959 he published a startling book on flying saucers, accepting their reality and interpreting them as signs and portents of the ancient gods, duly returning to change our way of thinking and initiate a new age. It was Jung's perspicacity, among other things, that led me in 1967 to write *The Flying Saucer Vision.* I just could not resist drawing attention to a phenomenon which, even though it was changing people's minds and lives—introducing new interests and perspectives—was scornfully ignored by the Authorities. It was not just state officials who hated and mocked at any mention of UFOs. Colin Bennett is quite right in what he says here, that in the world of art and literature, during and after Adamski's time, talk of UFOs and related subjects was in no way cool, hip, PC or the proper thing. Right-wing types disliked it for upsetting established patterns of thought, while the intellectuals saw it as a plot to divert attention from their revolution. This has always been considered a radical subject, and for good reason, and that is why writers of Colin Bennett's quality are attracted to it.

I really enjoyed this book, the author's wit and wisdom and the spirit in which he deals with the great events of our time. His story is about the current revolution in cosmology—the way we understand the world—and the switch from the old categorical judgmental approach to a more accepting and inclusive view of reality. He begins with George Adamski, and why not? He was an impressive old rogue, like Madame Blavatsky and in the same tradition. Such people, according to Plato are the kind whom the gods choose to enlighten us. I am sure that is right, and that changes in our minds are brought about by the gods, in their due seasons and often through highly dubious characters.

John Michell

Introduction

In 1952 a Polish immigrant who worked in a restaurant on Mt. Palomar, California, claimed that he had made contact with an extraterrestrial being in the Nevada desert. It wasn't the first time in history that a human being had made such a claim, nor would it be the last. But this particular meeting has reverberated to this day, influencing the very core of our contemporary culture.

The immigrant's name was George Adamski. Over the years that followed he would document his claim with photographs of flying saucers, dozen and dozen of photographs, in fact, and three books on his quite fantastic adventures. The first of these, *Flying Saucers Have Landed,* published[1] in September 1953 in conjunction with the British writer Desmond Leslie, quickly became a bestseller and brought Adamski worldwide fame.

Flying Saucers Have Landed is a masterpiece. It is a story of about our perception of history, the nature of technological power, and just who or what exactly governs the forces of modern belief. Its textual planes are like the distortions of a mediaeval map. Just one of its achievements is that it makes the ordered Cartesian perspectives of conventional literature look as if they have a similar distortion. In doing so, it suggests that perhaps the UFO itself lives between the folds of such cultural warps as did the sea serpents of old maps, appearing on most unsuitable and inconvenient occasions to baffle, hypnotize, and infuriate.

To understand the Adamski phenomenon, we must ask whether a text is a mere something enclosed between pages, written by clever people with refined skills, or whether it should be considered as a life form in itself. One thing is certain: if we ever lose such bad and mad books as those of George Adamski, we will lose a delicately-balanced psychic pond-life as holy and valuable to us as the rain-forest or the midwife toad.

Many people who met George Adamski commented on his considerable charm and his good appearance and address. These things certainly helped him on his world tour of 1959, during which he met Royalty and leading figures in military and intelligence, and acquired a mass of followers in many countries. He managed to enter power structures with ease, just as did the travelling astrologers and alchemists of old. The occultists Paracelsus, Agrippa, and Albertus Magnus, all tell that when one world

Jacket of book published in 1953.

enters another and goes out again, after no matter how brief a stay, it is never possible to get the furniture back in place. That is because thinking never really ceases to be a form of dreaming. For good or ill, when we imagine, we create a form of life, that is a seeding of pictures and possibilities, a watering of secret hopes, private fears, and hidden ambitions.

Despite his often comically hypocritical denials, Adamski was a classic magus. In this, he was right in the center of a war not of facts versus fiction, but of possibilities and allowances. In the million acres of nonsense published about occultism, few realize that nothing is created by the sorcerer so much as allowed. It is a dim soul indeed who does not want to see the world turned upside down. There can be such a hidden subversive pressure built up in psychic realms that there is seepage of part-worlds through a membrane to a social realization. Using these ideo-associative forces, an almost penniless Adamski pulled together high-level folk in a manner almost impossible to achieve by any other means. The occultist, like the pornographer, merely sets fire to imaginations. He knows what people really want. In this, the occultist is a ruthless salesman.

Adamski's experience was the first modern powerful suggestion, with early technological trimmings, of a prototype "pan-dimensional" reality, and we had better get used to that situation, because a hybrid state of affairs is the microcosm of our Entertainment State.[2] The thousand-channel consumer society hardly deals with the mechanical objective realities of the previous hard-wired society. The death of a soap character is just as important a "causation" as economic need or social stress. In this intermediate state, live aliens, the prototypes of which are the "Space Brothers" whom Adamski met in the Nevada desert.

It should come as no surprise that he angered the scientific establishment of his time. He was accused of being a compete impostor, yet time and again that cap would not stay on his head, being always thrown off by some impossibly bizarre sighting, curious incident, or magnificent coincidence that would somehow, inexplicably, give his extraordinary theories and claims some shred of credence.

Yet, despite the success of his books and his rise to fame, by the early 1960s Adamski had become a deeply disappointed man. Through scandals and accusations of every kidney, his worldwide support had dwindled, and many of his closest friends had deserted him. He died aged 74 on the 23rd of April 1965.

Did Adamski really encounter an extraterrestrial? Or were his first and his subsequent contacts and his many films and photographs all hoaxes? Was Adamski an impostor, or indeed a madman, who was out to fool the world? Or did he trip into some parallel reality that we are only dimly aware of? This book contends that whatever the truth of the matter—and the truth is not as easy to untangle as the skeptics would like—the influence of George Adamski's claim was enormous, and the term flying saucer will be forever associated with his name.

Just one of the strange things about these strange aerial forms is that is that a half-century after his death, they are still with us in the form of the UFO, or Unidentified Flying Object. The crescent-shaped disks that American pilot Kenneth Arnold first saw flying by Mount Rainier in 1947, make flying saucers older even than Rock n' Roll. Strangely, the flying saucer has not aged with this world.

Though Adamski received ridicule in plenty for claiming to have contacted beings from other worlds, nevertheless, his dome-shaped flying saucers, along with the bikini bathing suit, remain with us from the time of the Truman Doctrine, the Marshall Plan, and the Korean War. It could be said that Shakespeare didn't do too badly considering he could not write about politics, sex, or religion. The UFO does very well therefore, considering it has nothing to do with Race and Class, Drugs, Economics, War, or Terrorism. It has, of course, always been strong on entertainment value, stronger even than science, and far less destructive. In the time since the birth of the UFO, everything has changed, from jokes to the color of socks, but not the battle-royal between believers in UFOs and scientists and skeptics.

This battle appears at times to be a fight between different sets of wall-papering circus-clowns, and fifty years later this rather simple extended joke does not show any sign at all of running out of steam. Few jokes last that long, and thus both saucers and bikini both are magically suggestive icons, pure unadulterated image-stuff which has triumphed in time. Both are beyond all sense, fact, and rationale, those tyrannical elements of an old and fading Industrial Time. The "facts" of the late 1940s and early 1950s are gone; the scientific theories have been largely superseded, the clothes, conversations and cars of over fifty years ago have vanished, but the "flying saucer" and the swimsuit shaped like a Pacific nuclear practice range is still very much with us.

Perhaps both the bikini and that which we now call the UFO stayed with us because we like reminding ourselves that the world is never quite completely real. To many who feel that they live under the claustrophobic oppression of a "factual" culture that is practically destroying all land, sea, and air, that is a comforting thought. We bind such things to our hearts like pressed leaves whose personal code tells us that both Matter and Experience are conspiracies. As such their plots can be subverted, and the good news is that there are rumors of guerrillas in the hills, tales of lights in the forest at midnight, and if we believe George Adamski for even a second, we may even see a White Rabbit or two, if we keep our eyes open.

Though Adamski has become a much-derided figure since his death, perhaps he will have the last laugh, if only because his doughnut and hamburger-shapes are still up there on a thousand and one nights of the world. It is as if the Mount Palomar restaurant of his life-long friend Alice K. Wells had exploded into the air and was still coming down with countless scores of the hot-plate favorites Adamski himself must have sold to many ankle-socked and short-panted school parties from all over America.

Some of these young visitors might now struggle to recall the face of the man whose dome-shaped flying saucers are like a rain of frogs. They still have housewives running into police stations, truck drivers consulting psychiatrists; they still produce anger from scientists, denials from governments, and very strange behavior from the Intelligence Services and the "disinterested" Armed Forces of the major nations. On occasion even, a blond male sylph of the kind to which Adamski appears to have been partial, still steps out of a landed UFO that has been detected by radar, leaves ground-impressions, and has been seen by multiple witnesses.

Adamski is therefore a battlement ghost from the immediate post-war world, appearing at the stroke of midnight to remind us of the disturbingly yet exciting possibility that what we call "reality" may be far more scandalous an affair than previously thought. This is both the awe and fear at the heart of the UFO experience. Frequently baffled and even insulted is that very intellect which gropes for its fundamental nature. As with the Oswald Syndrome, the UFO reveals events and implicit connections, movements of people, materials, and ideas, which hint at a world-order so outrageous it is almost beyond all belief. The UFO culture that thrived after Adamski still reminds us of the night-side of both Man and Nature: we experience a phenomenon that is infuriating, subversive, and quite impossible in its behavior.

But ultimately what it most important about George Adamski is that he structured one of the most blatant acts of visionary cheek of the twentieth century. Far cleverer men have done far less. Though towards the end of his life he became a confused man, and was driven to making up lots of stories, he sounded many alarm bells within deep cultural bedrock. In telling such tales, like many world-shakers, Adamski broke all the rules, and the world couldn't quite get all the pieces back again.

In this sense history has extremely difficulty in getting rid of Adamski and his deliciously silly stories. We haven't done with him yet. We need him if only because his views are quite wonderfully absurd. He is therefore nearer the truth of Salvador Dali, Andre Breton, and Alfred Jarry than the truth of the strange form of Theosophical Christianity that he followed. While the UFO is with us, we are stuck with him as one of the Founding Fathers of Ufology. Like the proverbial tin-can tied to a cat's tail, he rattles through our dreams, shaming, embarrassing yet thrilling us still with a perverse intellectual eroticism which is absolutely irresistible. Such folk as he are healthy reminders that the truth may not be nearly as sober as we would like it to be. He suggests to us also that the old box of tricks we call "reality" may prove finally to be that fraudulent old rascal we always secretly knew it was.

The question might well be asked as to why, in an age dominated by democracy and scientific rationalism, hasn't all this nonsense about flying saucers been put into the museum, along with the Left, the Twist, the Class-War, the Revolution, Punk, and Flower Power? From one point, at least, its attraction holds no secret: most of us love to see Authority baffled, chasing its tail, its tools of control and oppression no longer of any use. The flying saucer, like the modern UFO, never held persons or places in great respect, appearing to a group of starving peasants in Mexico just as readily as to an airline pilot over the Atlantic. It is also still capable of generating new interest sectors, new shapes, and new roles of its developing self, such as different kinds of abduction scenarios. As soon as media or the various military or technological establishments either ignore it, or put it down, it streaks across the sky, frightening motorists and cows in fields. It appears on radar, leaves ground traces, and as soon as comes the scientific denial, it is seen by policemen on bicycles, pilots in the Gulf, and housewives pegging clothes on a line. One thing is sure: the UFO greedily dines off all explanations, whether earth-lights, searchlights, little green men, creatures from other dimensions, super-bees, or intelligent cabbages.

When we view the shattered life that Adamski weaves between his books, we glimpse multiple dimensions of establishment and military intrigue, and Intelligence allied with conspiracy. Like many visionaries, his life was finally a broken affair, fragmentary and incomplete, and almost as unbelievable as a Cottingley fairy photograph. But if humanity ever loses such heroism born of Adamski's deep refusal to believe in the world as received, it will be lost forever. If he had ever looked down from his tightrope, he would certainly have fallen, another victim of the breathless cheek of the sheer intellectual eroticism of all prophecy and vision. If most people are terrified by the unusual, those whose lives are committed to thought (as Adamski's life certainly was), are equally disturbed by the everyday mundane scale of affairs. They see any social conformity as a vast imposture, just as evil as more obvious moral demons.

Adamski had something in him of the dark genius of the covered wagon and riverboat rascals of Mark Twain and Herman Melville. Like Howard Hughes and L. Ron Hubbard, he brought down fire, if not from heaven, certainly from an elemental somewhere. But unlike Hughes and Hubbard, he didn't make any money, and so America ignored him. But America will have to face Adamski sooner or later, and bring him, if reluctantly, into the pantheon of scarred American heroes.

Like many with a streak of genius, he didn't really know the difference between work and play, dream and religious impulse, inspiration and rational thought. But his faulty intellectual grasp saved him: it allowed him to play with all these things, and in playing he chanced upon something that talked to him. But like Francois Seurel in Alain-Fournier's novel *Le Grand Meaulnes,* Adamski was to lose the enchanted house in the forest that once he saw. Like Ahab, the quest finally consumed him, and like Hemingway's Old Man, he was left with only fragments of wonder as a magical defiance of time and decay.

When we say that what Adamski saw was created by his "imagination," we show how far our world has fallen, not progressed. We seem to have forgotten that there is nothing at all which is not conceived by the imagination, and that includes "fact" in itself. In forgetting this, we have lost the long trail between the ravings of visionaries in back rooms, the launch of a space station, and the death of a President. If Adamski's life can do anything at all, it can teach us how to rediscover that trail.

CHAPTER 1

When We Imagine, We Create a Form of Life

George Adamski was born in Poland on the 17th of April 1891 of parents Joseph and Frances Adamski. When he was two years old, his family immigrated to Dunkirk, New York, where he grew up in poor circumstances. An FBI memorandum to J. Edgar Hoover of the 28th of January 1953, mentions three sisters,[3] but no brother. This is odd because on occasion Adamski talked of a younger brother who he said was a priest, and who came to Palomar Gardens to see him occasionally.

Adamski had little education, and he took what was one of the few options open to him, and joined the army. Most sources mention that from 1913 to 1916, he served with K troop of the 13th US Cavalry in the Mexican war. This was probably the last war in which romance and heroism played against a landscape and climate full of the excitements of revolution and high adventure. His early youth was charged therefore with overwhelming excitements and they may have permanently supercharged his later life and created a need to relive some of its vital inspirations. He was certainly blooded by a fantasia of historic names. He pursued Zapata and Pancho

UFO contactee George Adamski

Villa no less, serving under General Pershing, whose aid-de-camp was a young second lieutenant by the name of George Patton. His Arlington gravestone mentions his National Guard unit, the 23rd US Guards, and his "active service" status is confirmed by the mention of World War I, although he did not serve in Europe.

As Hemingway might have said, a man who fired the old Springfield rife at the dusty hordes of Villa and Zapata is a man to have a drink with. Certainly, as one of the last horse soldiers of America, Adamski would have looked good and menacing on a cavalry steed patrolling the Mexican border in the years just before the Great War. His features, staring out from black and white photographs of the era, are more Greco-Florentine than Polish, and in a good light, he could be Tommy Lee Jones doing Aristotle Onassis in a new episode of *The Godfather*. Adamski's face is a piece of interesting simulation in itself; he looks like a desert man—his sinewy leonine body and his Indian-chief's features match the desert rock and scrub in which he would make his first contact with a "spaceman." In grainy photographs, he looks risen from the desert itself. As a young man, in the many Italian restaurants of the young Al Capone's bootlegging America, George Adamski might well have been quickly and quietly ushered to the best table, be given no bill, and asked no questions.

On Christmas Day 1917 Adamski married Mary Shimbersky, a devout Catholic. After his marriage, in that same year, he was honorably discharged from the army. In 1918 he worked as a government-employed painter and decorator in Yellowstone National Park, and also in a flour mill and in the cement business. Part-time, he served also with the National Guard until 1919.

During the time of the Prohibition (1920-1933), Adamski claimed that he bootlegged alcohol, which if true, is a claim that puts him in some very good company indeed. "During the Prohibition I had the [Royal] Order of Tibet," he would tell contactee Ray Stanford a quarter of a century later. "It was a front. Listen, I was able to make wine. You know, we're supposed to have the religious ceremonies; we make the wine for them, and the authorities can't interfere with our religion. Hell, I made enough wine for half of Southern California. In fact, boys, I was the biggest bootlegger around.... If it hadn't been for that man Roosevelt, I wouldn't have [had] to get into all this saucer crap."[4]

This was almost certainly an example of Adamski's rough humor, which according to Lou Zinsstag, the co-author with Timothy Good of *George Adamski: The Untold Story,*[5] he had in plenty. There are dangers in being too puritanical about human beings. A priest in a private and relaxed moment is surely free to say that he could have made a lot more money if he had put some of his congregation on the streets instead of in the pews.

"When asked about his profession or means of livelihood," wrote Zinsstag of Adamski, "he replied that for some years before he settled in Mount Palomar he gave popular lectures on astronomy and philosophy, in New Mexico, Arizona and California. He called himself a kind of wandering teacher, visiting settlements during the winter months, when farmers had little to do and were pleased to see him. 'There was no TV then,' he said, "and people were grateful for lectures or entertainment of any kind."

In the late 1920s Adamski settled at Laguna Beach, California. Here he taught a form of oriental mystical philosophy combined with very strong Christian fundamentalist overtones. This view was based partly on the Theosophical teachings of both Madame Blavatsky and Annie Besant, who was President of the Theosophical Society from 1907. This view was influenced also by Rudolph Steiner, who taught a Christianized view of Theosophy.

Adamski called his particular version of his kind of belief "Universal Law." The spaceship chief he would meet during one of his trips into space claimed to have been carefully watching him during his formative years, and was therefore fully aware of the kind of spiritual teaching he developed during the inter-war period. The chief addressed him as a "prodigal son," referring to what Adamski himself called "Universal Law," this being a kind of cosmic moral paradigm which binds together the entire animal, mineral, and vegetable universe: "As Earth men consider this law, they will see and understand how all is working from the low to the high, which is the universal purpose; and not from the high to the low. Yet the power expresses from the high even unto the low that the low may have the strength to rise unto the high. There is eternal blending, but never division."[6]

A further example of the Sunday school content of these lectures illustrates what Adamski thought was a "scientific" approach to "philosophy." The big chief speaks: "In the full conception, all manifestations of all forms are like beautiful flowers in a vast garden where many colors and many kinds bloom harmoniously together. Each blossom feels itself through the manifestation of another. The low looks up to the tall. The tall looks down to the low. The various colors are a delight to all. The manner of growth fills their interest and intensifies a desire for fulfillment."[7]

If we feel comfortably superior to this kind of simple-minded philosophizing, it must be borne in mind that there is considerable evidence that Adamski practiced successfully as a healer. There are three examples of this given in Gray Barker's *Book of Adamski,* showing that he certainly gave great comfort and spiritual uplift to many stricken with often fatal illnesses. Lou Zinstagg also gives an example of Adamski correctly analyzing a young boy's eye defect in the presence of a doctor, who was impressed.

In Adamski's own words, his life was dedicated almost entirely to "metaphysics, psychism, and religion." In this he was certainly a prototype of many hippie-style teachers who were to come after him in the 1960s. The "Natural Law" principles that he formulated were rather like our own "New Age" conceptions though mawkishly expressed, more often than not. At worst Adamski was a time-waster, at best he showed good environmental sense, reflecting the views of Rachel Carson's *Silent Spring.* He mirrors also the early "green" view of such writers as Jack Kerouac, the American novelist, and the occultist and chemist Jack Parsons, one the founding fathers of the Jet Propulsion Laboratory who wrote *Freedom Is a Two-Edged Sword.*[8]

Though he was not a particularly clever or well-educated man, Adamski blended a strong intuition with limitless enthusiasm and a powerful commitment to a hybrid belief system. He had also some rare characteristics for a deeply religious person: a passion for evolving technology, accompanied by a good grasp of scientific politics at a time when the two were not seen to be connected. In his time, Christianity was still essentially a pre-industrial belief system. The language and metaphors of mainstream Christianity in the 1940s and 1950s were still those of the Book of Common Prayer, and even young preachers were hardly one remove from an Eighteenth century pastoral society. Though somewhat naïve, and desperately unconventional, Adamski was nevertheless one of the very first writers to think about modern space science and ancient theology in Christian terms.

If some of his "spiritual" writing in connection with technology appears daft beyond belief, then at least he was one of the first people to think about such connections at all. He knew his Bible back to front, and was certainly the first to offer the kind of religio-scientific speculation that was to launch hundreds of books after his time. He discusses the UFO visions of Ezekiel some ten years before Joseph Blumrich's *The Spaceships of Ezekiel* and Von Daniken's *Chariots of the Gods* appeared. A passage from his third book, *Behind the Flying Saucer Mystery,* shows the techno-theological view Blumrich and Von Daniken inherited: "Evidently the early church came to believe the cherub was an angel because it was described as flying on wings. They had no knowledge of the nature of the space travelers and assumed that the ships were fire-breathing animals of some sort. They couldn't conceive of mechanical constructions made to navigate the heavens. I imagine the automobile would have been described as another type of angel or cherub, or perhaps as a demon or devil."[9]

It is as well to remember here that the idea of "objective reality" is a late and rather callow arrival on the historical scene. Certainly Shakespeare would not have understood it; for him Mind and Nature were a seamless robe. The important thing to realize here is that Adamski, despite his love of what he called "science," lived quite happily for the most part in the visionary anthropomorphic world of the Old Testament, in which the idea of "fact" had not arrived. Thus the accusations of "impostor" which would later be thrust upon him are neither right nor wrong: in his terms, they were meaningless. If in William Blake's eyes, John Milton's sin was to make the Bible more glamorous and dramatic, then in modern eyes, George Adamski's sin was to try and update it. And in doing this he certainly convinced many of his followers that the forces that bound together the Ancient world for millennia still existed, but in a fragmented and broken form that indeed mirrored the pattern of his own life.

Perhaps Adamski felt a little like Moses when he came down from the mountain: the rawness of the "actuality" was perhaps too potent. This pure concentrate had to be staged, lit, and produced in easily digestible episodes. Thus did media begin. In choosing to tell stories, Jesus as a teacher did exactly the same thing. Thus we do not have that old steam-age "factual contradiction," beloved of simple-minded skeptics, but a belief system whose developing processes are spread over a wide and extremely fuzzy spectrum. Adamski got there, and then the event slipped through his fingers. What is a man to say of such an experience?

A comment by Gray Barker, in his *Book of Adamski,* sheds light on Adamski's transparent homespun Christian honesty on the one hand and the source of some of his fabrications on the other: "Something real, though weird and fantastic, happens to an individual and he tells the world about it. People come from miles around to hear the story, and then want to hear more. The saucer 'contactee' may similarly concoct further accounts, not wishing to disappoint his public."[10]

The consequence of accepting such a situation means that we must recognize a new kind of event in the universe. We might call this kind of event a *fast transient.* Acceptance of such an event means that we may replace the old yes/no paradigm with "perhaps" and the working/not working paradigm with "working/not working very well."

There was never a man and woman born who did not at some time tell a tale about themselves, elaborate on a personal experience, if only to put themselves in the best possible light. If we do not have some love for ourselves as well as other people, we often become sick in body and mind. All thought begins in the great Imagination, and in the context of evolving life and experience, every single one of us can be caught out by a past statement, opinion, letter, or even publication. As weary researchers in Artificial Intelligence sadly admit, the mind does anything but reason by "facts." It "reasons" by hypocrisy, downright confusion, mistakes, selective amnesia, and often monstrous self-deception. The ultimate nightmare of the democrat and rationalist is that when all this anomalous noise is filtered out, the mind becomes little more than a car park papered over with ancient copies of *TV Guide.* When that happens, the living are indistinguishable from the vast hosts of the dead.

There is a photograph of Adamski taken in the inter-war years showing him preaching from a lectern and surrounded by plaster images and paintings of Christ that by most standards would be called *kitsch.* Though he looks certainly like a young carpetbagger about to abscond with the collection box, by any and every account of friends, associates, and co-workers, his craggy and formidable looks belied his nature. From his thousands of followers over the years, there has not been a single complaint of the vicious physical and financial exploitation we have now come to expect of many of fringe-religion preachers throughout the world. Yes, his co-author Desmond Leslie remarks on his more than occasional stubbornness, Lucy McGinnis his secretary for many years, talks of his ego, and Zinstagg is often suspicious of many things he said and did, but it doesn't amount to much as criminal fraud and deception are concerned.

Adamski's first book, *Wisdom of the Masters of the Far East,* was published by the Laguna-based Royal Order of Tibet in 1936. This was the first in a series of booklets and pamphlets he was to write, and despite their often naive thought and expression, they gave him quite a following. *Telepathy: The Cosmic or Universal Language* and *Science of Life Study Course* were both developed continuously after 1936 and sold as a mail order course of 12 lessons, one per month. Much of this material was broadcast by local radio stations KFOX Long Beach, KMPC Los Angeles, and various Beverly Hills stations.

In 1940, being beyond the age for military service, Adamski moved with his wife and a group of his students in "Universal Law" to Valley Center Ranch, which was along the route to the foot of Mount Palomar, whose peak is the site of the world-renowned 200-inch optical telescope. There the group, united by a common religious interest, formed a small self-help farming community, hoping to grow enough produce to support themselves and sell to others.

Adamski continued to lecture, often drawing large crowds. But in 1944, the Ranch was sold and he and his friends, followers, and "Universal Law" pupils "moved a few hundred feet up our mountain" to live a candles-and-kerosene existence. Life was very hard in these mountain communities of the American West; given the war situation, every possible resource was either in short supply or restricted. But Adamski, if not all that practical (Desmond Leslie remarks on his "technical inability"), was anything but a shirker, doing manual work and any odd jobs that came along.

Perhaps the only equivalent Britain had to this kind of community in those days was the Findhorn community in Scotland founded by Peter

Caddy and his wife Eileen in the 1950s. "There have been stories in the press about a small community where the elemental world of plants and animals co-operate with fairies, elves, and gnomes in creating a land where nothing is impossible and legends are reborn," commented Paul Hawken in his book *The Magic of Findhorn.*[11]

In the Adamski context the "Don Juan and Tolkien combined" atmosphere sounds familiar. But for the Palomar community there were to be no 40-pound cabbages, 8-foot delphiniums and roses blooming in the snow, as at Findhorn. The wonders were late in arriving, but arrive they did. "Often we see the Saucers flashing overhead," wrote Adamski in 1955, describing what could be seen from his mountain home. "In fact in recent weeks the space ships have been seen by many in neighboring towns and cities. We are content to know that they are above us, and in the skies of our earth. We hope that in the not too far distant future all peoples in our world may see and know them for what they are; and we hope that many of those whose words we would convince, who do know now and would keep silence, will speak out in the interest of all mankind."[12]

The mountain commune cleared rough virgin land, and constructed some basic accommodation for the many people who came up the mountain to see Adamski and hear his lectures. After much effort, a kibbutz-style kitchen and living unit were built, the former cut into the side of the mountain, and equipped with "outdoor chairs, benches, and picnic-style tables" and a charcoal grill. In the early 1950s, there was as yet no electricity or water, but a freshwater stream, which ran down the side of the mountain, was tapped and piped into a pool with an outlet. Eventually lavatories and electricity arrived, courtesy of a friendly contractor.

Adamski also worked with his wife selling ice cream, hot dogs, and hamburgers in a restaurant owned by his close friend and follower, Alice K. Wells. This restaurant served mainly the visitors and tourist parties who were going to Mount Palomar Observatory high on the mountain. Lou Zinsstag makes the apt comment that she never understood "why, in a democracy, this fact did so much to damage his image." Perhaps the world still thinks as Shakespeare thought, that only those on the top of the social scale are capable of having intensely significant experiences. Certainly Adamski was conscious of his social and personal disadvantages in early 20th century America. Just as today, if you are somewhat swarthy, have a strong foreign accent, and sell hamburgers, you are nobody, whether you believe in flying saucers or not.[13]

"Although I have lived in America since I was one year old, I still have an accent," wrote Adamski. "And I have no college degrees. Then, too, there is much manual labor to be done around Palomar Gardens, and I did it. Some people cannot associate such things with a scientific atmosphere, nor see that the practical can make a very steady basis for scientific and philosophical outreaching. So they try to discredit me. But I have never been deterred."[14]

Naturally enough, Adamski was always very sensitive about the "hamburger vendor" title some popular newspapers had given him. Even as late as 1999, the British *X Factor* magazine condescendingly refers to his "hot dog stand." From this remark, we assume that for sound philosophy, first-class restaurants are absolutely essential.

None of the apocryphal accounts of Alice K. Wells' modest establishment square with the description by Lucy McGinnis of the café as a place where "hundreds of people from every part of the world came and went, month in, month out."

Adamski says in *Behind the Flying Saucer Mystery* that even if the four-seat tale had been true, it would not have been to his discredit, for "America is built upon the little fellows who made good." Though he protests in the same book that he was not "employed in any capacity at the Palomar Gardens Café," there is evidence that he certainly helped out there quite often if not actually being "employed," since the commune he lived in hardly supported such a relationship in any case. He certainly lived on the café property with his wife, and the owner Alice K. Wells was a woman dear to his heart who helped create the George Adamski Foundation. He felt obliged to defend her and her enterprise: "Palomar Gardens was far from being a 'hamburger stand,' for it had been twice publicized in *Holiday* magazine." Be all this as it may, the restaurant was quite obviously the center of his social life, if only because his two telescopes were nearby.

In *Behind the Flying Saucer Mystery*[15] Adamski gives a cameo of his life at this time as he acted as an unofficial public relations officer for the Palomar Observatory. "The observatory had no one to give out information, so many people would ask questions at the café in regard to its operation. I often conversed with guests in the café dining room, on astronomy and other topics. When the spacecraft arrived, I was in a position to answer many questions and to give free lectures for service clubs."

Between working at the restaurant and doing his duty as a first-aid air-raid warden during the Second World War, he continued his lifelong interest in astronomy, and a 15-inch telescope came his way, which he housed in a slotted cupola. This Newtonian reflector was a miniature version of the great telescope on the top of the mountain, and financed by pupils' donations, sales of his books, and lectures and broadcasting.

But the telescope he used to shoot most his famous flying saucer photographs was a much more useful tripod-mounted 6-inch Newtonian reflector. This had been given to him by a "friend and student" some time in the late 1920s, and the firm which made it, Tinsley Laboratories, was long gone by the late 1940s. The bulky plate-camera attached to it was therefore ancient but nevertheless still fine technology for its day. This telescope often stood in the parking lot by Alice Wells' cafe. With it he recorded things that the great telescope far above his hotplate either could not, or even did not want to see. As far as Adamski is concerned the accusation of being a "fantasist" comes usually without reference to those operational 19th-century fantasies without which Palomar observatory could not have been built in the first place.

Although Adamski states specifically in *Flying Saucers Have Landed* that he was not associated in any way with the Palomar Observatory, both his miniature equipment and his preoccupation created a peculiar and undeniable symbiotic relationship between himself and Palomar. Perched on "our" mountain he acted as a warning sprite on a path of initiation to the machine high above him.

Writers on any subject at all must not only take into account bare "facts," they must be aware of simulacra and the alignment of symbols, the cross talk between irony and image. All these things make up the vital fabric of individuals and events. Students of complimentary simulacra might well take note of the contrast between the face of a human being and the face of Palomar Observatory. Undoubtedly, Palomar has what Norman Mailer would call a WASP face: nothing could present a more clean and respectable bourgeois face than the serene white edifice of the world's largest optical telescope. At 5,600 feet, it rules over the landscape of California, a mighty Apollonian symbol of reason and mechanical triumph over Nature. Compared to this powerful image, the gypsy features of Adamski are of Dionysus as Joker, with a hint of the sulphurous alchemical features of chaos and old night. If these pan-dimensional matches have anything at all to teach us, it is that we must learn once more to read the long trails of cross-referencing metaphors. The almost-falsehoods of this trail will lead us away from the almost-truths of economics, finite social function, and scientific purpose.

The Palomar telescope itself, with its 20-ton Pyrex mirror, was quite obsolete before it became operational in 1948. It cost six million dollars, took 18 years to complete, and it stands now in the 21st century rather like a gorgeous 19th-century folly [16] It is a veritable cathedral of early industrial-age technology, beautiful as Chartres, yet as useless as an old mineshaft beam-engine, or a Communist five-year plan. But certainly in 1953, before the age of computers, space, and radio astronomy got into their stride, there was nothing to challenge Palomar as the supreme symbol of clean-limbed scientific and technological success. The great observatory represented the unsullied innocence of the science of 17th century optics brought to almost decadent perfection. It was one of the last great white hopes before oiled sea-birds were to litter the globe, the nuclear clock neared midnight, and "big" science was pitched headlong into its first polluted mid-life-crisis and not a few greasy fingers were caught in the scientific till.

Those post-modern thinkers who reason by metaphor and simulacra rather than by linear "factual" propaganda, will have noted this conjunction of the great Palomar observatory and George Adamski. Little did this powerful symbol of rationalist aristocracy know that it had a blue-chinned knave toiling away at a hot grill below-stairs who was going to half blow it away. For all the world, it was as if the great house of Palomar had given birth to an unwanted son and had ordered him to the castle-kitchen to cook burgers for visitors to the great dome on the hill. Apparently there were moments both confusing and amusing when tourists from far-flung domains encountered Adamski's cupola, his pseudo-Palomar, and were offered cut-price deals on frankfurters and cola by what many assumed to be the Chief Astronomer.

The opinion the Palomar astronomers had of Adamski is reflected in an FBI report of 1953. The unnamed astronomer condescendingly refers to Adamski as an "astrologer," and mentions that during World War II, Adamski called himself a reverend and conducted Easter services in the valley. As with the blinkered "mere seller of burgers" remarks, the attitudes so well portrayed in Thomas Hardy's novel *Jude the Obscure* are still alive and well. C.P. Snow in *The Physicists*[17] mentions that Otto Hahn, the German physicist who split the uranium atom, and who stayed behind to work with Heisenberg, once called Einstein "the butler."

Adamski is one of those individuals quite common in history whose "facts" don't add up. Like Adolf Hitler, he was a kind of metaphysical Pied Piper, though fortunately on the reverse side of the moral coin. It is not of much use to find a lie Adamski told in 1946, a tall tale he told in 1952, or a re-editing of experience that he published as "real" event. Like Hitler again, he is both phenomenon and man, and in his tumultuous wake follow extraordinary events and ideas, strange people, and bizarre conflicts and accusations that still rage today. In this sense, George Adamski was a most extraordinary individual who drew to him forces that were equally extraordinary.

It seems that right from 1949, hamburger vendor or not, his life and opinions aroused military and scientific interest quite beyond all normal levels of expectation for a penniless man. Perhaps a man should never assume that he is so small and harmless that he has not been registered on the screens of Big Brother. Military men and scientists couldn't resist him, if only to savage his reputation. In drawing antagonism out of all proportion to the threat he represented, he was a living representation of that strange homeopathic theory which states that the more diluted the mix, the more effective is the power of the application.

But perhaps those who create new metaphors that Authority does not like are infinitely more dangerous than those who plant bombs.

On the 9th of October 1946, Adamski with a group of his followers observed a "gigantic space craft" hovering above the mountain ridge south of Mount Palomar, towards San Diego. A local radio station that broadcast sightings confirmed the observation by others. A few weeks later he met a "large group of people" from San Diego in Alice Wells' cafe, and a discussion began about this sighting. Six "military officers" (he does not say which branch of the American Armed Forces) were dining there also, and they listened intently to the discussion. One of them spoke up, saying, "It is not as fantastic as its sounds. We know something about this." Adamski asked what they knew, but they would not tell him. Yet "they assured us all that the ship we had seen and were discussing was not of this world."

The much-publicized Kenneth Arnold sighting of June 24th 1947 quickened Adamski's interest. A few weeks after this event, accompanied by four friends, he watched scores of lights turn, bank, and maneuver in the night sky. The lights would reverse their path, and on occasion "appeared to have a ring around the central body, or dome." One light became stationary, shooting out two powerful beams of light, one towards the south and San Diego, the other North toward Mount Palomar. Another light appeared to be acting as a kind of leader before they all faded away like a squadron of passing aircraft.

Tony Belmonte, a soil conservation employee who was living in a trailer on the same property, said he counted 184 of the lights or objects. He also told Adamski that a group of men from the Dempsey Ranch in Pauma Valley on the west side of Palomar had counted 204 of these lights or objects. Shortly after, two scientists on the way to the observatory came to see Adamski and asked if he had seen the lights, and he told them he had. They told him that Tony Belmonte's count was accurate. Adamski commented that "They would divulge little more than to assure me that all indications pointed to them being interplanetary, because they did not belong to our government."[18]

On a rainy day late in 1949, four men came into Alice Wells' restaurant. Two of the men, G.L. Bloom, and J.P. Maxfield, were scientists from Point Loma Naval Electronics Laboratory. The other two (one in uniform, possibly naval), Adamski does not name, but he does say that they were from what he terms "a similar set-up in Pasadena."

These men told Adamski that although they had 48-, 18-, and 12-inch telescopes, they wanted to see what he could do with his six-inch one. Though they said that this would be voluntary unpaid work, they did mention the Kenneth Arnold sighting, and pointed out a specific area of the moon, which they said they would like Adamski to concentrate on.

"They asked me if I would co-operate with them in trying to get photographs of strange craft moving though space," wrote Adamski, "since I had smaller instruments than those at the big Observatory. They said they were going to the top and ask for the same co-operation from the men at the big Observatory."[19]

Thus right from the start of the post-war period, big systems and organizations, both military and scientific, were beginning to get interested and involved in what people like Adamski were saying and doing. Thus encouraged by the attention he was getting from serious and responsible folk, he bought new film and started a new watching regime. It was not long before he succeeded in getting two good pictures while observing the very area on the moon originally pointed out to him by the scientists.

It was professional editing practice in these early days of books on flying saucers to dramatize real-life situations in a lurid B-feature script manner, quite unlike the cold and clinical technique common today. Donald Keyhoe's earliest books, for example, are full of over-scripted purple passages. While Adamski's books are not nearly as bad, the following scene from *Flying Saucers Have Landed* is straight from a Dashiell Hammett film script of the time: "I cannot remember the exact day except that it was during the time radio reports were being broadcast of a flying saucer landing in Mexico City." While we struggle to beat that for an opening sentence, we read on: "I had just tuned in the 4 p.m. news from KMPC, Beverly Hills, California, when Mr. Bloom stepped into the place. He sat down beside me, next to the radio, and told me to be quiet and listen. After it was over, he made an odd remark. 'They did not give all of the truth. There was more than that to it.'"

Adamski continues in a style that has been parodied countless times over half a century of films, radio, and television: "Then I knew that he knew more about it, but he would not talk." He then says that he met some "government men" in Mexico a year later and they told him that indeed a space ship had landed, but the story had been suppressed because of fear of a rising panic amongst Mexico's "superstitious" population. Before Bloom left, Adamski handed him prints of the two photographs he had taken, asking him to let his colleague Mr. Maxfield have a look at them.

On the 21st of March 1950, some months after the Bloom visit, Adamski gave a lecture to the Everyman's Club in La Mesa, California. Sanford Jarrell, a reporter from the daily *San Diego Journal* was present, and gave the lecture a front-page report the next day. However, he did not mention the two prints the Point Loma scientist had taken away with him, a matter he had privately discussed with Adamski. On the 22nd, the San Diego *Union* and *Tribune* smelt out the story, and contacted Adamski, who in turn referred them back to the Point Loma scientists. The newspapers could get nothing from the Navy Laboratory, and so they asked the Pentagon. On the 29th of March, by way of Copley Press Leased Wire from Washington, the Pentagon denied everything.

The two scientists concerned were important enough to have full autobiographical entries in *American Men of Science,* 9th Edition, Volume 1. In 1957, the then editor of *Flying Saucer Review,* Waveney Girvan wrote a letter to the employment superintendent of Point Loma asking about the whereabouts of Maxfield and Bloom. The reply stated that the former no longer worked at the laboratory, but Bloom was currently employed. A further letter inquiring of Bloom personally whether he had indeed been interested in trying to obtain photographs of saucers in 1949 remains unanswered to this day.

After his success with two good photographs, Adamski got virtually nothing for the next year and a half. Often sleeping in a hammock slung nearby, he describes very beautifully, in terms of temperature, climate, and animal and bird life, the nights he spent watching during these many months. From the summer and fall of 1951 through 1952 he took something like 500 photographs, of which only a few were suggestive of any kind of craft. In July 1951 *Fate* magazine published an article of his, which helped him financially and also initiated many inquiries about his pictures, for which he reluctantly asked a small payment.

To this day, there is no proof that any of these photographs were forgeries. Adamski says himself that he "had no desire to prostitute so profound a subject nor make a mockery out of so unprecedented a happening." In any case, the plates he used were very old-fashioned plates even at that time, and the obsolete equipment he used did not easily lend itself to experiment without leaving over-obvious traces of interference. All his print developing (or "finishing" as it was called then) was done by an expert on this vintage equipment, a Mr. D.J. Detwiler, who lived in Carlsbad, about 40 miles from Palomar Gardens.

Through 1951 and 1952, Adamski began to receive reports of saucers actually landing in desert areas not all that far from Mount Palomar. He made many trips to such areas, but without result until at last his patience was rewarded. It was about 12.30 "in the noon hour" on Thursday, the 20th of November 1952, that Adamski said he met a man "from another world." Six months later, after plenty of time for reflection, all the witnesses to this encounter signed affidavits as to the truth and reality of this event before a Public Notary in the Arizona County of Navajo.

CHAPTER 2

Meeting in the Desert

The Californian desert on the 20th of November 1952. Two cars speed out from Desert Center down the Parker Highway. Lucy McGinnis, Adamski's secretary, is in the first car, together with Alice K. Wells, the owner of the much-abused restaurant. Lucy McGinnis was to part from Adamski some years later in a welter of profound disagreements, but Alice K. Wells was so impressed by the desert encounter that she was later to help form the George Adamski Foundation that exists still today.[20]

George Hunt Williamson[21] and Al Bailey are with their wives in a second car. Though Adamski does not know the two married couples very well, all are manic saucer enthusiasts and Adamski admirers. The party are on a saucer hunt. They intend to visit places where it is rumored that saucers have been seen both in the air and landing. Just after a pleasant picnic lunch prepared no doubt by the industrious Alice Wells, the group sights "a gigantic cigar-shaped silver ship, without wings or appendages of any kind." Their wonder is increased when they see that many very earth-like aircraft surround this ship. With his mind full (even in 1952) of daunting rumors about abductions (which he calls kidnappings), Adamski tells the others to stay back. He is sure the occupants of the ship are trying to contact him, and he does not want them scared off, and neither does he want his friends exposed to possible danger. Lucy (together with Al Bailey), drives him to a spot about a half-mile away, which he feels is a suitable spot to set up his camera. Al Bailey helps him set up his 6-inch telescope on its tripod, and Adamski also prepares his own Kodak Brownie camera. Lucy and Al Bailey then drive back to where the rest of the group are observing events through binoculars.

Soon after the "spaceship" disappears, Adamski notices a "flash in the sky" and a "beautiful small craft" appears, "drifting through a saddle between the two mountain peaks and settling into one of the coves about half a mile from me." As quickly as he can, he photographs the object with his telescope-camera, separately loading 7 films. He puts the sealed frames containing the exposed negatives in his pocket, and tries for further shots with his Kodak Brownie (aperture a slow 1/25th of a second). The first Brownie shot he published in *Flying Saucers Have Landed,* and shows the craft just before it took off.

With yet more conventional aircraft circling round as if looking for the saucer, Adamski takes another three shots with his Brownie, more to capture terrain than anything else. After he has done this, he becomes aware of a human figure by the entrance to a ravine about a quarter of a mile away. The figure beckons to him, asking him to come over to where he is standing.

Adamski goes up to the figure under full observation by his companions, although they were some distance away. Alice K Wells looking through binoculars, sketched the figure at the time, and this drawing is reproduced in *Flying Saucers Have Landed.*

The communication with what Adamski calls "a human being from another world" was by hand signals and telepathy. Adamski regarded telepathy as an acquired skill, and had taught it as a technique for nearly thirty years. Given this method plus a few spoken words, a surprising wealth of information passed between the two. Circling the sun with his fingers, Adamski indicated the nearest orbit of Mercury, the second orbit of Venus, and the third orbit of Earth, pronouncing this name as he did so. The "man" (whom we shall now be called Orthon after the name given him later by Charlotte Blodget, one of Adamski's followers and the editor of his second book, *Inside the Spaceships*[22]), then indicated the second orbit of Venus, and this is the very first indication of anything Venusian. Adamski then pronounced the word "Venus," and Orthon, speaking for the first time, repeated this name. He therefore either accepted Adamski's name for the planet, or acknowledged that he knew that this was the name humanity had for the planet.

There then follows a familiar exchange. Orthon "says" that the coming of extraterrestrials is in friendship. He indicates that they are worried about nuclear bomb tests in the atmosphere, and says "Boom! Boom!" without being prompted by Adamski. The images then communicated become religious, and the thoughts of Orthon on this subject are curiously similar to Adamski's own ideas on "Natural Law."[23]

Fortunately this aspect of the conversation does not last very long, for Adamski does not write well when talking about his favorite subject. When he becomes objective however, he does show a talent for deft, clearly factual description, reminiscent of the classic naturalist's style of the nineteenth century. This is most evident when he describes Orthon's clothes and figure, and when he describes the scout-ship. It is "translucent and of exquisite color," and its shape is more like "a heavy glass bell than a saucer." He describes the three-ball landing gear, how the hull flashes prismatic colors in the desert sunlight, and also how the craft (which appears to be rather light in weight), rocks in the wind. He is aware also of shadows moving within the ship, and for a "fleeting second," a "beautiful face appeared and looked out."

Orthon bears an almost exact resemblance to many such beings seen in similar circumstances in the fifty years that have gone by since that time.[24] "He was round-faced," wrote Adamski, "with an extremely high forehead; large, but calm, gray-green eyes, slightly aslant at the outer corners; with slightly higher cheek bones than an Occidental, but not so high as an Indian or an Oriental; a finely chiseled nose, not conspicuously large; and an average size mouth with beautiful white teeth that shone when he smiled or spoke."[25]

Adamski is quite overcome to the point of embarrassment. His previous careful objectivity suffers melt down. He waxes lyrical: "…the beauty of his form surpassed anything I had ever seen…I felt like a little child in the presence of one with great wisdom and much love, and I became very humble within myself…from him was radiating a feeling of infinite understanding and kindness, with supreme humility."

Orthon refuses a handshake, but places the palm of his hand against Adamski's hand: "The flesh of his hand to the touch of mine was like a baby's, very delicate in texture, but firm and warm. His hands were slender, with long tapering fingers like the beautiful hands of an artistic woman. In fact, in different clothing he could easily have passed for an unusually beautiful woman…."

Adamski ignores a warning not to get too close; his right shoulder comes slightly under the bottom skirting of the machine, and his arm is painfully jerked up as if by an electric shock. In pulling him away, Orthon somehow slightly injures his own hand, and red blood flows. Fearing for his precious negatives more than Orthon's injury, Adamski takes the frames from the right-hand pocket of his jacket. Orthon, seeing this, asks him if he may have one of the frames, and Adamski agrees.

Orthon then goes into the ship via a sliding door. Adamski then hears fragments of a kind of conversation with another being "and the voices were as music, but the words I could not understand."

The craft takes off, and Adamski, with an almost completely numb arm, signals to the others to come over to him. Almost speechless with astonishment, they pack up the equipment and prepare for the journey home, George Hunt Williamson taking his famous plaster casts of the Venusian's footprints in the sand. Again, while they are doing this, numerous conventional man-made aircraft remain present overhead. A giant USAF B36 jet bomber, of all things, joins them[26] This was probably out from Edwards Air Force Base.[27] A half-century later, Edwards has acquired as many UFO rumors as Area 51 at Groom Lake.

The planes circle, turn and bank, and their motors "resounded in the still desert air," coming so low that they cast shadows on the ground around the group. If these shadows included that of the B36 then the combined sound must have been quite a devastating experience to this group of people, who had absorbed enough excitement for one day.

George Hunt Williamson and Al Bailey asked Adamski's permission to give an account of the whole business to an Arizona paper, and they all agreed. *The Phoenix Gazette* and the *Oceanside Blade Tribune* ran stories of the encounter in November. Photographs were included of the footprint-casts and of the group, but unfortunately Adamski's photographs did not turn out well. We can reasonably assume that these accounts by newspapers were the original sources that encouraged a friend of the British writer Desmond Leslie to suggest that he get in touch with Adamski.

About stories such as this, analysts always chant the "facts" mantra. They like their "realities" to be old industrial things, easily separable into fact and fiction. But the desert contact scene is pure Carlos Castanada:[28] the desert, the waiting initiates, the magician, and the vision in the sky. Linking all these things is that string of complex deceptions of many shades, from "solid" to aetherial needed to mount transformation of belief and certainty within both group and individual. The dynamics of this situation are much older than "fact."

Adamski himself comes out of it all just as surprised as everyone else. Perhaps his first thought was of how the trading society he lived in would react to his claim that he had just got something for nothing.

Perhaps he had also the Castanada-like thought that he had started something he might not be able to finish.

Twenty-three days later. Early morning on Saturday the 13th of December 1952. The day dawns bright and clear over Palomar Gardens. Adamski, acting on a hunch, takes time off to prepare his 6-inch telescope. Again, he hears the sound of military jets as they zoom overhead. At nine o'clock, he sees a flash in the sky, and focuses his telescope upon it. In a sky suddenly empty of planes, he sees an "iridescent glass-like craft flashing its color in the morning sun!" He quickly shoots four pictures with the craft hovering within a hundred feet of him.

A very strange thing then happens. A "porthole" opens and *a hand reaches out* to drop down the negative frame taken by Orthon on the first meeting on the previous November 20th. Not exactly a hi-tech gesture, not very well mannered, nor respectful, to say the least. It was a gesture certainly not caring of damage to the negative, which bounced off a rock, denting the carrier! All Adamski gets after that is a very slight wave of the hand before the craft leaves.

The jerky frames of this incident would do credit to a Charlie Chaplin film; one can imagine Adamski's face as he stood by his old-fashioned plate-camera telescope watching the hand reach out as if throwing away kitchen-waste from the porthole of an ocean liner. His sentimental romanticism does not seem in the least disturbed by the rather off-hand treatment. But this absurd comic touch could be a measure of the truth of the occasion. Perhaps all thinking entities have a touch of Chaplin, whether they live in caves or spaceships, or whether they look like lizards, owls, or moths.

One cannot help thinking that if Adamski were making all this up, he would have made his story more plausible. It is notable that this incident contradicts the cozy view of "sublime" beings obeying his "natural law" of charitable boy-scout principles. Absolute seriousness means robots, and thankfully, both Mind and Matter may be fuzzier than we ever like to think. Both thinking and behavior are always near a chaotic absurdity. On this incident alone, some have condemned Adamski as an impostor. But the last thing a real smart operator wants is trouble. Yes, he wants to win, he wants to utterly convince, but he knows also that he will be destroyed by the law of diminishing returns if his story becomes just a little *too* fantastic. If this part of the Adamski story was designed, it was designed not to sell.

But sell it did.

Although it was a Saturday and the demands of the restaurant were pressing, Adamski asked to be taken (presumably by car—he did not drive himself) some forty miles to Carlsbad to hand his plates over to his photographic finisher, Mr. D.J. Detwiler, who unfortunately was out at the time. But Mr. Detwiler's wife took the negatives, promising that her husband would develop them that evening and return them himself to Palomar at noon the following day.

Both Detwiler and Adamski must have been absolutely astonished when they saw the prints. Adamski had succeeded in capturing images that despite fifty years of controversy have entered cultural bedrock. A half century has gone by, but even ten-year-olds scream for toys much like Adamski's three-ball-undercarriage "bottle-cooler" UFO which he photographed on this date, December 13, 1952. Despite all that has happened since that time, these black and white images are still hauntingly beautiful, symbols of mysteries beyond mysteries that have entered the universal imagination.[29]

Adamski kept the print in the dented frame for a few more days before having it developed by Mr. Detwiler. He was surprised to see that his original shot had disappeared, and the print showed a strange writing and a cross-section of a saucer-shape with, strangely, a reverse swastika to that on the right-hand shoe-print cast take by George Hunt Williamson.

There were even stranger events on the 13th. Referring to the immediate departure of the craft, Adamski says: "Dropping below the treetops, its path of travel took it very close to the well and one cabin on the upper part of the property, and there it was seen and photographed by others whom I had previously alerted."[30]

There may have been "others," but the only one we know of is ex-sergeant-instructor Jerrold E. Baker. He was then a young Palomar wannabe, newly discharged from the USAF. Adamski, for once dropping his Mary-on-a-donkey voice, said later of Baker that he was behaving "like one of the family" and "helping himself to everything, freely and in abundance, but without money to pay for anything." Now that's the George we like, hurt out of the back-bedroom Day-Glo chapels of his mind, and getting ready to kick the ass of a freeloader.

With a hint of trouble in Paradise, our interest is revived.

According to Adamski, young Baker arrived "late one night" in December 1952. On the 13th of that month, using no doubt his USAF training, he arranged with Adamski to try a UFO shoot with his Brownie at the same time as Adamski shot with his famous six-inch tripod-mounted camera-reflector, some distance away. Two very different cameras from two different positions registering the same phenomenon would be evidence as good as any.

According to Baker's signed statement made on the 13th of December and published by Gray Barker, his sighting lasted two minutes, and it appears that he shot exactly the same machine as Adamski describes above. During this time, he observed that the machine had portholes and the three-ball "undercarriage" now familiar the whole world over. He stated also that it made no sound, moved as if under intelligent control, and had a slight odor, probably of ionized air or ozone, a common feature reported by other UFO witnesses. Baker stated: "I saw a circular object skim over the tree-tops from the general direction of the area where the Professor was located…it then hung in the air not over twelve feet high at the most, and about twenty-five feet from where I was standing. It seemed as if it did this knowing I was there waiting to photograph it. I quickly snapped a picture and as I did it tilted slightly and zoomed upwards over the tree faster than anyone can almost imagine."[31]

Baker got one shot himself, reproduced in *Flying Saucers Have Landed,* and Adamski says he got four, three of which are reproduced in that same work. According to Baker again, the pair hurried to Carlsbad to Mr. Detwiler, who always developed Adamski's pictures

Oddly, Baker's account indicates that the pair were very close chums, but in *Flying Saucers Have Landed,* Adamski's late 1953 account of the 13th of December 1952 *contains no mention of Baker, or his shot.* This is strange, since Adamski chose to publish Baker's photograph in this same book and give Baker credit for it in the text accompanying the published photograph.

There then begins one of the first great celebrated Ufological controversies containing a great a spectrum of confusions. James Moseley, in the October 1957 issue of his *Saucer News,* gives the fullest detailed information on the Baker saga. Moseley, who for years has been one of the brightest commentators on the UFO scene, discusses the rather suspicious Baker's friendship with the very suspicious Frank Scully,[32] who wrote the legendary 1950 book *Behind the Flying Saucers.*[33] Scully appears in the Appendix to *Flying Saucers Have Landed,* and we shall meet him later, where his adventures and friendship with the equally suspicious Silas Newton are described by writer Karl Pflock.

Baker wrote to Moseley, and Moseley acquired Baker's letters to Scully, and also to Desmond Leslie. He published parts of these letters together with a statement by Irma, Baker's wife, in the October 1957 issue of his *Saucer News.* From this evidence, Moseley concludes that George Adamski was a con-man, a master trickster who hoaxed pictures, books, stories, and just about everything else. But as far as Moseley's great regard for Baker's evidence is concerned, Moseley reprints a paragraph from one of Baker's letters[34] to Frank Scully that shows Baker's deep and complex uncertainty about the whole and entire business.

We might well compare Baker's previously quoted statement of December 13, 1952, with the following, made on January 29, 1954, and published by Moseley in the October 1957 issue of his *Saucer News:* "He [Adamski] has taken the most astounding photographs obtained thus far on the elusive saucers. This man claims he has spent untold hours watching and waiting, both day and night, to obtain the pictures. This is not true. I know that he knows exactly when a spaceship is coming, and is there at the precise instant to snap the picture. It is a planned, purposeful action, not the mere chance which he implies. Why the necessity of the deception? Is it as he claims? Perhaps yes; but more likely no."

Surely the absolutely astonishing thing here is that Baker admits that saucers appear and Adamski photographs them! Whether Adamski *knows* if they are coming or not is surely of secondary importance. How Moseley, no fool by any means, could base his negative arguments against Adamski on such evidence by his major witness is quite astonishing. Moseley of all people should have known that when in the ring with an opponent like Adamski, the last thing to do is hesitate.

Baker's question—"Why the necessity of the deception?"—has a haunting poetic ring to it, and it is a question which still burns as fiercely today as it did a half century ago. He might well have asked himself about the necessity of his own deception. In another statement published by Moseley, Baker claims that Adamski took the Brownie shot himself and offered it to him, saying that he could become world-famous with such a picture and could write a book. Baker in a letter to Desmond Leslie (August 4, 1954) says, "I readily admit that I fell victim to a hoax."

Baker, for one reason or another, became steadily more suspicious of Adamski after the 13th of December 1952. He made matters worse by forming an alliance with one Karl Hunrath, another Palomar wannabe, who had arrived soon after Baker. Hunrath claimed to be an inventor, took residence, and announced according to Adamski, that he was staying "indefinitely, with no money to pay for his expenses." Hunrath had been one of Adamski's more intelligent correspondents for some time, but he appears to have fallen in life, and had decided to take his last sacrificial offerings (in the form of various electronic inventions) to the mountain, in best biblical fashion.

As the atmosphere became worse amidst the mountain group, Baker and Hunrath stalked around looking for models that Adamski might have used for trick-photography. They did not come across one, but found a curious circular wooden frame lying around behind Adamski's cabin one day. The crude frame had one-inch strips of copper hammered to it in a circular fashion. But the pair must have been disappointed when Adamski told them that this was his TV aerial. It certainly sounds like one of the crude TV aerials of the time, some of which were sold in self-assembly kits and looked just like the object described.

Model or not, we are now getting to a stage where things on the mountain are rapidly deteriorating. Relations are re-aligning, falling apart, and there is bitterness and intrigue. Tempers are so high that even bits of wood and copper are suspect, ready to be transformed into countless UFO confusions, rather like the donkey's head of Bottom in *A Midsummer Nights Dream,* which is quite a suitable play for the Palomar community.

In all likelihood, the truth about this business is that Adamski, who was certainly at least bisexual, developed early on a strong physical affection for young Baker that was spurned. When Baker aligned himself with the rather nasty woman-hating Hunrath, and rejected Adamski lock, stock, and barrel, the multi-level affair blew up in all their faces, made probably worse as far as Adamski was concerned by Baker announcement that he was getting married. The result was that an angry and blushing Baker (who, in turn, may have been equally uncertain about his feelings as Adamski), took it out on his former friend, claiming that he was an imposter. If Adamski did take the Brownie shot and offer it to Baker, it was in all probability the act of a dazed and confused would-be lover to an equally confused protégé. In any case, the uncertain mess produced terrible guilt feelings on both sides. Adamski, a somewhat lonely bisexual, was looking for a familiar—an androgynous sprite to put his arm around, and an angry and insulted Baker fled to the side of the unpleasant Hunrath, if only for protection.

We notice that Baker is angry about the Brownie shot alone. He doesn't say anything about the photographs Adamski took by himself about the same time on the 13th of December.

As we shall see later, just one of the wonderful things about the study of the UFO phenomenon is that it spreads such a wide spectrum of confusion and uncertainty that what is commonly called "reality" appears to be shot through with holes like a French cheese. It also defeats the strongest of oppositions. For example, the fairy webs created by the magus Adamski settle on the eyes of skeptical arch-demon Moseley, who after meeting Adamski personally, places a first foot square into the enchantments of a very slippery slope: "I have been convinced that he [Adamski] is a kindly man who would do no harm to no one…his book has entertained thousands, and injured no one." In typical accordance with the Adamski effect, Moseley's other foot follows rather quickly. Astonishingly, just like his chief witness Baker, Moseley lets Adamski off the hook: "I am not saying—nor is Mr. Baker, that George Adamski's account is necessarily untrue."[35]

Well how about that? The shrewd and clever Moseley has to admit that in the case of the UFO, even a thousandth of a swallow would make for infinite summers on countless mountains.

Moseley, like many UFO researchers, makes a most basic mistake in his methodology. He is delighted when Al Bailey, one of the original desert witnesses, says that he didn't see Orthon or Orthon's ship. But the point is surely that Al Bailey says he DID see the big "mother ship" that appeared minutes before Adamski's contact. If such unbelievable things exist, why spend so much time arguing about the "authenticity" of Orthon and his ship? If the contact was a hoax, then again we ask Jerrold Baker's question: *why the deception?* And perhaps we ask ourselves an even more terrifying question: Are the deceptions and the appearances linked?

As our journey through the life of Adamski continues, there will emerge strong indications that they are.

In the days following the 13th of December 1952, the plot thickens yet again. George Hunt Williamson was also in residence at Palomar at this time, and the three men—Hunrath, Baker, and Williamson—had resolved prior to this date to form the George Adamski Foundation. This was a measure of how close this group of men were in the first halcyon days of their friendship, and how much at first they believed in the claims of George Adamski.

However, apart from his growing difficulties with Baker, Adamski soon found out that Hunrath's gifts to the gods took the form of electronic equipment, with which he said he could attract saucers and make them crash. Adamski blew a main fuse, and ordered Hunrath off the property immediately. Hunrath in turn ordered Adamski off the property, and for a minute it looked as if blows might be exchanged, but Hunrath thought better of it, probably because, as Baker's wife Irma recalls, Adamski was much stronger and bigger than Hunrath. According to Irma, Hunrath was a violent and hateful misogynist, and probably resented deeply the affinity between Irma and Baker as much as did Adamski. Adding to the conflict was Adamski's ill-concealed liking for intense relationships with young men such as Baker, who according to Irma, had rather a weak personality. Irma says[36] herself says that Adamski at this time was "like a woman scorned."

Yet another problem was George Hunt-Williamson, who despite entertaining everyone with Indian traditional dances, was in a deeply depressed state. He had temporarily deserted his pregnant wife for "psychic" treatment by Adamski, who was supposed to rid him of low spirits. For much of December 1952, Hunt-Williamson lay prostrate, with "Indian spirits" speaking through his vocal chords.

This witches' brew bubbled over early in 1953 with the departure of all three original founding fathers of the George Adamski Association leaving the mountain in a cloud of accusations and counter accusations involving possible theft of mail and money. According to Irma Baker's account, there were tearful, paranoid, and almost violent scenes. Hunrath, when collecting the mail from Escondito, was almost attacked by Adamski's faithful secretary Lucy McGinnis, and the police were called to the incident.

In the middle of this divine comedy involving flying saucers, psychics, saucer-zapping machines and good old human hatreds, Lucy McGinnis called Irma on January 12, 1953, and asked her to call the FBI to Palomar Gardens. Lucy said that she was terrified that the three founding fathers would return to do "the Professor," Alice Wells, and herself much harm, as well as downing some USAF planes in the bargain.

That very evening men from both the OSI and the FBI arrived. Little did they know that sixteen days later they would again trek up the mountain to admonish Adamski, who had been boasting in Alice Wells' restaurant that his views on flying saucers had been sanctioned by the FBI.

According to Irma, the agents listened astonished as an angry Adamski showed a side of his nature very much removed from the "kind and loving man" reported by Jim Moseley. For once Adamski acted consistent with his looks as he poured scorn on Hunrath, Baker, and even George Hunt-Williamson. His accusations against Hunrath were straightforward national sabotage, which no doubt the "government men" (as they were called at the time) fully understood. But they possibly were somewhat baffled by Adamski claiming that in addition, Hunrath was practicing "occultism," and had been possessed by a "beast." To add to this delicious Fortean mix, Adamski accused Hunt-Williamson of being a "fake" psychic. While trying to take all this in, the agents had also to cope with Adamski's suggestion that young Baker was possibly a secret agent, one of their own brood, no less!

These mountain scenes are the *gestalt* of the UFO: men and women wrestle with both ideas and themselves; they struggle for command of both technology and spiritual elevation. All these things were part of the magical Californian summers that were to come. The battle between Adamski and the founding fathers had all the rainbow spectrum of Californian inspirations. In the generations to follow, machines and madness, inspirations and visions would fill almost the entire West Coast with millions of Orthons, many with long blond hair and a good number indistinguishable from one another in both appearance and gender. By simulacra again, if the aggressive and nature-despoiling Hunrath is the coming American holocaust of Vietnam, George Adamski is part of the American mountain bedrock, and the guardian of his saucers in his lair, for all the world a fallen Prospero.

Eventually, Baker was to leave his mountain and live a mundane life, probably dreaming forever of summers lost. As for Karl Hunrath, in 1953, he found a new partner, one Wilkinson, for his saucer-zapping activity. Apparently the pair went to Mexico, and like many of the young mountain-sprites of the coming Summers of Love, they were never seen or heard of again.

Fifty years later, these flying saucer contacts of George Adamski still intrigue. The incidents of the 20th of November and the 13th of December 1952 still have something in them for everyone. The phenomenon has even produced its own "objectivity" to satisfy the most discriminating of interested parties. Of late, Timothy Good has unearthed information that supports Adamski's claims. *In George Adamski: The Untold Story,* Good tells us:[37] "On the 3rd of August, 1956, the U.S. Air Technical Intelligence Center, in reply to an inquiry from researcher Richard Ogden regarding the Desert Center Contact of 20th November, 1952 (during which Adamski and the other six witnesses had said that Air Force planes were flying over the area at the time), stated: 'In response to your letter of July 18, 1956, we are enclosing a summary of Project Bluebook Special Report No. 14, which was released in October, 1955. The full report statistically covers all reports up to that date, including a report by an Air Force pilot on November 20, 1952, from the general vicinity of Desert Center, California…."

Later Ogden wrote another letter requesting further information, but was told by Major T.J. Connair Jr., USAF Adjutant, that it was not Air Force policy to release details of its UFO investigations. As a result of his inquiries Richard Ogden was rewarded with a visit from the FBI."[38]

Good then quotes from a USAF Project Bluebook file, which relates to a Teletype message concerning a sighting at Salton Sea, California, on the 20th of November, 1952, which was the second year of Captain Edward J. Ruppelt's reign as the director of Project Blue Book, the official Air Force investigation of UFOs:

UNIDENTIFIED OBJECT SEEN PILOT LOCKHEED AIRCRAFT B50 5626, ON A ROUND ROBIN FROM DAVIS MONTHAN. OBJECT SEEN AT 2005 MOUNTAIN TIME 10 MILES EAST OF SALTON SEA, ALTITUDE 16000 FEET. AIRCRAFT WAS ON A HEADING OF 275 DEGREES AND SIGHTED OBJECT AT 1100 O'CLOCK TO HIS POSITION. OBJECT WAS STATIONARY AND WAS CHANGING COLOR FROM WHITE TO RED TO GREEN. STARTED IN MOTION IN N.W. HEADING AND DISAPPEARED LIKE TURNING OUT A LIGHT. THERE WERE NO [word not legible] OR PROPULSION OR LOCOMOTION AND THE PILOT WAS UNABLE TO DESCRIBE THE SIZE OR SHAPE.

NOV. 22, 1952

It must be borne in mind that at 16,000 feet, practically the whole of California can be seen. That this "unidentified object" was in the same area on the same day as the Adamski sighting suggests it might well have been there at "12.30 in the noon hour," when the Adamski party made their historic sighting.

Many juries have convicted on lesser circumstantial conjunctions of time and space.

CHAPTER 3

Saucer Nights on Palomar

After these close encounters, the shooting of photographs, and the angry confrontations, it must have been somewhat unnerving for any uninitiated visitor to hear Adamski and the members of his group talk about utterly fantastic things as if they were talking about bags of groceries.

"I wonder how many realize that he (Adamski) was a member of the interplanetary Council," says Alice K. Wells, in her obituary.[39] "This is a group of men of high Cosmic Conscious Awareness that evaluate the conditions of our system and keep their representatives informed of the changes. The Brothers who travel in ships and those here on this planet are liaison men that carry this information. Due to George Adamski's unwavering loyalty in carrying out his every commission, the Council decided to grant him a new body through which to work."

Undoubtedly, these cloud-worlds were as real to the group as wages and economies were to others. Fred Steckling, a friend and colleague of Adamski, and author of *Why Are They Here?*[40] was no exception: "I have had the pleasure of talking to some of the space visitors. They were introduced to me while in association with George Adamski. These people, men and women, are physical human beings. Their bodies are identical to ours from the medical point of view. The only difference between them and us is that they are more enlightened, living according to natural laws, and not by man-made standards and ideas, as we do."

Even the highly perceptive Desmond Leslie, Adamski's co-author on *Flying Saucers Have Landed,* was vulnerable, and steps onto the same enchanted ski-run as Fred Steckling. Leslie in his tribute,[41] says that Adamski "believed that he had reincarnated from another planet through karmic reasons to give his teachings, and I find that quite acceptable."

It is a measure of the power Adamski had over people that he got the tough-minded, strong-willed and brilliantly intelligent Leslie to "accept" the anodyne reasons why the spacefolk did not take him on a trip in a saucer. "He refused to ask me on a 'contact' with him," writes Leslie, "and at the time it peeved me greatly. But I realized later that I was in no fit spiritual state for such an experience and had I been taken aboard a saucer I doubt if I'd have been a very successful prophet afterwards for my ego is highly susceptible to spiritual aggrandizement. Many who have genuine contacts have gone very odd, forming new religions and in fact doing everything the Brothers desire least."[42]

From most accounts, it sounds as if Adamski claimed many more visits from the space-folk than are mentioned in his books. He drops them into remarks and conversations as if they were visits to the local library. He told the Danish writer Hans Peterson[43] that in December 1958, while his train was delayed near Kansas City, a spaceman picked him up in a car, and drove him a short distance to where a craft hovered above a grove of trees. According to Peterson, Adamski said: "I had the experience to be (sic) lifted up into the space craft while the ship was hovering. It feels as if something is surrounding you like a transparent or plastic curtain, yet you can't touch it and you don't see it, and like a magnetic force, it lifts you just like an elevator into the ship."

When we say that some people live in other worlds perhaps we mean that such worlds are not really "far away" but are worlds ancillary to ours, structures which fit almost, but not quite. Two worlds or more existing at one and the same time within a single person's consciousness can be a difficult situation to manage. Lee Harvey Oswald (with his many observed doppelgangers) had trouble doing it, so did the "thoughtphotographer" Ted Serios,[44] the poet W.B. Yeats and the magician Aleister Crowley, to mention but a few.

These secondary worlds are plausible, coherent within themselves. But when they struggle for prime time, their temporary domination makes them appear as perfectly naturalistic localizations, but in a totally absurd setting. Nothing more suggests Dali's melting clocks than Adamski's meetings with people from Mars and Venus. And perhaps nothing more suggests what a wartime B-29 bomber looked like to a Melanesian mind than the following, which if done deadpan before a single microphone in a Lennie Bruce club of this era after midnight would have been a riot. It also might have convinced Adamski that he was in the wrong business: "During the year 1958, I had the pleasure of attending a meeting comprised of people from Mars, Venus, Saturn, Jupiter, Uranus, and Neptune. It was a friendly get-together, devoted mainly to discussions of some of our everyday problems. The subject of eating was introduced, and I asked for more specific information, since so many questions regarding this topic are coming to me. Their answer was simple and precise. They told me they usually purchase the cheaper cuts which can be boiled with vegetables like my mother used to cook when I was a boy."[45]

Adamski spent the 1950s delivering such stuff all over America. When radio and television stations were not asking for him, he did the rounds of clubs, institutes, and professional associations. He would speak between showing his slides, photographs and sometimes his moving footage, and the results more often than not were a dreadful mess because, as Desmond Leslie points out, Adamski at most times "tried to say too much at once." But then he was a lot better at taking questions from the floor:

Question: How can I meet a space person and get a ride in one of their ships?

Answer: I honestly cannot answer this question. I am met when and where a meeting is to the advantage or convenience of the Brothers.

Question: Do the space people use money as a medium of exchange on other planets?

Answer: No. Their means of exchange is a commodity and service exchange system without the use of money...

Surprisingly, there was an enormous appetite for this kind of thing, both in America and abroad. After 1953, Adamski established a vast worldwide network of correspondents, admirers, and other contactees. Most joined his "Get Acquainted Program," the "acquainted" part of this meant forming relationships and dialogues with the space-folk. He launched a regular newsletter for updates on cosmic contacts, and many groups in different countries were formed to discuss his views and disseminate the latest information.

While many derided him, the photographs and the moving footage would make them think again. Those contactees who did not have such an extensive collection did not stand nearly so great a chance against criticism. Howard Menger for example, though he claimed a few photographs, did not succeed in rivaling Adamski's fame.

Throughout the fifties, life was never dull when Adamski returned home to Palomar from his travels. Many lost souls would take the spare beds, and would-be sorcerer's apprentices and other wannabes would arrive and beg to work with "the Professor." Just like Baker and Hunrath, prototype hippies arrived to empty the larder and spend their time contemplating the infinite rather than work. This was the time of Ken Kesey[46] of course, and if Adamski had not been of a different generation to him and his followers, perhaps lights and amplifiers would have strewn the sides of Mount Palomar.

But not even Ken Kesey had spaceman dropping in uninvited for dinner.

Time: an evening in the early 1950s. Place: Mount Palomar. Adamski's extended family are about to have dinner. A light knock on the door announces the arrival of "tall fine-looking man" who, says Adamski, "stood there asking for me." After an hour of perfectly normal conversation, mainly about space matters from an Earth perspective, the spaceman reveals things which Adamski says no one on Earth could have known about space except, of course, he himself, who had been there in the ships. After the man leaves, others present say that they do not think the man was a spaceman and so the matter is dropped.

For once, it is good to know that there were some skeptics on Palomar Mountain. However, sometime later, Adamski says that during "a recent meeting with the Brothers" (showing again that he was wont to meet them more than he ever let on), he had met this same man and learned a little more about him. This man "was in charge of the schedules on which ships from Saturn arrive." In other words, he was a kind of interplanetary bus-garage manager. But we are not told about the interesting aspects of such a fascinating job, since even a list of Saturnian commuter timetables would dwarf all possible Earth interests. We can imagine the reaction of harassed Earth folk in a busy passenger hall if the schedule-clerks spoke like this: "The reason you identified me at that time was not so much from what I said but because your soul and your mind were as one and it was your soul that recognized my soul."

One asks: do the space brothers ever take time off from this rubbish? Do they ever give anyone a break? Do their toilet attendants and whores speak like this? Or their criminals, policemen, or the grocers who sell them their always wholesome food? If they do, then their more "pure" world contains a level of boredom that would atrophy the testicles of a woolly mammoth.

With a senior staff like this, asking where your baggage has disappeared to in a Saturnian departure lounge would be like the Dormouse asking the address of the Mad Hatter.

Equally interesting were the visits of the numerous very human beings who were drawn to Adamski's domain. In 1960, Henk Hinfelaar, a New Zealand co-worker from the "Get Acquainted" program published a letter concerning one of many USAF pilots who came to see Adamski in the early 1950s. Lucy McGinnis had written this letter originally to Hans Peterson, the co-worker in Copenhagen. She says: "A young pilot who had been to the café a number of times and had talked with GA, came in for lunch one day. He told about piloting an American plane to Australia where he landed on a vast airfield. He said that a gigantic spacecraft was already there. He was introduced to a group of scientists from another planet and told he was to take them to a scientific meeting in Scotland."[47]

Undoubtedly, Adamski made Mount Palomar one of the Magic Mountains of America, something the great telescope above him with its vision of an empty lifeless universe had failed to do. Up they came to see him: the dreaming and the free, the credulous and the criminal, the eccentric and the walking wounded of America. One wonders if a call goes out through Nature to subvert the very foundations of machines and kingdoms whose time has come. Like human beings and like kingdoms, machines too can suffer the death of a thousand cuts. Few now believe the 200-inch-telescope story of a dead heavens any more. The great machine is now a mass of almost useless clockwork. Its successor, the Hubble space-telescope, produces passable bathroom wallpaper pictures, but none are as fascinating as those of George Adamski, nor as fascinating in turn as some of those who made their way to his domain.

CHAPTER 4

Enter Desmond Leslie

Desmond Leslie was an Irish aristocrat who owned a castle in Ireland in which he had lived for considerable periods of his life. An ex-fighter pilot, he was a second cousin of Winston Churchill, and he was both a novelist[48] and a playwright.

According to Bryant Reeve, the author of the 1957 book *Flying Saucer Pilgrimage,* Leslie told him that he first tried to write a fictional account about his own conviction that aliens had contacted Earth many times in the past, and had left definite traces of their presence. But as soon as he started the research, he became convinced that

Desmond Leslie

what he had found was not fiction, but fact. Leslie, in his own account in *Gray Barker's Book of Adamski,* said that he sent his manuscript to many publishers who promptly rejected it.

It so happened that at that time, a western US newspaper publicized Adamski's meeting with a man from Venus. Adamski had originally intended to write up the details of his contact in a series of "small booklets" in order to try and respond to the many inquiries he was getting from all over the world. Leslie heard through a friend about Adamski's desert contact a week after it happened, and he wrote to him immediately. This letter requested also copies of Adamski's photographs that Leslie said he would like to use for his book. Adamski sent a selection of his photographs (including the controversial Baker photograph), refusing all payment for them, at which Leslie was astonished. A few weeks later, Adamski sent his manuscript, asking Leslie to suggest a publisher. By that time, Waveney Girvan, who worked for the publisher Werner Laurie, had accepted Leslie's book. Leslie suggested that it be a joint work with Adamski, and Girvan, though worried, agreed to publish it. Though the two writers were not to meet until 1954, *Flying Saucers Have Landed* duly appeared to much acclaim.

The book's two narrators—Leslie writing Part 1 and Adamski a brief Part 2—could not have been more different in style, approach, and content. Leslie could have written his Book 1 of *Flying Saucers Have Landed* in a library; his views are historical and academic. He makes no personal fantastic claims, and neither does he tell us anything at all about his own past life. Here lies the strength of the book's strong set of ironies: few other UFO books published since have anything like the quality required to stand alone as literature. In California, Adamski had found his landscape; he was no longer an immigrant Pole with an accent. Leslie, on the other hand, though he found a new world intellectually, remained as he always had been, both socially and personally, forever the astute and fastidious observer.

On the other hand, the whole flesh and blood of the flying saucer dimension permeated Adamski's very being; his internal and external landscapes contained almost nothing but a titanic struggle to grasp the phenomenon and to tell of its nature.

Thus two narrators, dramatic participant and observer, are cross-referenced by two vastly different textures and many dimensions of two widely differing personalities. Adamski is complex, Leslie is straightforward; Leslie has an extremely high intelligence, Adamski has something far older; Adamski has found what he is looking for, Leslie is still searching. The men also differ therefore in culture and social class, in nation, personal circumstance, and indeed in age itself.

The highborn Desmond Leslie was close to very high-powered groups of British leaders who had in the 1950s made significant comments on the subject of flying saucers. The members of this group, some of whom we shall meet later, were to be strongly influenced by *Flying*

Saucers Have Landed. The book served not only as an organizing focus for many disconnected thoughts and influences, it represented also the first modern chance of a possible reply to burgeoning rationalism, then in 1953, reaching the very highest level of social-scientific confidence.

The book also had what might be termed an annoyance factor. With Adamski's 55 pages of bizarre experiences tacked on the end of it as the somewhat intimidating Part 2, *Flying Saucers Have Landed* was guaranteed to drive scientists (never popular figures at the best of times), into a frenzy. An editor might have thought that this could well provide an amusing spectacle to a nation never enamored of its very own and quite unique progeny. There might also have been the consideration that both books gave some feeling of magical revival to a pre-sixties world which lived with the real threat of nuclear holocaust before it had been given time to recover from a holocaust made by conventional weapons.

In his book, *Gods and Spacemen in the Ancient West,* Raymond Drake looks back from 1974, and well expresses the atmosphere in which Leslie and Adamski wrote their prophetic book over twenty years previous. The following text is rather like a piece of reconditioned linguistic circuitry in which a battery of Left dialectics have all been replaced by a new metaphysical view:

"The legends of spacemen warring with fantastic weapons evoke within our souls some atavistic memory beclouding our secret lives...elated we gaze at the familiar world around us with new eyes, tired old Earth glows in heroic splendor, the fragments of ancient wisdom synthesize into a marvelous, exciting panorama...All we have learned appears inadequate, as though down through the centuries the truths of our universe were willfully suppressed, leaving us conditioned by dogmas sadly out of date. Conventional histories recording the follies of mankind now seem trivial, the squabbles of rival religions become sterile; those classical authorities founding our Western civilization misled our fathers as our modern culture misleads us today...we demand our cosmic heritage to attune our souls in thrilling to those Celestials from the stars.[49]

Drake's view might be compared with the following passage by Leslie from *Flying Saucers Have Landed* which shows us Desmond Leslie's vital inspirations at the time: "...it comes as a rather painful shock to any who rashly peruse the more ancient literature of races that perished tens of thousands of years ago, to find a strong suggestion that there existed previously not one, but several humanities greater, wiser, more moral, and more advanced in certain aspects of natural science than ourselves. Now what, in the name of this Age of Darkness and Superstition, has all this got to do with flying saucers?

"I think it has lot to do with it.

"Can you see, in imagination, a highly developed being in his space vehicle uttering the correct vibration which will make the propelling forces obey and thrust him through the void to out atmosphere? He uses gentle, harmonious forces that do not push and shove and heave and rend. And when we have won a little more true knowledge we may be able to do likewise; at the moment we have only learned how to kick things out of the way."

Publisher Werner Laurie certainly took a risk. The first manuscript pages of *Flying Saucers Have Landed* could not have looked very promising. The first part, Book 1, contains a trumpeting and rather pretentious Foreword, and a Note, which mentions the works of H.P. Blavatsky and Annie Besant. Daunting names, with Annie Besant almost unknown in Britain and Blavatsky viewed as a formidable and dangerous woman rumored to be a complete impostor. The titles of their works mentioned by Leslie must have been even more off-putting: *Secret Doctrine* by Blavatsky, and *Man, Where, Whence, and Whither?* by Besant. Book 2, by Adamski himself looked even more risky as it contained a description of an actual contact with a space "god" who stepped out of a flying saucer!

But in those long-gone days, just before television took the larger part of the reading public away, editors could afford to take risks, and the gamble worked. Most probably it was the more user-friendly titles of the separate parts of Book 1 that started the 17 shillings and sixpences flowing. In the harsh British winter of 1953, half-crowns and ten-bob notes flowed into bookshop tills that looked like small juke-boxes and which rang bells and clacked like large Victorian typewriters. But after all, facing a 1953 winter with coal shortages, ration-books, all able youth in uniform, and the increasing threat of nuclear conflict, what dull soul could resist chapters entitled: "The Flying Saucer Museum," "Flying Saucers Before The Flood," "Power and the Great Pyramid," and "The First Space Ship on

Record"? For those still unconvinced, there was "Saucers in Celtic Prehistory," "Saucers in Sanskrit," and the fascinating question "Are Vimanas Flying Saucers?" "Vimanas" being the airborne form of the Hindu god-chariots, no less. It all made a change from listening to "talks" on the BBC Light Program, which broadcast the traditional British radio fare about vicars, bicycles, and last year's carpet slippers. *Flying Saucers Have Landed* could also be read while looking forward with infinite patience to the first black and white television sets becoming available, when vicars, bicycles, and carpet-slippers and other British wonders might actually be seen in all their glory.

Thus for 1953, *Flying Saucers Have Landed* was a somewhat advanced prototype multi-dimensional text and with a quite original and refreshing transatlantic feel to it. A thread links two narrators of differing nationality, culture and education, across a great gulf of personality, education, and society. Leslie's Book 1 has many dimensions compared with Adamski's Book 2: though it is historical and essentially speculative, it brought together revolutionary and tremendously exciting new views of world history and human culture. This inspired firework display of new ideas was a successful counterpoint to the very simple straightforward telling of an experience by Adamski, who did not claim to be a writer in the fullest sense of the word. This strange combination worked: the reading public of late 1953 put down Graham Green's *The Third Man,* Norman Mailer's *The Naked and the Dead,* James Jones' *From Here to Eternity,* and innumerable War memoirs, and read *Flying Saucers Have Landed.*

In 1953, many were hooked immediately on Leslie's unprecedented mix n' match style, which at times comes near to a kind of literary vision of a much later multi-media age. We have history, and the closely focused present day in terms of a burst of spleen against Dr. Donald Menzel (the prototype for today's super-skeptic Philip Klass). We have a scream about politicians, accusations about a conspiracy of silence, topped up by sightings from those who possessed good sane bourgeois credentials.

Leslie quotes seven well-authenticated UFO sightings published originally by *Time* and *Life* magazine international on the 5th of May 1952. He combined successfully his skilful re-editing of the ideas of Charles Fort[50] with the power of a new prestigious mass-market magazine. The fully referenced information also impressed a very literate readership. The seven sightings Leslie gave as examples were all from groups of well-educated technologists. The first example was to become one of the classic UFO sightings, retold in great detail many times since 1952. At 9:10 pm on the 25th of August 1951, Dr. W.I. Robinson, professor of geology at Texas Technological College, stood chatting to two of his colleagues in the backyard of his Lubbock home in Texas. They were Dr. A.G. Oberg, professor of chemical engineering, and Professor W.L. Ducker, head of the department of petroleum engineering.

On a night which was clear and dark: "Suddenly all three men saw a number of lights race noiselessly across the sky, from horizon to horizon, in a few seconds. They gave the impression of about thirty luminous beads arranged in a crescent shape. A few moments later another similar formation flashed across the night. This time the scientists were able to judge that the lights moved through thirty degrees of arc in a second. A check the next day with the Air Force showed that no planes had been in the area at the time. The scientists agree that in order to explain the silence of the objects, it must be assumed that they were at least 50,000 feet in the air; in which case they were going not 1,800, but 18,000 m.p.h."[51]

Other sightings are given by a leading American astronomer, a group of five technicians from the Office of Naval Research, some technical writers for the aerophysics department of North American Aviation, the captain of a DC3 airliner, and the crew of a B29 bomber over Korea in 1952.

Up to this point in *Flying Saucers Have Landed,* there are no signs of mystical Tibetans, secret doctrines, or sparks of cosmic fire. But they arrive with a vengeance in "Flying Saucers and Sound," "Saucers for a Song," and "Saucers over Atlantis."

All this disparate matching, texture, and direction resulted in a book quite unlike anything written prior to 1953, apart from Charles Fort's 1919 *Book of the Damned,* which has by 1953 become an obscure out-of-print book. Like Fort's book, which has now been rediscovered, *Flying Saucers Have Landed* has the right to claim masterpiece status, with textual planes rather like the distortions of a mediaeval map. There is also the early warning of a "post-modern" nature, that the ordered Cartesian perspectives of Ordnance Survey may almost certainly possess similar distortions. As Charles Fort pointed out, many anomalies of which the UFO is but one variety, live between the folds of such cultural warps as do the banished sea serpents of old maps. These still appear to baffle, hypnotize, and infuriate. This is of course, the traditional fairy role, as pointed out by Jacques Vallee in *Passport to Magonia,*[52] and Patrick Harpur in *Demonic Reality.*[53]

Clara John was the editor for *Flying Saucers Have Landed.* She was certainly a master of her profession. Even though by different and some-times unacknowledged hands, the Notes to each chapter and Bibliography are fully integrated, and refer to one another rather like a prototype com-puter menu. Given two very different writers, and a subject that is moving in all directions at once, securing such a tight organization for the book was no mean achievement. The Notes at the end of each separate Chapter refer to Adamski in the third person, and were almost certainly written by Desmond Leslie for both Books 1 and 2. These Notes also form part of a commentary on the main text which act as a kind of sub-textual stabilizer to Lesley's often wild speculations; they ground him by means of good solid references. Thus the whole editorial apparatus contributes in no small way to the impression of the book as a fascinating mix of ever-vary-ing planes of reference within past, present, and future. Within this mix there is a cross-referenced fine shading between "fact" and "fiction" com-bined with objective references from many authors, both past and present. The Notes to each chapter contain a brilliantly inspired mix of ancient his-tory, contemporary newspaper reports, quotes from mystical tracts and non-Christian religious texts. This was a heady cocktail for Britain in 1953, where some streets were still lit by gas-lamps, some direct-current public mains electricity still existed, and the nearest thing to an avant-guard author was Terence Rattigan.

This technique was lifted by Leslie almost whole and entire from Charles Fort, but to give Leslie his due, in the Foreword he does acknowl-edge his debt to this author. What Leslie did (which Adamski would hard-ly have been capable of) was to take Fort's occasionally cumbersome style and give it a popular update. The result was a reader-friendly streamlining in which John Worral Keely's perpetual motion machine and the mystical power of the Great Pyramid follow breathlessly on the heels of saucer sightings over American atomic weapons establishments.[54]

In a special sense, *Flying Saucers Have Landed* is a book about books. The bibliography alone is a treasure house of lost, forgotten, out-of-print, and abandoned texts of a beleaguered underground culture. Just one of the charming things about Leslie and Adamski's book is the way it sent book-hunters in droves looking for such titles as Alice Bailey's *The Consciousness of the Atom* (1922). Other titles for dedicated bibliophiles included Noah's Ark by W.J. Crow, *Some Human Oddities* by E.J. Dingwall, and *The Self and its Sheathes* by Annie Besant, who was always a sucker for wonderfully unconscious titles. Other books are about the "riddles" of prehistoric Britain, Atlantis, Indian religious mysticism, *The Egyptian Book of the Dead,* and the obligatory "Tibetan" religious teachings. Many of the books mentioned may have been on Adamski's own shelves, including the Theosophical Publishing Society's *The Solar System* by A.E. Powell (1930), and *The Pyramids and Stonehenge* by A.P. Sinnett (1924).

Throughout many generations the ideas in such books had retreated before science and industry like fairies and elves had fled before Christianity. There they remained half-glimpsed forms beyond the outer rim of the cave-mouth fire of the mainstream culture. There, like frozen viruses under polar ice, they waited their opportunity for a climate change. When it came, narrow streams of such obscure and almost forgotten books[55] moved rapidly towards the delta-mouth of Leslie and Adamski's creation as if they were masses of Charles Fort's damned and rejected knowledge under sudden marching orders.

Flying Saucers Have Landed literally reincarnated such fustian material, brushed off its tomb-dust, and introduced it to the brave new world of what we now call image-bites. As such it was one of the first New Age books, and without it such influential books as Bergier and Pauwels' *Morning of the Magicians,* John Michell's *Flying Saucer Vision,* and Robert Anton Wilson's *Iluminatus* would have been impossible. To a large extent, Leslie did what Charles Fort did some forty years previously, but Leslie was a far better salesman. He goes at breakneck speed for almost every piece of whimsy at once, literally showering such gems like free gifts at a supermarket convention. No wonder Leslie got on with Adamski. In essence, the dynamic young ex-fighter pilot was an American *manqué;* there was to be no fustian British thought for him.

Much of the source material used by Desmond Leslie to build a new vision of the world had lain almost unnoticed in mainly limited editions and privately published works, the annals and collections of papers of obscure folk-societies and occult groups, and individual students of all matters eso- teric. The Nazis had looked in these same directions too, and had found power there, but used it for evil and destructive purposes. Many of the peo- ple who were involved in this obscure literary undergrowth were almost unknown 19th and early 20th century scholars or academics. Quite a few of these books were written not by professionals, but by people of private means, many of whom abounded in a very different age to our own. These people were in the main like the optical astronomers of the Nineteenth cen- tury, looking for particular orchid-gardens in a leisurely manner rather than being pressured for results as is the way in our own society.

Therefore rather as Shakespeare used Holinshed, and Chaucer used Plutarch and Boccaccio, Leslie's achievement was not only to bring together this most obscure material, but to synthesize it dramatically, and in his case, relate it all to the modern technological manifestation of the "flying saucer."

In 1954 the British publisher Frederick Muller issued *Flying Saucer From Mars,* an extremely well-written book[56] by Cedric Allingham that included photographs of an Adamski-type saucer, which he said that he had taken near Lossiemouth Scotland on the 18th of February 1954. Allingham shows that he also was influenced by the books of Charles Fort and his work is one of the earliest discussions of *Flying Saucers Have Landed.* He was one of the first to appreciate what Leslie and Adamski were talking about, particularly the connection of Leslie's material from the past with Adamski's "contact" story. *Flying Saucer From Mars* is use- ful again because there is a discussion of some immediate reactions to the publication of *Flying Saucer Have Landed* the previous year. Though the top American scientist Donald Menzel had published the extremely skep- tical *Flying Saucers* in 1953, Menzel didn't stop the idea of saucers just catching the final era of what Allingham calls the " the music hall comedi- ans," who sang of "flying saucers, teapots, and other phenomena." There is perhaps is no single modern phenomenon that is still looked upon as futuristic, yet can be traced back to the time of the "music hall."

Here is Desmond Leslie, writing in the 1970 revised edition of *Flying Saucers Have Landed:* "Ever since the cliche 'flying saucer' was coined, the greatest and most exciting mystery of our age has been automatically reduced to the level of a music hall joke. The comics of Vaudeville and the comedians of State and Science banded together, most successfully, to encourage humanity in its oldest and easiest method of escape—to laugh at what it does not understand."

It is interesting to note that of all people Arthur C. Clarke, writing in the *Journal of the British Interplanetary Society,* made a strong attack on *Flying Saucers Have Landed,* calling it "deplorable," and "a farrago of nonsense." Clarke, then hardly known as the famous fiction writer he would become in later years, thought the photographs were all faked. However, he added: "If flying saucers do turn out to be spaceships Messrs. Leslie and Adamski will have done quite a lot to prevent people of intellectual integrity from accepting the fact." In other words, the tribal chiefs want to get their hands on the cargo first. In another passage Clarke says that the perspectives in the photographs are wrong. But Allingham points out that by that time Leonard Cramp in his classic *Space, Gravity & The Flying Saucer*[57] had shown undoubtedly that the proportions were without a doubt correct. The then young radio astronomer Professor Bernard Lovell (he of later Jodrell Bank fame) suggested that the best thing to do with the complete edition of *Flying Saucers Have Landed* "would be to take it up as ballast in the first space-ship and dump it overboard in space." The reigning Astronomer Royal, Sir Harold Spencer Jones FRS, who wrote an article entitled "Now Bury These Flying Saucers," endorsed this opinion. In this, he said, "it is time the question was closed forever."

By comparison, the review in *The Observer* of the 4th of October 1953 by Charles Davy was intelligent, well-balanced, and left the question of truth or falsehood open. A letter of October 11th from G.G.J. Cooper introduced the question of lampshade similarity. Charles Davy replied: "One might have thought that anyone who wanted to support a tall story with faked photographs would have managed to make them look more plausible—more like an imagined 'space-craft' and less like a lamp."

The material in the longer Book 1 by Leslie quite overwhelmed the provincial and conservative British scientists at the time. Neither the education nor the scholastic background of these very British scientists had prepared them for such wide and original thinking. One can appreciate their difficulty. The harsh public schools of those days and the experience in many cases of two World Wars were experiences enough. By the time of the 1956 Suez disaster, and the utter failure of the first British space program, the aging senior British scientists of Adamski's time belonged to a totally exhausted generation. Given such reactions in Britain, it is strange therefore that interest in *Flying Saucers Have Landed* took root in what appeared to be somewhat infertile soil. But as always, the surface of a society is deceptive. Even in dour Britain, there were live underground streams running rapidly towards the more receptive times of the 1960s.

In the 1950s, interest in occult philosophy, fringe religion, and metaphysics in general was perhaps at its lowest ebb in European history. Many valuable libraries, manuscripts, and much historical material had been destroyed by the two Wars, and the gradual cultural marginalizing of all matters esoteric had been going on since the decline of 19th century spiritualism and the public perception of the behavior of such characters as Aleister Crowley. The young men and women who came out of the armed services and voted against Churchill in the 1945 election formed the rump of a new class whose practical and rational views were mainly left-of-center.

Even those who were not of this political persuasion, nevertheless believed in science and thoroughgoing rationalism as tools with which to construct a new society. Neither Left nor Right wanted anything to do with esoteric matters, which in Britain in particular had never been liked nor understood. To almost all of this generation, the occult was a standing historical joke, hardly entering serious British discussions; at best, it had something to do with Catholics, upper-middle-class eccentrics, tanned faces well south of Calais, or at its worst, it was associated with the Nazi philosophy of mystical racism. With Crowley and Blavatsky long booed off the cultural stage, the talk after 1945 was of economics and socialism, of "realism," and the demystification and demythologizing of elite social structures and antiquated Victorian ideology.

The first phase of this decision to change experience as received was brilliantly successful. In Britain, there arose the Welfare State, a quite revolutionary concept of socialism and society. It seemed that in the face of this achievement alone, applied scientific thinking was indeed historically triumphant, and many of the old ghosts sowing historical and philosophical confusion had been banished forever.

But the deeper reason for the success of *Flying Saucers Have Landed* was that many utilitarian rationalists still had bad dreams. The problem was the Nuremberg trials of 1945. It was impossible to describe Nazi crimes by conventional legal concepts. The events as examined could not be rationalized, could indeed be called hardly "criminal" at all. There was therefore hesitancy on behalf of the prosecution (exploited by the still defiant, if somewhat deflated, Goering) for two reasons. The first difficulty was that most of those on trial appeared to be genuinely bewildered by what had happened, as if they were coming out of a dream. The second was that as the trial proceeded, it became very clear that a highly astute native German intelligentsia (including some men of genius such as Walter Heisenberg), had been involved in forming an operational ideology that had caused the death of over 30 million people.

Plainly, what was on trial was not violence as conventionally accepted. The Fabian utilitarianism of even brilliant men such as QC Hartley Shawcross hardly equipped them to examine motive, when that motive involved intellectual corruption of an order whose scientific "objectivity" was a new kind of demonology, although previously Churchill, with his usual far-sighted vision had described Nazis science as "perverted." Perverted it was, if only because it justified the sort of medical experimentation on human beings that can hardly be described, and that was quite invisible to the normal processes of Law. Such a thing was also invisible to the normal processes of historical examination as expressed by traditional academic historians such as Trevor Roper or Alan Bullock, with their extremely limited social-democratic view, and even the far more venturesome William Manchester and William Shirer, who both thoroughly despised metaphysics. Concrete empirical methods were no tools for analyzing an inspirational force that passed through all moral walls as easily as Strontium 90, which by the time of Nuremberg, was steadily entering the bones of both the guilty and the innocent alike.

This feeling of unease as the Nazis were tried and hanged almost as simple-minded horse-thieves, was a justification for Desmond Leslie to take a second look at esoteric matters that had long since been thought historically dead. Though it was certainly not directly intended as such, *Flying Saucers Have Landed* can now be seen as part of a counter-culture reaction against Marxism and the puritanical terrors of the beginnings of the Cold War in Europe. Both Right and Left were against all free creative imagination, whatever form it took. Though the Nazis accepted the power of imagination via Wagner and Neitzsche, they perverted it, while the Communists attempted to destroy it utterly. Thus like *Alice in Wonderland, Flying Saucers Have Landed* has an implicit political background.

Though Leslie lacked Charles Fort's depth, range, and literary skill, he had nevertheless an ability to combine complex irony with bizarre humor. Other highly influential books such as *Morning of the Magicians* and the books of Brinsley Le Poer Trench were inspired by Leslie's achievement in turning obscure folklore into modern cultural dynamite. The whole approach in *Flying Saucers Have Landed* is bright, lively, and most informative, though the book lacks Fort's poorly hidden political anger and bitterness at non-recognition of his undoubted genius. Certainly it struck a brilliant light in those depressing pre-1960s days, which were a kind of "no-man's land" between the end of World War 2 and the far happier world of the 1960s.

Although sophisticated books on UFOs such *Flying Saucers Are Real* by the American writer Donald Keyhoe had begun to appear in 1950, Leslie's approach attached the saucer phenomenon to history and the development of ideas. This was something that Keyhoe, as a very dour and practical ex-Marine pilot, was not inclined to do. He rejected all contactee claims as outrageous lies, and threw Adamski out of the group he headed, the National Investigations Committee on Aerial Phenomena.

Leslie's book was also much more dramatically appealing than *The Riddle of the Flying Saucers,* the first British book on flying saucers by Gerald Heard published in 1950. Heard's otherwise intelligent and interesting account is marred by his theory that the crews of the flying saucers were nothing less than intelligent bees! Believing this, Heard, unlike Desmond Leslie, could hardly include contact stories or abductions. For the same reason, he could include no historical background, and the reaction to the suggestion that the pyramids were built by super-intelligent bees can be imagined. These were just a few of the reasons why in comparison, *Flying Saucers Have Landed* became by far the better seller. This tells us something about humanity in general and avid buyers of such books in particular: abductions by humanoid forms perhaps, but by bright bees, no!

At the end of Leslie's Chapter 20, "The First Spaceship on Record," the time is ripe for the entry of one of the most celebrated White Rabbits of the 20th century, one George Adamski. After quoting from the Brahmin Tables, Desmond Leslie gives George a build-up straight out of *Ben Hur:* "I now hand over the tale to George Adamski, who is the first to be able to give us a documentary record of his experiences and impressions on coming face to face with a man from another planet. Adamski was not afraid when he saw the shining vehicle come down, nor when the tremendous realization burst upon him that he was standing face to face with a living spiritual being, a man like ourselves, a human brother from another globe of existence.

"And so we who are of the same flesh and mould as Adamski can look up with joy, rather than fear, when from time to time other fragments; other people; Sparks from the same FLAME, flash for a moment into the orbit of our perception, knowing that, like ourselves, they are working out the full lesson of their worlds in the slow, aenonic, struggling ascent towards union in the Central Mystic Sun."

Finally, the man himself comes on stage: "I am George Adamski, philosopher, student, teacher, saucer researcher. My home is Palomar Gardens on the southern slopes of Mount Palomar, California, eleven miles from the big Hale Observatory, home of the 200-inch telescope..."

In contrast to Leslie's florid descriptions and often quite breathless enthusiasm, is Adamski's almost monosyllabic style. Such a contrast had hardly been achieved before in one book, at least with such aplomb. The cool and calm nature of Adamski's entrance (after such an introduction), comes as a pleasant surprise. Expecting some kind of crazy monster of a mad eccentric, instead we encounter a home and a life; we meet friends and acquaintances. Again, in contrast to Leslie, we meet many folk of differing opinions. Present is the landscape and atmosphere of the California mountain communities; there are cameos of its life and characters; its weather, climate, and atmosphere are well drawn.

From the very beginning Adamski raises an almost aboriginal sense of something about to happen in this region of the world. And UFOs apart, after 1945, something tremendous did happen. From Los Alamos to Los Angeles, there developed what was tantamount to a new Renaissance in culture and scientific thinking. Brains drained off from bone-headed traditional cultures whose speed of thinking was at the rate of cavalry before the advent of the tank.

The bizarre contrast of personality, background and style of the two authors is surprisingly effective. The Adamski experiences come over as an intense personal dramatization of one of the historical periods described previously by Leslie. The result is a surprisingly successful unity: read Adamski and you have to take Leslie with you, and vice versa. It creates an intriguing tension in the reader; the ideological jumps of Leslie we can handle, but the physical jumps of Adamski, well, perhaps we are not nearly so sure.

But Adamski writes surprisingly well. His voice is clear and extremely matter-of-fact. He was obviously a stable person, almost devoid of hysteria, depression, or the schizoid-tensions of fundamentalist believers. When he describes his first contact with what he believed was a man from an extraterrestrial spaceship, the mystic in him is awed into silence, and his description is plain and naturalistic, deft, and most careful. His point-of-view is outward looking; he mentions people and places by way of illustration; there are meetings with a wide social range, and opinions are exchanged. He travels, corresponds, and has good personal relationships. He has, for the most part, a balanced temper and a patient and scholarly disposition. He lived very happily within a busy commune-style society, of which almost all spoke well of him; neither does he appear to be devious or secretive.

Thus there is no psychological base for saying that Adamski was the kind of unscrupulous fraud he has been accused of being by many who have not given him his proper due. He was simply not complicated enough for the kind of sophisticated multi-dimensional duplicity involving many photographs and films of what would certainly have had to have been extremely sophisticated electromechanical models. Neither was he technically devious enough to accomplish the simultaneous and complete deception of no less than six witnesses to his initial desert contact. We must take note here of a good rule derived from Charles Fort, and not make any explanations more fantastic than the thing they are trying to explain. However, by his description of the desert contact, we can see the source of the problems that were to plague Adamski for twenty years, and bring him near to poverty and despair. He was simply an absolutely appalling optimist, and a rather camp sentimentalist to boot, amongst other things.

But he related a tale that the world was never to forget.

CHAPTER 5

Orthon's Shoes and Mr. Silas Newton

F*lying Saucers Have Landed* does not end with Adamski's story of the original desert contact on the 20th of November 1952. Both the Postscript and Appendix contain a mix of mad comedy and intrigue, and the latter contains unexploded bombs, some of which have only just detonated after ticking away for half a century.

The Postscript certainly sounds as if it was written by Adamski. It gives an account of the prevailing situation regarding the interpretation of the marks on the soles of Orthon's shoes, of which plaster casts were made by George Hunt Williamson at the time of the desert encounter. As ever Adamski is wonderfully unconscious of himself as a human being. He says without the least hint of comic irony that great efforts have been made to interpret these marks, as well as the strange writing on the photograph whose frame was dropped from the spaceship's porthole on the 13th of December 1952. And he adds without the slightest blush: "I learn that not one of the workers feels within himself that he has been fully successful in learning the messages to be passed to Earth men."

It takes some nerve to initiate a crazy game of interpreting the marks made by the shoe-soles of a being who claims he came from Venus in a flying saucer. It must have taken even more nerve to believe in it himself, as Adamski did, certainly. Though his sense of humor was not all that strong, it is difficult to believe that he did not smile to himself on occasion as he introduced this game to the world, and sat back and watch the world work on it. The mad metaphysical comedy he created in three dimensions is straight from the pages of Joyce or Sterne, with a touch of Edward Lear. Had the whole thing consisted of such, then at least we would have had a classic that could have been put on the shelf alongside *Ulysses* or *Tristram Shandy*.

But *Flying Saucers Have Landed* was a book that refused to be put into a passive role. Part of its appeal was that it was a fabric of living expression more than a simple text that could be hung on some "literary" wall as a decoration. It took from an out-dated context what some saw as traditional fairy stories and placed them centrally in fighter-cockpits and returns from aerial radar. It therefore made the fantastic haunt the glistening new instrumentation of the post-war age, connecting ancient sightings with modern rocketry and spaceflight, and ancient mysteries with contemporary scientific speculation. To add to this considerable achievement, month after month scores of "objective" verifications of the claims of the book were appearing in the outer world like a kind of supertext springing from its inked pages.

Thus with increasing sightings of UFOs themselves, the book was being updated as it was read and absorbed. Adamski's deft style helped this assimilation. Its disarming effect was ideal for leading readers up that garden path which is the entrance to the drama of Orthon's shoes. The following passage from the Postscript, for instance, is naïf Borges: "...the footprints with their markings, and a photo of the dropped print with its markings is being included here, with a partial list of suggested books, including the dictionary which gives very modern definitions of the individual marking as they are named in mathematics, astronomy, and other sciences."

No one appears to have noticed, but as a sideline, on the evidence of the above, George Adamski appears to have invented Trivial Pursuit!

The intellectual eroticism of all this delicious insanity was quite irresistible. With books flying into the sky and back, and dictionaries being brought in to shed light on shoe-soles, the Orwellian machinery predictably turned its head from screaming about communist dangers, and chanted automated denials about the flying saucer phenomenon. But it was no good. Like all good subversives, the saucers turned up in strength and in places where they were least expected.

During his tour of Europe in 1959 Adamski showed a film of the development of a "gravity-canceling"[58] motor said to have been made from interpretations of the "instructions" on the back of Orthon's shoes. A certain Basil Van Den Berg, a South African engineer, claimed that he had successfully constructed such a motor. When interviewed by South

African writer Philip J. Human (sic), Van Den Berg showed an impressive folder full of calculations and blueprints, and also some mechanical parts. He claimed to have been inspired by a man from Venus who visited him at night, and to have seen through a magnifying glass that the marks on the boots were holographic. This effect was visible even on a copy that Adamski had sent to him at his request. Major governments were interested in Van Den Berg's device; Mexico, for instance, offered him unlimited money and resources, but like many such an inventor, Van Den Berg disappeared never to be seen again.

Even the Appendix of *Flying Saucers Have Landed* does not let up. It consists of a description of an official USAF "briefing" in a Quonset hut with, among others, a confidence crook, a magnetic mystic, the author of a famous book on flying saucers, and the cameraman who filmed *The Ten Commandments,* no less! As Cecil B. De Mille himself might have said, could we ask for more?

Adamski is very much the shadow-guest at this conference. He threads through the lives of the main guests in one way or another. The heading is worth quoting in full:

Meeting at Veteran's Administration Bldg., Quonset T-26.
1 June 1953.
Air Force Reserve Officers.
Object-Briefing on flying saucer activity.
Led by Al. Chop, former Public Relations Head for Project Flying Saucer for Air Corps, Washington, D.C., also Public Relations Head for Pentagon having to do with release of all publicity and official statements re flying saucers.
Meeting for purpose of briefing these officers on known facts re flying saucer phenomena and to instruct officers on kind of information and observation the Air Force is seeking.

The date of June 1st, 1953, puts this "briefing" smack between Adamski's desert encounter of November 20, 1952 and the publication of the British edition of *Flying Saucers Have Landed* in late 1953. But Adamski was not at this conference (he is referred to in the third person) and neither was Leslie. Therefore a reader does not know who wrote this

Appendix, or what sources (other than memory) were used in its compilation. It sounds very much like an eyewitness account, and written up by someone who knew his or her job. Frank Scully was certainly there, and he could have given a written report to his friend Adamski for inclusion in Adamski's forthcoming book, whose publication must have been common knowledge by this time. If Scully did such a thing, then he had to do it very quickly because Adamski's manuscript had to make its way across the Atlantic almost immediately in time for Werner Laurie to include the report on this meeting as an Appendix. But again, if it was written by Scully, it is odd that he was not credited, as the inclusion of the name of this well-known author could well have increased the sales of *Flying Saucers Have Landed.*

For a "briefing" for "Air Force Reserve Officers," Quonset hut T-26 certainly contains an odd bunch, even by Scully-Adamski standards. One Harold Sherman is there, described as a "metaphysical teacher and lecturer." Harold was a "channeler," this being a receiver of psychic messages. He belonged to a council of "elders" who were connected to U.S. "contactee" circles at this time, and who held meetings at Giant Rock.[59] One Harry Myers, an "Instructor, Hollywood High School," is present, together with Gene Dorsey, a "Hollywood business man."

If all these people were indeed "Air Force Reserve Officers," then we have here an intriguing view of the air defense personnel of America at this time!

Giving a marvelously American touch to the proceeding is no less a person than the aforementioned cameraman, Pevernell ("Pev") Marley, who was married to Linda Darnell, a famous Hollywood film actress of the time. Marley had been a combat cameraman during World War II, and he showed some of Adamski's photographs to Al Chop. Marley is quoted in reported speech, as saying: "Adamski's pictures, if faked, were the cleverest he had ever seen, rivaling a Houdini. Marley pointed out that the shadows on these saucers, and also on the ground, corresponded to such a remarkable degree that they could not be faked, and that to fake such pictures would require costly equipment which Adamski, obviously, does not possess and which, even then, could not assure such a result."

Jim Moseley's October 1957 special "Adamski expose" issue of *Saucer News* contains the following comments by Moseley about this meeting: "Mr. Al Chop, who, it has been noted, is quoted at length in the appendix (sic) of the book, told me (Jim Moseley) in a personal interview that he is misquoted, and that he has considered suing Mr. Adamski because of this fact. Similarly, in a phone conversation with me, Pev Marley denied having made the statements attributed to him, and also denied the rumor, circulated by Adamski and a few of his admirers, that Marley had blown up one of the Adamski 'scout ship' photos and, found, in the blow up, the head of a man looking out of one of the 'portholes.' "

This kind of ufological Punch-and-Judy show still runs on its metalloid ways of time past and time future. With regard to heads out of portholes, Adamski himself replied, in *Gray Barker's Book of Adamski,* to a correspondent who claimed that he could see faces in the portholes of one of the ships shown in one of Adamski's photographs. Adamski says, perhaps tongue in cheek, that in his opinion, these heads are in the correspondent's imagination! Thus we have almost-heads almost looking out of almost-portholes in what some people say are almost-photographs. It is the "almost" component here which is far more interesting than any old iron-age "truth" or "falsehood."

These head-and-porthole sketches of fragile human concepts are pieces of pudding thrown out of the nursery windows of human consciousness. Where and upon whom they land is anybody's guess. The trouble is that the grown-up concepts of quarks and Big Bangs are equally good dumplings, and they most probably come from those same mad and unhygienic nursery-kitchens that serve up all human certainty as *bombe superb.*

Somewhere in the pushes and pulls of these intermediate states[60] is the mystery of the UFO. Perhaps the terrible truth is that since humanity at large can act in a way that is as daft as the proverbial brush, then we can well expect other conscious life forms to be just as crazy as we are. Our puny instrumentation will not register that, of course. Any alien phenomenon may have a thriving entertainment culture running alongside, or even replacing a techno-scientific one. That is just one shock we will probably have to brace ourselves for should contact be made. To be revealed as mere toys on a screen would not do wonders for our ego. We may not be offered up for slavery, exploitation, experimentation, or even food.

We may just be used as a joke.

Perhaps the most fantastic character present at the briefing is one Silas Mason Newton, the "magnetic expert" mentioned in Scully's book. Thanks to the research of writer Karl Pflock, we now know a lot more about Newton, who was a friend of Pev Marley, and whom Pflock reveals as "one of the great unsung con-men" of the 20th century. Newton was in the Adamski loop, and he most probably conned Frank Scully over the alleged Aztec crash. In December 1952, due to *True* magazine's revelations about his activities, Newton was arrested by the Colorado authorities and charged with fraud. In December 1953, six months after Chop's briefing, he was convicted, and could therefore possibly have read a first edition of *Flying Saucers Have Landed* from his prison cell.

Newton was thus between the Devil and the deep blue sea at the time of this briefing. However, true to his doubtful profession, he appears relaxed he as he corrects Chop when Chop replies to Marley saying that if Adamski got photographs of UFOs, then Palomar should have got them too. Newton points out that the Palomar telescope could not cover the low-altitude areas covered by Adamski's instrument. He adds that, in his opinion, the flight of the saucers is along the San Andreas fault-line and these vehicles are utilizing the earth's magnetic field as a form of motive power.

Newton was a clever and sophisticated individual with both humor and vision. He certainly had enough nerve to play the UFO game for all it was worth and see where the game led. But perhaps in doing this, he got more than he bargained for.

On July 11th, 1998, Pflock met an anonymous source who handed him 27 pages of lined paper "torn from a bound journal or school copy book" on which was a spidery handwriting.[61] The source said that this was Newton's hand, and dated from the last years of Newton's life in the early 1970s. The source added that Pflock could read the manuscript in his presence, take notes, but not make a copy. On a later occasion, Pflock compared the manuscript with the handwriting on Newton's will and they were identical. Newton says that the whole Aztec story[62] in Scully's book was a hoax initiated by him and others. The reason for this hoax was apparently to try and get a whole lot of new investment interests in claimed bits and pieces of stolen alien technology from crashed ships. Interested parties would be told that this technology could locate oil.

But as his tale continues, Newton realized that he had unwittingly aroused interest sectors quite beyond his expectations.

Sometime during the year 1950, two men visited his office. They claimed that they were with a "highly secret" government agency. They laughingly poked holes in Newton's saucer stories, but told him to continue his storytelling, as it just might help him with his legal problems. According to Pflock, taking evidence from the manuscript before him, Newton took this to mean two things: "…the big brass had something they wanted to hide and my game would help them to do it. Those fellows sure wanted me to think it was a real saucer and I did think it was and still do."

Newton was of the opinion that since the FBI deferred to state and local authority, he was helped by the mysterious organization the men said they represented.

The last time Newton saw these two men was on December 9th, 1953. They again asked him to stick to his saucer story. Newton responds: "I told them I knew there was something to all that flying saucer business and I was so sure I would keep using it. What I did not say was that I could see plenty of opportunities for games to work with fellows like Adamski and the others. Sure, I would play along."

This kind of thing was what made an essential part of Adamski's life rather like an echoing canyon built of stories.

Authentic modern mysticism[63] is now hardly to be found in established religions. The churches, rather like a major portion of the literary and arts sector, separated from the technological culture long ago and lost the game of intermediate states. Secular mysticism is found in such fleeting sprites as those seen by Adamski, summoned almost by some enactment of metaphor alone. Pale transients, like Woody Derenberger's Mr. Indrid Cold, or John Keel's Princess Moon Owl, or Adamski's Orthon, appear to come from paper-thin temporary almost-worlds. As characters, they are like a painting by numbers with some of the numbers missing, just like a text file that has been stored in the wastebin of a hard-disc for some time. Like Keat's Psyche of his poem of that name, many of these part-forms don't appear to have enough energy to keep up the schedule of proper world-appearances, and die as disintegrating systems-doodles. Like Keat's Psyche again, they are possibly intercultural, not interstellar, that is if the concept of interstellar is not intercultural in the first place.

Western thinking in general has great difficulty with these intermediate forms and partial states of being. Such an order of matter is excluded (rather than unknown) from science, banished to those far regions (either microscopic or interstellar) where rationalists always locate their mysteries, if only to daunt inquisitive heathens, the uninitiated, and, of course, the great partly-washed.

But the spiritually aware would also like their mysteries far-off, at some similar conceptual distance, held in some Hindu or Tibetan fastness; there they can be romanticized and managed. But rationalists and mystics both do not like unbelievable things in the air immediately above an Air Force Base. In that embarrassing situation things have got beyond all control, and that would never do.

CHAPTER 6

Cargo Perspectives

In the pre-Internet age that Adamski lived in, it would have been difficult to conceive of the UFO phenomenon as a species of live viral information using all the tricks of metaphor-screens in order to stay in business for as long as it could. Ideas of Artificial Intelligence developed since the 1950s have given us today an intriguing idea of what an alien "intelligence" might be like.

The African stick insect knows how to imitate the rhythmic march of a line of termites in order to avoid annihilation. It knows that this coded rhythm governs all dimensions and shades of its enemy's psychosocial cognition. It knows also that time will eventually run out; there will be noticed something slightly odd about the information-matching of its false march, and it had better move fast whenever a good opportunity presents itself.

Similarly, the UFO phenomenon as a species of information most likely creates a partial-objectivity to stay in business for as long as it can. Like the stick insect, Orthon's "task" may have been to create and hard sell a certain kind of wonder as screen for whatever were his complex intentions. Any downtown salesman would understand. As performers, "they" or "it" (and we may even have to eliminate even this differentiation), need an audience for whatever purpose. As Harvard psychiatrist John Mack, UFO abduction expert Budd Hopkins, and experiencer and novelist Whitley Streiber have pointed out, with the UFO we are dealing with an animal whose make-up is of such subtle evolving part-fictions as to smash all our conceptions of what an advanced intelligent lifeform may be. There may indeed have occurred evolution to a mere part-disembodied tissue of information.

In this sense, "contact" may indeed be an experience that transcends all and every notion of biological, anthropological, and indeed genetic prediction and expectation. In all likelihood therefore one of our biggest mistakes in searching for "alien" life may be that we expect "them" to possess a serious and straightforward WASP intention. That "advanced" beings might not see us as threatening so much as comic, would be psychologically devastating. In the colonial past, we gave natives top hats, umbrellas, and whisky and watched them dance. It could possibly be that given evolution, seriousness itself has become a Darwinian casualty.

This would certainly disturb those humans of sober mien and proper expectation. The highest level of information imparted by aliens thus far supports this idea. We might have to live with the intellectually uncomfortable idea that a peculiar something may not be so much deceiving as trying to make good guesses, and making an unwittingly comic hash of it. If this is the case, then we should rejoice: *they* might have their own comedians, and their own mistakes, and that would make the "aliens" really interesting!

Rather than being "true" or "false" (these being old industrial divisions prior to the thousand-channel society), a theory of catastrophic guessing would explain why most of the information imparted by "alien" entities would hardly do credit to an off-peak commercial break. We shouldn't be in the least surprised at such a thought. After all, we have done it to others in similar ways. It is the height of intellectual optimism to think that the compliment will not be returned. Instead of serious creatures of traditional sci-fi, we may encounter something guessing, laughing, and deceiving, rather than something physically violent. Science fiction and fantasy films usually avoid that possibility because it is not very complimentary to our warrior consciousness. The macho ego is least equipped to deal with that. "They" may even be blushing, just as we ourselves did when we sent a plaque into infinite space showing a naked man and a woman with no pubic hair, and no genitals at all shown on the female! What missing bits we may be sent in return is anybody's guess.

We may have to face the idea that in asking for and expecting profundity and high seriousness, that those concepts themselves might well have vanished through differing levels of cosmic evolution, just as they are vanishing rapidly from our own multi-media society. For aliens, the idea of such complex play might well have replaced any labor-intensive goal-oriented linear "progression." Thus "contact" might well smash all our rationally oriented and scientifically informed work-ethic paradigms at a stroke.

In this Internet age, we may well have to extend our idea of a life form far beyond cells and molecules and conceive of the flow and counter-flow of information itself as a form of life. Assuming that such an artificially structured process as "contact" will be democratic and politically correct is the height of bourgeois intellectual optimism. Just as our own so-called "real" intelligence, such a pseudo-intelligence, in imitation of the basic laws of verisimilitude, might mock and mimic, confuse, and deceive for the almost-preservation of its pseudo-life. Indeed, just as does our canny stick insect, it might well manufacture quasi-objectivity, made up of almost-substance of the almost-event. Should anyone not know just exactly what all that means, then they should pay more attention to the evening news on television,[64] or examine the quasi-objectivity of the Y2K fiasco, or the equally "virtual events" of the recent British and American National elections. Like the Gulf war, none of these "events" have the traditional "solidity" of the old industrial world.

Thus the idea of some extraterrestrial creature "sending" most serious messages across "intergalactic space" by fiddling with electromagnetic apparatus is a delicious Victorian idea. It was perfect for the age of great lighthouses. Our own universal use of the present tense when referring to cosmic events might well amuse the UFO phenomenon enough imitate such an elemental crudity as signaling, if only for momentary amusement, such as touching a spider's web to see the spider run out, no doubt puzzled at the absence of dinner. George Adamski's rather old-fashioned idea of a chummy colonial-style greeting might well hide such a joke.

Distancing Adamski's best expectancies, let us imagine for a moment a Polynesian island in the early 1900s. A longboat pushes ashore from a three-stacker tramp steamer. It does not contain Marx and Freud, Tennyson or Dickens, all bearing the glories of the 19th century. The island, if it is lucky, gets a psychopathic Boson, a mad Cook, a crippled Mate, and a couple of young Portsmouth deck-boys both with sore hindquarters. This motley crew will want water, fruit, vegetables, and women and fresh boys, though not necessarily in that order. After that, they will burn the entire place down as a gesture of we know not what.

We have also to bear in mind that for hundreds of years a standard procedure to clear hostile natives off landing beaches was for crew to wear bizarre masks and strange clothing. Richard Hakluyt (1552-1616) reports crews as saying that after they did that, in most cases, no natives were seen within miles of the landing. Later crews in sleeker ships than those known to Hakluyt tell that these disguises gave them great negotiating power over those few natives who were daring enough to approach. Of course such contacts would possibly not be repeated for many generations. Ships of a different design again would call, this time full of a very different "kind" of men, some of a very different skin color and race, and who did not wear the "false" masks whose images had by this time gone deep into tribal oral and artistic traditions.

The kind of moral, behavioral, and psychological confusions experienced by Adamski would all be experienced by natives of this earlier epoch, together with similar deep religious convictions and "cargo-cult" expectations. Even within our own time, within Melanesian tribes, some of these utterly confused beliefs have proved impossible to eradicate or "explain." Since the Resurrection alone can hardly be "explained" even to ourselves, Christian missionary zeal adds (and is still adding) yet more mythological confusion. We would be very silly to assume that such confusion could not be sown amongst ourselves in turn. They could be the very cause of the kind of cultural uncertainty the "advanced" West is experiencing at the present time.

If we read *abductions* for slavery, then we put our modern concerns and ourselves in a most plausible framework.

In this respect, George Adamski's hopeless romanticism did not serve his contact situation well. When he meets Orthon, the precise and healthy objectivity with which he opens Book 2 of *Flying Saucers Have Landed* melts into multiple fantasies and confusions about the planet Venus, and the dangers of the atomic bomb. He is not in the least suspicious of the man from "Venus" who according to Adamski communicated by hand-signals and telepathy. Adamski is quite overcome; he speaks of the "beautiful waves" of Orthon's hair, "glistening more beautifully than any woman's." The last thing in his mind is the idea that something or someone has made a damn good guess at what might appeal to his fundamentally bisexual character.

In accepting all this, Adamski reveals that he was a tragic innocent. He simply is not in any way aware of the difficulties of the quadruple-takes that can occur in translating complex ideas between different levels of Earth culture, never mind possible alien societies. To trust the waving of arms (and alleged "telepathy" in the bargain) so literally and precisely as Adamski does, contains far more risks than say, trying to translating the "Friends" TV series into Eskimo. A bottle of brown HP sauce on a Blackpool boarding-house table in the North of England is a symbol that is the entry to an entire universe; how do we begin to translate such a thing to a Turkish fisherman, still less a Peruvian herdsman? An interesting consideration is that if Adamski were practicing a deception, he would surely not have left himself and his actions so open to ridicule. A more devious man would have cleaned up the entire act, and made it more convincing. The highest probability is that a man who so willingly risks making himself the laughing-stock of an entire civilization is telling it how he saw it.

This is just one example of the kind of game that snared Adamski. These things make the whole of his experience rather like an early three-dimensional model of a "web" world in which old-fashioned space and time have been replaced by a gaming information-flow. In this medium, "up and down" and "truth and falsehood" have been replaced by the kind of scale of hard and soft fantasies, as portrayed by the film, *The Matrix*. There are those scientists who think that a really advanced "intelligence" might well exist in a semi-disembodied game-world in which that old industrial analogue we called "objective reality" might be replaced eventually by virtual simulations. Fifty years after this contact we are in a much better position to understand how an apparently serious and profound experience is just as much a series of double-takes, screen flashes, and cultural advertisements as is any other kind of experience, including the so-called "objective" scientific experience.

During the Second World War, the natives of the Melanesian islands built decoy airstrips in the bush, complete with bamboo radio shacks sporting wooden aerials to receive messages regarding delivery of goods, that is "cargo." Often GI radio commands such as "Roger, out" were preserved as an oral tradition, and telephones made of white flowers became the objects of ritual obsession. On many Pacific islands, the ejected wing-tanks from World War II fighters became objects of veneration, as did B 29 propellers and even tins of jam left behind in abandoned USAF stores. Research anthropologists also report that fragments from ancient US Army rations are still used as a kind of host in "cargo-cult" ceremonies.[65]

What are we to think of the designs on Orthon's shoe soles, knowing that happened?

Stuart Swezey, writing in the *Amok Journal*,[66] comments on the reaction of Melanesian natives to the sight of black American troops on active service towards the end of World War II: "These black men could operate the radio transmitters which beckoned the falling cargo from the ancestors and seemed to the oppressed islanders to be dealing with the white man confidently, and on equal terms. *Life* magazines brought by the GIs contained photographic proof that in America people lived surrounded by refrigerators and cars in the kind of consumer paradise that the islanders had been striving so far unsuccessfully to obtain."

These observations provide an intriguing view of Adamski's comically confusing claims about the "fertile" planet Venus. They also make us suspect that our iron age "fact versus fiction" differentiations may eventually become largely meaningless. In *Inside the Spaceships,* on one of Adamski's trips into outer space, Ramu, who has spoken English from the very start (what we would give to hear the accent!), describes a city on the moon. This is a perfect "cargo" picture: "We have to construct a few hangers near the cities for convenience in landing with the supplies we bring to the population here—everything not available locally for their needs. In exchange, they furnish us with certain minerals found on the moon."

This trading-mechanical view of the activities of what is most probably a super-intelligence do not so much prove Adamski wrong as being his way of trying to interpret what he is seeing in comprehensible terms. We might compare Edward Rice's transcription[67] of a Melanesian "interpretation": "Before the war an American was hauled very high in the sky in a net. He came to Vila. He spoke American wisdom. We didn't understand what he means, true or untrue. He stood on something white, like a plate. In a minute, two minutes, he went to America. We didn't know his name, but we called him Nabnab, Mr. Nabnab, which means fire, Because always, he's just playing with volcano smoke at Tanna. When the wind blows that cloud somewhere, he's just sitting up on that cloud."

Any contact with a different kind of intelligence will show such distortions, if only because all thinking is constructed of such projections. A Melanesian native does not "see" a tiny computer chip with 32 legs any more than we do not "see" a moon with cities on it. Anyone who has ever been a professional teacher at any time will know that trying to make certain people see what they are not mentally capable of seeing is a daunting experience. That richness of connection that enables conscious recognition of a spectrum of resources varies greatly. We have a complex technological and scientific culture built on the mysteries of magnetism, electricity, and radiation, the fundamental nature of which remains completely unknown. No matter how we try therefore we surely cannot help recognizing that what we live amongst are mental structures most of which are certainly as comic as Mr. Nabnab.

Adamski exhibits a kind of Old Testament literal acceptance of the situation he was undoubtedly faced with. He is not in the least suspicious or frightened when on their very first contact Orthon admits to him that humans have been abducted, just as were slaves in the past. This violation of human rights does not seem to worry either himself or Orthon; the golden glow and the overall feeling of wisdom and clear cosmic certainty remain. Neither does it occur to Adamski that he might be in very grave danger, although he gets a hint of trouble when he touches the rim of the ship and is badly shocked as if by contact with a high voltage.

After all these years, the truth about the Adamski experience is becoming gradually more clear. It was almost certainly the classic cargo-cult situation, with humanity for once in the "inferior" position. This of course no more denies the "reality" of Orthon to Adamski any more than it denies the "reality" of the black troops to the Melanesian natives. As Harvard psychiatrist John Mack has pointed out, to Westerners "contact" would represent "a Narcissistic blow of unimaginable proportions" that the ego would do anything to avoid, even when faced with undeniable evidence. That may well be the best single reason for not only the subsequent cover-ups, but also for many of Adamski's confusions that disappointed many on his very last tour of Europe in 1963, which was not a happy event for him. On that tour, he was asked in understandable human cartoon fashion, what Orthon was going to do next, when would he contact again, and where was he now? He was in the impossible position of natives asking (many years after World War II) just *when* the B29 Superfortresses were going to return to the island with free tins of US Army rations.

The natives were not in the least bit interested in the B52s making sky-trails above them. Because a B52 didn't look anything like a B29, and didn't land in any case; they were looking for a piece of that America that was born with Glenn Miller and died with President Kennedy. Goodness only knows what they would think, say, if a modern film unit on location in their area shot a mock-attack by a reconditioned Japanese Zero fighter on a privately rebuilt B29 say, for a TV advertisement. A full understanding of this situation would be very difficult, if not impossible for the natives. They would have to interpret vast social, economic, and technological changes all of which moreover are dust to ourselves in any case. The Japanese and American societies that built both the Zero and the B29 lasted for less than decade, and as live cultures once upon a time, these societies have vanished forever.

Therefore while watching such possible filming, to the Melanesians, the events observed would have "reality," but from our own point of view, they would have no "reality" at all. The events described are to us manufactured events, and Melanesians have no concept of the idea of manufacture in the sense we understand it. In addition, the idea of "advertisement" and the idea of filmed reproduction, actors, and airborne props would add to the confusion. Such an observed "mock" combat with no real damage done would perhaps lead Melanesians to the idea that they were seeing some kind of advanced ritual dance. In terms of Western consumerism of course they would be right. But of course that would be as far as they would get. After a little thought, most of the confused natives would surely come to the conclusion that everybody was telling outrageous lies to everybody else, which is as good a definition of consumerism (and media) as anything else.

Time, technology, and belief were compressed into an even smaller spectrum by other Polynesians who preferred the B17 Flying Fortress as a god-vehicle. The B29 Superfortress that succeeded the B17 became a "false" god, one that was faster and higher and far less frequent. The front-line combat life of the obsolescent B17 in the Pacific theatre was no more than some nine months. Slices of world-history do not come much more narrow than that. Thus the Polynesian "god" came and went in an almost imperceptible flash of light and inspiration before thousands of the Boeing B17 "deities" were piled up on uninhabited islands awaiting the pre-war cutting torch. Of course, venturesome natives in outriggers would come across such islands and would return to tell the weirdest tales that the gods were dead. However, in wandering amidst the wreckage they would come across the occasional tin of plum jam, sausages, or even bread. That these things could still be eaten proved the immortality of the gods.

Ten years later, anthropologists found fragments of fossilized pork sausages being offered up as hosts in religious ceremonies while congregations prayed for the future return of well-stock B17s to the island.

To this day these isolated Pacific cultures run their societies on such assumptions. Though "false" to ourselves, many Polynesian societies run smoothly on these beliefs, and they have gradually transformed all traditional moral, legal, and social norms.

That such patent falsehoods have become psychological and sociologically operational is a very grim reminder that such things may have happened to humanity in the past and indeed are still happening.

Such a psychology of confusions must be considered when approaching claimed contact and abduction experiences. Almost all of these experiences have a common element of deep absurdity that cannot be approached by the simple-minded skeptical eugenics of seeing such things either as real or unreal.

Thus just like a character in a novel, Adamski was put in a position where he had to create follow-through stories cut to fit human cartoon "what happens next" expectancies. His story book universe was hence complete, inside and out, echoing the Elizabethan playwright Marlowe's version of Mephistopheles' answer to Faust: "Why this is hell, nor am I out of it." That, of course, is the only answer to a request from a Melanesian for an explanation of why neither the B17, the B29, nor the Zero are any longer seen fighting it out in Melanesian skies, or why there are hundreds of dead gods on scores of islands.

In turn, our biggest mistake with regards to "contact" may be that we expect a recognizable *scientific* culture. There are no prizes for anyone who suggests that science, being a culture amongst other cultures, will decline, inevitably. An even bigger problem with "contact" will be the alien 2, 3, and 4 ad *infinitum* situation. There is a bewildering variety of known human Earth cultures, all in different stages of any and every kind of development, including decline. By simple analogy, it is more than reasonable to expect the same variety within more "advanced" beings. It follows that the relationships between the differing levels will again mirror this same wide variety. It is therefore extremely unlikely that "contact" will necessarily be with a single isolated strand of alien life. For ourselves the time between sails and funnels was a long time, and the cultural difference between crews of sail and steam (never mind the coming aircrews), is profound. But for the Pacific tribes in their pre-industrial setting, it was no time at all. The various "crews" of different vehicles of different ages were to a Melanesian a set of different *images,* not *products* in the Western sense. Each image for them is not necessarily a function or a logical consequence of a preceding image, as is the case with a structured "product" that has a technological development in industrial time. Images to a Melanesian are associative, not sequential. Therefore, we have to consider that a truly "alien" psychology may have no sense of simple sequential Western "constant improvement" time, just as a Melanesian does not reason that a sail crew came before or after a steam crew.

This is not completely unfamiliar to us. The 1960s culture looked *back* to a pre-industrial age, and science itself looks *forward* to a time when a great "everything" is explained. These are modern myths, quite identical to Genesis in form, content, and psychology.

Neither is the Melanesian idea of time and change as mere scene-shifts in a universal theater unfamiliar. Wartime airplane crews on temporary stations scoffed at being asked by Melanesians if they personally *knew* a certain white man who had "come out of the sea" long ago. According to missionaries, the story of this (probably shipwrecked) man had been told for several hundred years.

But like mirrors placed face to face, there are mutual astonishments. When Captain Cook's reports eventually came back to 18th century England, the excitement aroused by Cook's descriptions of idyllic native life in the far Pacific[68] was a spur to burgeoning ideas that would form the Romantic Movement. Even Rousseau threw away his watch when he heard of a life without tasks, structures, interpretations, or even discoveries. By the 1960s, many of the long-haired sons and daughters of the scoffing bomber pilots were all looking for the secrets of the Melanesians as the Melanesians looked for the secrets of their fathers.

Being alive means to a large extent being confused. Confusion defines both the thinking process itself and the highest intelligence. Those who are not confused to some degree are not thinking. Only the skeptic and grocer are certain, with their finite inputs and outputs, their profit and their loss. But both maintain certainty only by ignoring the advertisements for the goods, and almost unconsciously neglecting to ask questions about where the goods come from.

The brain "reasons" not by old industrial ideas of "objective facts" but by mistakes and amnesia, by images and suggestion, by the most outrageous self-advertising and by hypocrisy and blindness. Out of such rubbish came both our morality that raises us above the animals and our creative imagination that gets us into such terrible trouble with the gods.

When contact occurs (if it has not happened already, even many times in the past, and perhaps is still ongoing), we will inherit "their" confusions and uncertainties as the poor things will undoubtedly inherit our own. This will make the universe appear not only very strange, but as the great biologist J.B.S. Haldane said long ago, possibly stranger than we could imagine.

With Haldane's thought in mind, here are two examples of almost Melanesian absurdity, high strangeness, and cultural confusion combined, but working all together in our own society. Timothy Good says: "…a German scientist who worked at a top-secret U.S./German space research center whose name I cannot disclose, alleges that the director of the center was himself an alien—and furthermore of specifically 'Venusian' origin. This knowledge was restricted to a quorum of scientists at the center, and my informant stated that the director provided them with information which proved invaluable to their research."[69]

Adamski himself had often claimed that Professor Hermann Oberth,[70] the pioneer space scientist whose students included Wernher von Braun,[71] had received direct extraterrestrial assistance.[72] The "space travelers" he says "work in industries and government positions throughout the world. They may also be found in the armed forces of every nation, working in divisions of science, communications, medical corps, etc. where they are not required to be trained for slaughter of their fellow men."[73]

To express such a positive sentiment in the same breath as he mentions name of Nazi fellow-traveler Oberth and ex-SS man von Braun, shows perfectly that mixture of childish innocence, optimism, and naivety with which George Adamski attempted to organize his beliefs and his life.

Concerning such cultural confusions, the ideas of Charles Fort,[74] that remarkable researcher and philosopher of the unexplained, is useful. Fort saw humanity in general, and scientists in particular, as deep-sea fish trying to account for the fall of wreckage from a huge ship that has exploded. The fish have no concept or a five-year diary, a wooden leg, an umbrella, or a split steel door of a cargo hold, never mind the myriad of other unidentified objects descending into their particular bandwidth of perception. Yet, as Fort would say, if fish think at all they will systemize, they will interpret, just like the astronomers; they will, like scientists, produce accuracies and certainties beyond the sun and moon. These will be based upon scraps of inconceivable cosmic wreckage, some electrical bits of which might even respond with a last bleep or two, producing endless fishy scrolls of prophecy and revelation concerning aquatic destiny.

What the reactions of a fragment of live coral, or a passing eel would be to such a Voice from on High is anybody's guess. "I'm in the state of mind," wrote Fort, "of a savage who might find upon a shore, buoyant parts of a piano and a paddle that was carved by cruder hands than his own: something light and summery from India, and a fur overcoat from Russia. The higher idealist is the super-dogmatist of a local savage who can hold out, without a flurry of a doubt, that a piano washed up on a beach is the trunk of a palm that a shark has bitten, leaving its teeth in it."[75]

CHAPTER 7

The Ufonauts are the Liars, Not the Contactees

It is rather strange that George Adamski chose to end *Flying Saucers Have Landed* in December 1952. He does not take the opportunity to include in the 55 pages sent to Werner Laurie describing what he says happened to him on the 18th of February 1953. It seems there was still time to update his manuscript that would be published in September of 1953.

However, he waited until the publication in America[76] in 1955 of *Inside the Spaceships* to announce not a "new" contact, but one that had occurred before *Flying Saucers Have Landed* was published some two years before. Paradoxically, this adds to the authenticity of Adamski's claims. A greater commercial advantage would have been gained if *Inside the Spaceships* had been conceived as a straight sequential "update" of the first book. But the man himself is at one with splintered planes of cross-reference: instead of telling what happened next, he tells us what happened before his last punch line!

There have been suggestions that Lucy McGinnis had a considerable influence on the writing of *Inside the Spaceships*. This is somewhat unlikely, considering the backspacing in time. If the conventionally minded Lucy had helped write it as a piece of faction, she would surely have tidied it up and made the events described a perfectly sequential commercial answer to any inevitable "what happened next?" question. Any other self-respecting editor would have screamed at Adamski to do this.

A serious investigator must never equate breaks in the consistency of received information with "untruth." Contrary to the view of the more behaviorist of artificial intelligence researchers, the mind works by very fuzzy paradigms, and not simple yes/no circuitry. Life would be far more simple than it is if we assumed that a congenital liar and a proven fraud could not have had a perfectly valid UFO sighting. Skeptics, we must remember, reject photographs because they are too clear on the one hand or too obscure on the other. It is therefore often more than useless to play slippery-slope "evidence" games with skeptics. Witnesses who have more than one UFO sighting also come under suspicion, as do those who have books about UFOs on their shelves. Few skeptics offer any ideas about how the things from the books get into the sky, and vice versa. Those who have seen a UFO[77] and who have had the misfortune to write about such things beforehand are also "unreliable" witnesses. But those who have a "tendency to believe" (what a wonderful and magical tendency that is!), well, they are the most "damned" witnesses of all.

A really sophisticated investigator must consider that such inconsistencies, and unlikelihoods as encountered in the Adamski story might well be a measure of truth rather than the reverse. If the stories of his encounters were being consciously rationed out for us, they would have been far easier to assimilate than if done in a less fuzzy manner. As the two books stand, however, Adamski's conceptual dyslexia (which we shall meet on other occasions), acts as a long camera-pull from the first book to the second, and the overlapping in time part-superimposes the two. There is no better example of the way in which his mind works. It sheds light on many inconsistencies encountered in his work. His confusions are an effective mirror of the interplay of mind and character, substance and idea, and the way such things communicate in terms of mimicry, self-deception, and simulacra.

A good example of this fuzzy process at work is the FBI report on Adamski dated January 28, 1953.[78] The mistakes and inconsistencies it contains could have been plain incompetence combined with a covert plan to catch Adamski out. Certainly there were those who wished to entangle him in contradictions and plain lies, in the manner of Silas Newton, who as we have seen, was certainly an FBI fellow-traveler and informant.

In the 1953 report, the agent records that Adamski said that a ladder descended from what appeared to be "a small stairway in the bottom of the craft," and a " space man came down the steps." However, researcher Karl Pflock[79] has pointed out that when *Flying Saucers Have Landed* was published some nine months later, there is no such stairway described, and the "space man" appears at first with no saucer in sight at all. When we think that this descending ladder would have made a far prettier story, we are left with two intriguing questions. First, if it was a better description why did Adamski leave it out of his later account?

Here the suspicion centers on the agent himself, because there is included in this same 1953 report an astonishing piece of misinformation. Either the agent concerned was superbly incompetent or he was making it all up as he went along, which is exactly what poor Adamski was accused of doing. The agent has Adamski saying that his wife Mary was with him during the desert encounter! For Adamski to say this would have been to lay up so much dynamite for himself it is well nigh impossible to believe that he did say it. Certainly the six witnesses who signed affidavits would have denied such a presence immediately, and Adamski knew that in making statements to the FBI he was legally liable. As has been said, Mary hated her husband's saucer interests, and was therefore the last person on earth to go on a saucer hunt. Again, if Adamski did say his wife was present, then he took the unbelievable risk of the agent asking to see Mary then and there, and having to face the direct consequences of denying her presence—if indeed at that time Mary was resident at Palomar at all.[80] There is a blanked-out section in the report before the phrase "…and his wife Mary," and all would be explained if "Mary" was the name of the wife of one of the two other men witnesses. However, their wives were both named Betty.

Timothy Good, in conversation with me, believes such inconstancies were mistakes made by the agent. But if so, they were rather blatant and quite consciously specific mistakes. The agent might have misunderstood Adamski's heavy Polish pronunciation of "Betty" for "Mary," but that is some assumption to make. In the light of this, how much credibility then are we to put on the report of the presence of the descending "ladder" mentioned by the agent and not mentioned by Adamski in the later published text? That these mistakes were also made in the presence of an accompanying USAF officer from the OSI[81] (who presumably made his own report) is even more difficult to believe. It would be interesting to unearth this separate report to see if this officer, in turn, made the same mistakes.

If this example illustrates the quality of material reaching Edgar Hoover, then much doubt is cast on the reliability of FBI reports. In the succeeding years, this situation was to effect American culture in many areas other than those dominated by the UFO.

Another example of how some think Adamski was so naïve as to risk total disaster within hours is afforded by a letter to the *Fortean Times*[82] from the Hon. Mark Dowding, the grandson of Lord Dowding. Mark Dowding claims that his father, Derek Dowding, told him that while giving Adamski a lift in his car, Adamski said, by way of passing comment, that he had fabricated the whole flying saucer story. The car journey must have been in 1959, and it must have been made to or from the station on the one night Adamski lectured in Tunbridge Wells at a meeting presided over by Lord Dowding himself. To have made such a devastating comment in passing to man he had only just met, and to have risked not being blown out of the water by such a remark, is almost impossible to believe, if only because at this time, Adamski was in the middle of his European tour. That Derek Dowding was an ardent skeptic (in reaction to his father, we suppose), and was also a Royal Air Force Attaché to the Pentagon in the 1950s, is very interesting.

Yes, the skeptics might indeed be correct when they say that such folk as contactees make mistakes, and suffer from all kinds of personal selectivity and psycho-social amnesia. But Adamski's personal witness burns its way through this fuzzy mess, as other testimony burns through the Roswell haze and the mysteries of events in Rendlesham Forest in Britain.[83] Something truly fantastic and significant happened in the Californian desert in November 20, 1952, as at Roswell[84] on July 4, 1947, and in Rendlesham Forest in December 1980.

There is, of course, a third alternative, which most baffled and skeptical researchers avoid. If a locus of lying witnesses and psycho-social fabrications can sculpt a part-reality complete with disappearing actors, partial events, and disappearing evidence, then we have a phenomenon which pales in comparison to the mysterious UFO. But perhaps in our Entertainment State, we should no longer try and "solve" mysteries, so much as try to enter their peculiar dimensions.

The same post-modern thought that what we perceive as "real" may, on close inspection, consist of countless incomplete scripts is only just beginning to enter ufological discussions. In this respect, *Inside the Spaceships* offers us a mystery to enter rather than solve. It is to enter a drama scripted by Kafka and Borges, filmed by Goldwyn-Meyer, and performed by the Marx Brothers. That Adamski was not at all Jewish is therefore quite remarkable.

We now enter one of the great fairy-stories of the 20th century.

Time: sometime during the early evening of the 18th of February 1953. A hunch tells[85] Adamski to leave the "quiet starlight and peace of his mountain home." He obviously does not think the world knows yet of the troubles on the mountain. He decides to travel into Los Angeles, a "city of lights and noise, of rush and restlessness". He tells us that he has not come to the city "for excitement," (as if he did not have enough of that on the mountain), but has been drawn there by "the kind of urgent impression described in *Flying Saucers Have Landed*."[86] He checks into a small familiar hotel, and from then on, the scene is pure *noire:*

"After the bellboy had brought my suitcase to the room, received his tip and departed," writes Adamski, "I stood uncertainly in the middle of the floor. It was only about four o'clock in the afternoon and since I literally did not know what had brought me here, I felt rather at a loose end. I went over to the window and stood staring out at the busy street. There certainly was no inspiration there."

Coming to a sudden decision, he goes downstairs to the cocktail bar. A waiter who knew him well, and who was fascinated by flying saucers, greets him. The waiter says that a number of people who knew Adamski from his radio and TV programs also knew that he stayed in this particular hotel whenever he was in town. In the manner of fans, they had asked the waiter to give them a call if he should appear. An almost reluctant Adamski agrees. A small crowd assembles, and he discusses saucer matters with them. He dines out of the hotel, and when he gets back, he decides to ring a woman friend he knows. The woman, a previous mountain-student of his, is glad to come and see him, for she says she has certain personal problems she wishes to discuss with her friend and teacher. He buys a newspaper, goes to his room to avoid being recognized again, but is restless waiting for the girl, as her journey will take an hour or more.

Humphrey Bogart should have done it. Adamski meets the girl, reassures her, and accompanies her to the corner where she takes a streetcar. His restless feeling persists. He looks at his wristwatch. It is 10:30.

What happens next is straight out of a prototype version of *The*

Matrix, and laugh as we may, it is a scene which has haunted the Western media imagination ever since—the Men in Black. Though he didn't create this archetype all by himself (rumors about such had been circulating since 1949), Adamski did have a hand in it, which is achievement enough, and let any scoffers try and do nearly as much. He probably got bits of this modern legend from his friendship with Frank Scully, and from knowledge of Alfred K. Bender's experience with his International Flying Saucer Bureau that was formed in 1952. Allegedly, three Men in Black smashed this organization to pieces in 1953, through harassment. But note that the following Adamski incident was certainly written before Gray Barker's 1956 book *They Knew Too Much About Flying Saucers* that was inspired by Alfred K. Bender's story.

Two men approach Adamski. They look like "average young businessmen." One is over six feet in height, has a ruddy complexion, black hair, and the "kind of sparkle that suggests great enjoyment of life." The other younger man is shorter, has grayish-blue eyes, sandy hair, and smiles as he addresses Adamski by name. This man extends his hand in a certain manner, and Adamski is overjoyed to realize that this is the very signal given by the Venusian he met in the desert on the 20th of November 1952. The younger man invites him to accompany them, but only if he has the time to do so.

The men, now silent, leave the lobby with Adamski walking between them, and turn into a parking lot. No less than a "four-door black Pontiac sedan" pulls up, at which point Adamski shows that he must be the most optimistic man who has ever been born: "They had not spoken during this short time, yet inwardly I knew that these men were true friends. I felt no urge to ask where they proposed to take me, nor did it seem odd that they had volunteered no information."[87]

Never has being taken for a ride by four silent strangers who say they are from outer space been so inspiring: "I sensed a power which made me feel like a child in the company of beings of vast wisdom and compassion." Eventually the taller man speaks: "You have been very patient...The speaker smiled and indicated the driver. 'He is from the planet you call Mars. I am from the one you call Saturn."

The bizarre group travel for at least an hour and a half along "smooth highways." It is dark, but Adamski senses that they are entering desert country. The car turns off the main road and travels along a rough track for nearly a quarter of an hour before the Martian says "We have a surprise for you!"

A spaceship comes down and soon standing there beside it, giving greetings to Adamski is Orthon, the man from Venus he met on his original desert encounter! Orthon is now speaking English more fully, "with only a slight trace of an accent." Since there is no such thing as English without an accent, we are left wondering what he sounded like, and how, in the three months between encounters, he learned almost perfect English.

There begins a series of incidents reminiscent of Jules Verne. Orthon says he has been doing some running repairs, and promptly empties out onto the sand what appears to be a small amount of molten metal from a small crucible. This is cool enough, however, for Adamski to wrap some in a handkerchief, much to the amusement of the space brothers. He claimed to have this sample to the end of his days.

Purely for the sake of convenience, Adamski now says he will name the rest of the space men. The Martian he calls Firkon, the Saturnian is named Ramu.

He now enters the ship.

CHAPTER 8

The Doll's House Machine

At first we are surprised and a little disappointed. Here are things we recognize and know. The interior is almost as mechanical-industrial as Jules Verne's submarine, *Nautilus*. There are hangars and power-supplies, lifts, ramps, and battery-chargers; there is even the charming touch of a small blacksmith's forge of all things, wonderful news for the nut-and-bolt theorists, although as an indication of the shaky stage-flat of a conspiracy, it is just as wonderful. There is no organ to play, as in Verne's submarine, but then this is not so much a space ship, more a doll's house full of early consumer expectancies. Adamski describes the chintzes and the glassware lovingly. It is as if he felt that they were the final compensation for the many years of his drop-out past, when he scraped a living preaching mainly in those trailer and clapboard communities that were the prototype communes of the 1950s.

At times his description of the interior of the space ship makes it appear like the reject footage of *South Pacific*. We suspect not so much his sanity, more his consumer maturity. Led by Ramu and Firkon and Orthon, our gullible hero enters a shopping center full of window-busts come alive in a kind of gay version of a Flash Gordon film. In this camp ship, ever-smiling male drones in ski-suits stand at antique Buck Rogers control panels full of buttons and flashing lights. The whole scene is a B-feature combination of the lurid post-war covers of magazines such as *Astounding, Unknown,* and *Marvel.*

But we before we dismiss Adamski, we again have to bear in mind that a Melanesian native taken aboard a cruise liner would likely suffer a similar distortion of critical-focus. When Yali, a native who had seen service in the Australian army during the World War II, saw ritual masks in a Queensland museum, he assumed he was in "Rome," and that the "gods" were being held prisoner there. Further confusions followed when Yali was shown a textbook illustrating Darwin's theories. After seeing this, he no longer believed the Adam and Eve stories of the missionaries. Neither did he believe in the work ethic because the "big men" he had seen did no work.

Now there's a clever one from Yali.

The struggle of Melanesian natives reflects Adamski's difficulties. They too tried to understand the web of lies and deceit often spun quite unwittingly (as well as wittingly), by Western contacts. The natives were equally as baffled by British Christian missionaries who themselves were at a loss to explain the Resurrection, magazine photographs of the Blackpool Illuminations, popular soaps, or the British Royal Family. If we smile at the loincloth folk, we had better remind ourselves of the quite impossible problems we ourselves have in explaining the differences between religion and culture in the Bronx, never mind Northern Ireland. In the Western world, the religious plea for "cargo" in Adamski's case (and for thousands of others since his time) is not a plea for goods. It is an asking for a "confession" by Authority that it has recovered alien craft and that it has the dead bodies of aliens still preserved at Wright Patterson Air Force Base.

Those UFO investigations described as "factual" are nevertheless linked to the process Carl Jung called "participation mystique." Somewhere along the line of that immaculate evidential line of reasoning called "objective research," things begin to go wrong. A burgeoning chaos sets in, and Authority, found lying, looks over its own shoulder at its own implicit distortions, like any baffled missionary.

Adamski became possessed by an atavistic fear equal to that of any island native. Finally, the show in the sky, though it whet his appetite, allowed him to enter the system, but only for a brief time. The reassurances and explanations given to him by his space folk lasted briefly before disappointment and paranoia had him trying to write further episodes all by himself. Historically, this is familiar ground, but to understand it fully, we have to dispose of our own modern crude ideas of what constitutes a "falsehood." Adamski's activity of "invention" is the direct equivalent to carving images of the gods. Such *mimesis* or *imitation* gave birth to Literature, the Arts, and indeed Science itself. Therefore, before we ridicule his "falsehoods," we must remind ourselves just how far our puny concepts of the alchemical idea of *imaginatio* have fallen. Certainly Shakespeare would not have understood our equally puny concept of "factual objectivity".

And he did well enough without it.

Adamski's fear is rather like that which possessed the Pythagorean Brotherhood. In a similar way, Adamski also was the victim of mysterious "silence groups" that made life difficult for him. To add to his fear, the first UFO casualties had begun to arrive. Perhaps we all get frightened when we realize that we really don't know where either goods or confessions come from. Most UFO casualties have occurred in that area where one turns into the other, and vice versa. This is a mysterious border country where the game-moves go right under the hill of dreams, and dreams matter. A country may have good natural trade routes, a temperate climate, and excellent natural resources, yet its culture is dust. It would be churlish and ungentlemanly to mention names. That "cargo" in terms of goods and products finally emerges from Western inspirations within a fantasy life as rich as any Melanesian native is a cargo-secret well preserved. Economists will never admit that. They see trading relations and goods and products as things quite separate from dreams, which of course they are not. Scientists of the older generations may think that the idea of the concrete has triumphed, but as any good general Store knows, knickers with no mystique are no knickers at all.

Once onboard, Adamski is introduced to two gorgeous pouting Russ Meyer hostesses, Ilmuth and Kalna. They are as nice as Bambi and twice as cute. A modern-day Eurovision song-contest might show them banging tambourines at the side of some twanging Lothario, singing about summer on the Costa Brava. They might have appeared in pre-pubic editions of 1950s soft-porn magazines, when bikinis were as thick as nappies, all the girls had fixed Jackie Kennedy smiles, and the rare nipple was in soft focus. In this bargain basement Adamski acts as if he were experiencing a synthesized blue-collar orgasm. In these first eye-blinks of the consumer society, eroticism has become part of the furnishings and attire. Here are myriad yearnings of a first post-war Sears catalogue, printed with uncertain color registration by out-of-practice young ex-dogfaces and grunts who have only just left their M1 rifles in deep grease at a depot near the 38th parallel.

Adamski's aliens are not the busy and dentist-like humanoid examiners of the Betty and Barney Hill encounter (who express astonishment at Barney's false teeth), or the disembodied space-voices of George King of the Aetherius Society. They are nothing like the river-dragons of Pascagula, the forest-trolls seen by Travis Walton, or the homespun creatures seen by Daniel Fry or Truman Bethurum. Like the "gods" of Howard Menger, Adamski's space folk are pure Disney-schlock, and their conversations have the mental content of a *Television Times* or *TV Guide* editorial. Portraits of Doris Day and piped favorites of the Mormon Tabernacle Choir oozing from the walls would not have been out of place. The effect is perfect for that lavish spiritual kitsch which is Theosophy.

This sample of early prime time comes complete with the kind of "spiritual" formation swooning which gives scalped gurus a bad name. The lovely blond Kalna, obviously no swinger, tells Adamski: "Our social dancing is usually of a group pattern…as the poem form in words can suggest deep feeling not possible to the prose form, so it is with the perfect rhythm expressed in the movement of a body dedicated in a dance of worship"[88] She is not the best of Saturday night prospects exactly, and a little later this young matron has even more depressing news about the birth of Rock n' Roll: "We could derive no joy from the kick, wiggle and hop we have observed on your Earth, during which a man and a woman clutch each other ferociously one moment and fling each other off the next."[89]

The worse this gets (and it gets worse) the more one thinks that the whole thing is genuine just as Adamski saw and experienced it, if only because no one could invent this. If they did manage to invent it, they would improve it, and make it more plausible, but our hero does no such thing. Again, the book is the man, and no other.

There comes a point when the choirboy in Adamski momentarily deserts him, and he asks if they have "parties." To which he gets a pretty depressing answer from the magnificent brunette, Ilmuth. Parties, she says are "simply a matter of inviting our friends to our homes that we may talk or relax together. Like yours, many of our homes have grounds that are planned with swimming pools and large terraces."

Poor Adamski. No chance of bop or a smooch on this bourgeois spaceship, never mind anything else. With these young matrons, he is on the wrong flying saucer. But we must remember that historically, the elemental is a great joker. If all this is rigged by the "space folk" then it could all just be a hint that they have a sense of humor, as distinct from our present "greys" and their boring and repetitious gyno-preoccupation. After this, we can imagine torn scarves, mad aunts and somewhere in hyperspace, poetry, autumn evenings, and infinite nostalgia.

Of course, many claim that Adamski wrote, produced, and cast this prototype soap opera all by himself. If he did so, then *Inside the Space Ships,* like the 1957 *Flying Saucer Pilgrimage*[90] of Helen and Bryant Reeve, stands as a masterpiece of early 1960s literary *art primitif,* but worth no more than 33⅓ rpm long-playing records of the *Monkees,* or wire-cassette recordings of early Bing Crosby radio shows. Certainly there is good evidence to show that Adamski's Venusians with their long blond hair were around in books, magazines, and motion pictures[91] some years before he claimed that he had met such creatures in "real" life.

The problem here is that in the 20th century we have lost the relationship between Imagination and Fact. For us, with our "objectivity," Fact and Imagination no longer seed and synthesize one another as they did for say the world of the Renaissance; they are somewhat "separate" entities, the first for "hard" truth, and the other for "soft" entertainment. These are ridiculous metaphors; certainly Shakespeare would have no problem at all with UFOs; they could be fairies, the transmigration of souls, the appearance of gods, witches in flight. The Court of his time was a kind of integrated mandala in which all these things were connected with destiny, with good and evil, and the moral, personal, and national consequences of high Tragedy. In this system, the anomaly (often pointed out by the Court Fool, and represented by Cordelia in *King Lear*) was a built-in system-destabilizer. As a culture, what dreary pictures we ourselves present at the side of this rich structure of different levels of belief and meaning. In this, compared to the age of Shakespeare (and indeed to cargo-cult tribes), the West lives in narrow confines of thought. For us, Imagination has fallen to Entertainment, and Fact emerges from the screams of billions of tortured laboratory animals.

In a revised and expanded edition of *Flying Saucers Have Landed,* published by Futura in 1970, Leslie took the opportunity to comment on each section of the original book. Looking back from a distance of seventeen years, he says of Adamski's Book 2: "How then, do I dare to have the face to republish this book in the light of current findings? Why do not I humbly admit that I was mistaken in adding his burblings to my otherwise more reasonable treatise that consisted purely of historical facts—facts that can be checked and verified? Why don't I quietly drop him from this volume and pretend he never existed? Why do I continue to stick my neck out?

"I have a long neck, and plenty of it. Furthermore, unlike most of his critics, I went to considerable pains checking up on him, his photos, his negatives, his equipment, his corroborating witnesses and any other circumstantial evidence I could find; and despite many blind trails and disappointments I was left with the disquieting conviction that the account of a landing on 20th November 1952 did in fact take place, more or less exactly as reported by those privileged to be witnesses and to give testimony of it."[92]

While Adamski's ludicrous encounters were easy enough to reject, his photographs and films were a different matter. Much of his filmed work has survived stringent authenticity tests to this day.[93]

Like Lee Harvey Oswald, and Ted Serios, who were two other men who could walk through twentieth-century walls, Adamski's life had never been easy. The spaceships as he described them contained worlds where perhaps he thought he might be happy and put his feet up for a while, away from the demands of both the hot-plate queues and his hectic lecturing schedule, for which he only ever claimed expenses.

The events on board appear carefully tuned to personalities. A clue is the choice of least resistance. The phenomenon appears not to want any hard questions asked, and certainly no piss-takers or troublemakers, or perhaps such do not get back to tell the tale.

The dialogue is all very much one-way. Adamski himself is never asked a question; his hosts conceal all curiosity of Earth, and he himself does not find the platitudinous condescension at all offensive. The ladders, decks, elevators, and cable-ducts hint at a structure masked off to all curiosity, a stage-set built and designed specifically to prevent questions being asked, and of course Adamski, quite enchanted, does not ask any.

The scene onboard the spaceship is rather old-fashioned. Most of the equipment is big and clumsy, and a good deal of it could have been found in 1900 on *Dreadnoughts* of the British Royal Navy. Thus even by the standards of a hundred years ago, much of Adamski's space-ship technology is out of date; it is all far too crudely electromechanical. The heart of the mystery is that it looks like somebody else's bad guesses rather than Adamski's. As we now know over fifty years later, the future didn't go that way. In the post-industrial society, the device is silent, invisible, indeed hovering on the verge of no physical existence at all, like the computer virus or the nano-engine.

We get an idea that Adamski was chosen because of all people, the kind of mid-to-low-grade goods on offer would, bless him, quite overwhelm him. He simply did not have the mind to want to know about causal links. This made him a perfect choice for traditional enchantment. He had no guilt about Wonder. He was the last person on earth to try and look backstage to see if any Peter Pan wires were visible. It look now as if he was the subject of a series of very bad guesses at a consumer-oriented theosophical nirvana calculated to go straight to Adamski's essentially sentimental heart.

The "reality" of the entire business is that the space folk appear to know their George Adamski pretty well. In this, a master Intelligence expert could not have done better in constructing a composite package for one particular person. The world of Adamski's space-folk could hardly exist: there is no wear and tear in it, no healthy conflicts, complaints, rows, disagreements that make life worth living. Just a curse from one of the pilot-drones, or a long-legged fart from one of the outer-space bunny girls would have brought it off.

Adamski is granted an interview by the big man himself, a kind of UFO Oral Roberts, who addresses him as "my son," and has the cheek to tell him that his viewpoint is extremely limited. The Leader's language and sentiments are suspended between the dehydrated prose of a sales brochure, and what might be termed a sanitized form of early Perry Como. After showing Adamski green fields on the moon, he says: " 'My son,' he said, looking deeply into my eyes, 'much of what our brother has been saying to you is in conflict with many things your people have been taught to believe as truth. This, in itself, is of no importance, since that which was learned yesterday serves only as a stepping stone towards the greater truth we can learn tomorrow. That is the law of progress. Once on the right path, it cannot be otherwise. It is essential always that men work and strive together with open minds."[94]

If this is spiritual enlightenment, then perhaps we should go down on our knees and praise the impure. On such occasions, Adamski as hero and likeable rascal both, disappoints us. In *Inside the Spaceships,* he actually puts the phrase "natural law" into the mouth of the Big Chief, not mentioning that "natural law" was taught by himself for thirty years all over California!

It is disappointing that Adamski took himself so seriously. He would have earned much more credibility if he had asked the paste-up old queen whether he did weddings and barmitzvas. The Big Chief is so awful he could be almost real. If Adamski wanted this kind of thing, he needn't have bothered with flying saucers at all. Downtown Los Angeles in the 1950s would certainly have catered to his needs. But certainly his readers loved this vapid setting, just as the man himself was impressed with the saucer's Turkish-brothel decor, the trailer-trash furniture, and the airport-lounge food and drink. The Star Trek chat about magnetic drives should have alerted Adamski just as the Melanesian Yali became alert to the duplicitous and confusing messages from missionaries.

After supper, the two robed geisha-girls do a kind of Muppet-dance, and then change to go on duty as pilots of the ship, if you please.

The only thing missing in this saucer is the pianist from *Casablanca.*

There is an early mall-quality about these early contactee experiences. Adamski's religious writings express a leveled-off spiritual profundity, "instant" as the new technology of frozen burgers in the new Bel Air ice-box, personally delivered by a man straight out of *Death of a Salesman.* Contactees of this period almost invariably talk about space "gods" as if they were neighbors just dropped in for mid-morning coffee. Fred Steckling, Adamski's number one preaching convert, claims he met spacefolk all over the world, and his words echo the voice of his teacher: "Our space brothers know so well how difficult it really is for us, the adults, to teach the little ones the value of life…our friends from other worlds never poison a child's mind as we so often do. By imposing our dislikes, opinions, and assumptions upon others, we violate the very basic law of Christianity!"[95]

This is cool mall-sanity taken to its limits. Emotionally, most early contactees were such wide-eyed mall creatures. They appear to have undergone transformations in which their higher feelings have become pure Muzak. Profundity is instant, sterilized and packaged; awe, being far too disruptive, is banned in the weather-proof mall of their new "consumer" beliefs; dread is banished from both its well-managed interior and the advertisements which hold the entire stage-set together. At times the whole Adamski personality becomes as gnomic as an evangelical text for a junior Sunday school. As a man, we cannot help feeling on occasion that a man such as he might have been programmed as the perfect prototype customer for the burgeoning consumer society. This "society" was beginning to flex its junior muscles in the early 1950s with a narrow-tuned bandwidth of response identical to that of the first television soap operas. With this in mind, we can now perhaps get a much better idea than Adamski what Orthon's mission was all about.

"Contact" may indeed be contact with a highly developed information field that has the power to change metaphor. An advanced intelligence may have evolved far beyond industrial "hard fact" into pure advertisement-stuff. This would be an infinitely more powerful instrument of persuasion and control than "fact." With our burgeoning experience of cyberspace, we can now see that this may well be the direction an advanced intelligence might take. Alien life blood may well be based on image-suggestion rather than exchange of factual information.

In accordance with the emerging "mall" nature of Adamski's era, the bland responses of the "space folk" exhibit as little radical curiosity as does Adamski himself. He would have been a difficult man to fool over the grocery bill, the tax demand, or the garage repair. But most contactees do not seem to mind that the "voices from space" seem to lack any old gods, idiot gods, or plain daft and silly gods, all of which the Greeks had in plenty. Neither do their gods have any chronically ill, or mad, or any difficult young; nor do they have any renegade souls, and they lack all sign of any downright bloody-minded subversives. They lack all humor also; Adamski's crews have an irritating Zen-like calm, and the "messages" given to him have the depth of the instructions on the back of a stir-fry pack.

Thankfully, there are a few hints of trouble in paradise, but this is expressed with the sort of emotional force that censors neighbors who do not clean their windows often enough or leave broken-down pick-ups in the road, jacked up on bricks, and minus a wheel or two. There are also hints as to what happens to those very few space-gods who have not seen the light. These misguided spirits are subjected to spiritual eugenics; Helen and Bryan Reeve, the authors of *Flying Saucer Pilgrimage,* speak of "housecleaning" in the "higher vibratory regions" of outer space as easily as talking of washing their curtains and chair-covers, and with just about the same range of emotions.

These "space folk" who speak so casually of "magnetic vibrations" and "etheric matter-transfer," are therefore nice chintz-cushion and flock-wallpaper gods. They are very definitely not the bleeding-to-death, treacherous, or kick-in-the-backside gods of Shakespeare, Neitzsche, or Mount Olympus; these "space folk" gods are the nice boy-scout deities of patio and lawn. They are the guardian spirits of regularly washed curtains, and neat hedgerows, the gods of a landscape tamed, and their rare petulant bleats could be from Donald Duck at extremely low ebb.

It is extremely odd that Adamski did not "contact" the elemental beings of his own mountain home. Given his early hippie prototype "New Age" views, this is surprising. The beings he meets are not from rock, cloud, or forest. They are mechanical-industrial and electromagnetic to a fault. They are the "gods" of an age that in Adamski's time was already was dying on its feet. Fifty years later with an intense suspicion of mechanistic science, we see that what Adamski saw was far too optimistic. The message was that the "future" would form a seamless blend between science and progress; his beings as projected are successful scientists who are "spiritually" advanced at the same time. None of this came about, and technology shrunk to invisibility.

If Adamski was duped, he was duped by feedback of his own best expectations.[96]

But his simple-minded romanticism sees no dangers in the absence of the tortuous paradoxes of all higher mental complexity. In the mall-like space ship, there is no blood on the paradigms. It would appear that

Adamski has entered his own gestalt, a kind of mall-simulation. All parties in the exchange appear to have become mall-products themselves. As shown in their book, *Flying Saucer Pilgrimage,* the Reeves in particular have almost shrunk their "gods" to medicinal house-goblins, who give moral precepts about as valuable as wart-cures. We are talking of course of the early 1950s, when the first malls were being built, and being built in prosperous America alone. Such things had not yet reached Europe, whose war-shocked consumer-gods at that time had not yet come out of the closet. When the early British "space gods" do appear[97] they are still the rather tired and weary rough-hewn deities of hill and grove, ready reluctantly to bow out somewhat reluctantly for Adamski's synthetic dolls.

Thus "contact" may not be in terms of either "greys" or spindly *War of the Worlds* machines spouting laser death-rays, but in the cool form of that powerful suggestion-virus called the advertisement. "Advanced" life might be indeed as vaporous as a mere power metaphor that dines on belief batteries as inevitably as cattle chew the cud.

Poor Adamski again. His hosts didn't ask him to sign his name in blood, they just asked him to believe in the clapboard frontage of their five-and-ten-cent store, and not ask who or what was signing the checks.

February19, 1953 at 5.10 am. The spectacular evening ends with Bogart back in his lonely room in the existential city: "I sat on the edge of the bed for a full hour," writes Adamski, "reviewing the experiences of the night. And even as they went through my mind I could not help but reflect on how fantastic the thing would seem to my fellow man. Nevertheless I must tell of it…I could scarcely believe in the reality of all that had happened in the past few hours. Yet I knew what my eyes had seen and my ears had heard, and that without doubt it had been a completely physical experience."[98]

As a man dedicated to Theosophy, Adamski might have born in mind Emmanuel Swedenborg's warning: "When the angels begin to speak to a man, he must beware, for they will prattle of such outrageous nonsense as would never be believed."

April 21, 1953. The same strange feeling. By this time, Adamski's manuscript must have been ready to fly across the Atlantic to Werner

Laurie. Same hotel, same chatty waiter. Lo, a smiling Firkon arrives, and like a chief scout, gives him a special code word. Adamski finds a cozy booth just for two, and Firkon orders a peanut butter sandwich on whole wheat, black coffee, and a piece of apple pie. Again, we wonder about Adamski sometimes in this respect. He seems to like being smothered by "well proportioned" young men, invariably handsome and with an air of confident superiority. In their presence, he is reduced to a wide-eyed child-ish wonder. All over the world, he prefers small out-of-town hotels for his accommodation, saying that these are suitable places to meet "the boys," as he always refers to visiting "spacemen."

Biographer Lou Zinsstag notes Adamski's ill-concealed excitement when, in a Swiss bar in 1959, he sees a tanned man wearing dark glasses with his blond hair brushed over his forehead. She checks discreetly on Adamski's hotel visitors, and finds that he has regular callers, all male. If we believe they were all spacemen, we'll believe anything, for after all, Adamski describes the space folk as "creative men and women who take a delight in styling and making clothes." There are other telling gems, such as the rather blushing admission from Desmond Leslie in the *Cosmic Bulletin of the Adamski Foundation:* "I don't suppose he will mind me telling this, now he has cast off the fine old body, but he once showed me the most extraordinary birthmark. His navel was not like a human navel at all. It was a huge solar disk with deeply cut rays extending out about six inches all around it from waist to groin. What this signifies I have no idea—unless it is truly the sign of a 'Child of the Sun.'"

Back in the Los Angeles hotel, the food may be good, but the conver-sation leaves a lot to be desired. Says Firkon, between bites: "We of other worlds who have been living unrecognized amongst you can see clearly how identity with Divine origin has been lost. People of Earth have become separate entities which are no longer truly human in expression as in the beginning they were."

Then into same black Pontiac. Different mother ship, but same dia-logue and the recurring Adamski theme: a greeting from a handsome man. This man he names Zuhl, and Zuhl is as disappointing as Firkon. He gives out more pasteurized talk about the Divine Father, some Barnum and Bailey bits about Jesus, and a haughty Martian "lady" speaks early-middle-Barbarella: "You Earth people do not desire to show such cruelty towards one another. This, as you have been told before, is merely the result of your self-ignorance, which in turn blinds you to the laws of the Universe of which we are all a part."

After that, more rail balconies and elevators come as a relief. Adamski, when he ceases his constipated religious mouthing, can be interesting. He describes a laboratory straight out of Mary Poppins, full of the kind of "control panels," "graphs," colored lights, and screens seen on the lurid covers of *Astounding* science-fiction magazine of those days. The control panel, from the days of the earliest railway signal boxes to the array in front of the "pilots" of the Space Shuttle, is a unique twentieth-century motif. One day, just like the gargoyles of Chartres and Notre Dame, the changing shapes and complexity of these ever-evolving desks and boxes will be read as indicators of the ideology of power and social control. They too will be seen as the shapes of thought and being, intellectual achievement and moral order of Nature as it was lovingly conceived once upon a time. Control panels are the religious relics and mythological tableaux of an age of technological uncertainty, just as the increasingly nervous late mediaeval universe was full of theological fear. The walls of Occam's enclosed universe were to fall before the trumpet-blasts of early experimental science; much later, Francis Bacon's "objective" view was greeted with the same kind of spleen Adamski-type ideas now still receive.

Very few authors can combine factional "techno" fairy-tales in the typical "naïve" Adamski manner, and make also a work of valuable literary concept art in that genre we now call pan-dimensional. Adamski's life and personality both are pure image-stuff, fodder for Warhol and Dali dreams. Like the contactees Howard Menger and Frank Stranges, he accepts without question ludicrously comic and deliciously crazy experiences. He does not laugh, question, or criticize, and never is he suspicious. On a screen in one of the space ships, he is shown a close-up of the surface of the moon, and sees a "four-legged and furry animal" scurrying around. He was a sucker for any programmatic agenda. Today he would perhaps be honored as a media-freak; he was just waiting to be filled up night and day with new dreams, and explode them all over the planet like metaphor-spores. If computers, mixed media, and twenty-four track mixing desks had been available, he would have dragged the lot up the mountain and blown the mountain apart.

If we roar with laughter, we might bear in mind that without human living rain forests like Adamski, we are all dead.

Of course, he went far beyond the stage of eccentric entertainer. His boxes of tricks did not stop traveling from faction, to fact via fantasy, and then back again by way of fiction. This process of discovery is a classic alchemical progress. In this, he achieved a collective discovery of himself. He didn't need acid or marijuana. He cared little for alcohol, money, or even fame; he tripped on new images alone. They were the manna of his intensely spiritual life. If he was chosen for this kind of experience, then this is the reason why.

As such, he took in anything and everything. He is a loincloth native fascinated by cheap trash as well as high mysteries;[99] the most elementary gimmickry has his eyes bulging. He praises seats that are raised by a foot pedal, the "pilot suits" of the women, the silent sliding doors, and the colored screens that are displaying information from the scout-discs that are roving the earth.

The spaceship nears the moon, which is shown on a "screen" to have fertile valleys. But when we are about to give up hope for poor Adamski, there occurs one of those frightening moments when he gets the technological future right on target. We must remember that he predicated the existence of the Van Allen belt of space-radiation, and later astronauts confirmed the outer-space "fireflies" he said that he had seen on his trips. Now this untutored cheeky chappie who broke all the rules almost gets it right about future computer programming, VHF telemetry, and digital communications.

There are remotely-controlled scout discs going in and out of the motherships, and six girls by means of "keys like an organ" feed "instructions and flight data" to them, which they retain. Pretty early stuff[100] for the time of the composition of *Inside the Spaceships,* whose American edition appeared in 1955.

But just as we are getting interested in all this, just as it begins to gain a little of what we might call verisimilitude, yet another "master" more camp than the first arrives to give more jukebox religion. But what this particular master said was to prove ominous for Adamski: "Now that we have been together in this way, you can the more easily at all times make contact from your mind to ours. Remember always that space is no barrier."

This means that there is going to be telepathic communication. This was the idea that was to drive Adamski nearly insane before he died, and cause the collapse of much of his worldwide support. But as far as any possible alien intelligence was concerned, the changes in metaphor had been initiated. The story-virus had spread throughout the world, and the world was not the same place after the appearance of *Flying Saucers Have Landed*. As for the conspiracy, it had disappeared, enfolded within a deception within a deception. Eventually Adamski was left high and dry with a few threads of possibility within possibilities. From this thin fabric, he tried to sculpt the faces of the gods and their tale of tales.

The Argentinean fantasist Jorge Borges, alive and well at this time, and not all that far away, would have loved all this had he come across this cutting-edge of a new culture, but if he knew of it, he ignored it. The great writers of Adamski's day ignored it also. They were absorbed in largely obsolete literary conventions and unaware of the "pan-dimensional" texts those "non-literary" writers such as Adamski were weaving out of myth, popular culture, and the newly emerging technological imagination. Thus did the very last generation of great writers miss out on the first wave of quite unprecedented changes in the world. Writers such as Norman Mailer and Tom Wolf are almost contemptuously silent on the flying saucer, as were Alan Ginsburg, Jack Kerouoac, and surprisingly, Timothy Leary.

CHAPTER 9

The Last Contact

September 1, 1953. Adamski feels that "great urgency" again. The publication in Britain of *Flying Saucers Have Landed* is only weeks away, but he does not talk about how he looked forward to that event. No, he is back in the same Los Angeles hotel, a glutton for punishment. He dines out again with Firkon and Ramu, but this time there is no apple pie, just sandwiches and coffee, and the jovial waiter is nowhere to be seen. They are served by a cordial waitress who interrupts only to fill their coffee cups. The coffee was certainly needed, for there is yet more consumer-metaphysics about Divine Laws, the Creator, and something called All-Knowledge. The content gets slightly more interesting however, because for the first time, Adamski asks hard questions about the death of Captain Mantell, a National Guard pilot who died chasing a UFO in his P51 Mustang,[101] for instance. But Adamski gets some evasive answers. By the time he returns to his hotel he is now a junky, and can't wait for his next fix of mall-religion, USA.

"Not long after" this meeting, he is again traveling to Los Angeles, filled with joyous anticipation like "a child before Christmas." But again there is the ominous note, now amplified: "The mental communications from my friends of other planets were becoming more and more definite as time went on."

Ramu greets him at the usual hotel. Firkon couldn't make it, and Ramu apologizes for him. Same Pontiac, same Saturnian scout ship, but this time, Ramu says that the visit has been requested by the master himself, and that the whole of the trip will be not a tour, but a long session with the master. In the face of this awesome prospect of another ball-breaking speech, Adamski must have been not a little relieved at meeting a posse of beautiful Saturnian women. But just as Ramu says "There is quite a bit of activity on the part of your air force tonight," the master arrives to break it all up.

All of Adamski's "masters" have a serious problem. They must be amongst the most boring and crass-brained individuals ever born. This one in particular wouldn't make the ratings at a downtown Salvation Army bun-for-a-prayer meeting just before the addicts and the drunks are thrown out and the cops are called. He is possessed by a kind of green blooming pond-algae of the mind for which a sock on the jaw might have come as a relief to him and all concerned. Here he is in full flight, giving all earthlings the usual kicking: "A great fallacy which has grown on the people of Earth is the custom of dividing into many parts that which should never be divided. You have multiple divisions in forms and teachings, many firm likes and dislikes, all of which serve only to add to the state of confusion on your planet."

In other words the master does not like those wonderful conflicts, paradoxes and tragi-comic catastrophes that alone make life worth living. His hostility to fuzzy-minded hairy-arsed humanity is a seamless piece of moral Muzac. If this candy was produced by a "higher intelligence," then it could be nothing more or less than a comic mimicking of Adamski's own religious philosophizing for the purpose of entertainment alone. These ruminations about the Earth, Man, and the Supreme Intelligence come to an end with the kind of sentiment that has led the world to absolute disaster on countless occasions. Ramu, speaking of the master, says, "he is one of the most evolved beings still functioning within our system. Just to be in his presence is to grow in love and understanding. We are all fortunate."

Adamski asks Ramu if the master contacted him telepathically and asked him to come along on this occasion. "Yes," answers Ramu, "your own ability to receive is growing."

We now know how "fortunate" this growing ability was for Adamski, because eventually, these space-chapel voices in his head were to almost destroy him, mentally, physically, and professionally.

All these mighty confusions were, as we shall see, the stuff of personal tragedy involving interaction with the great visionary and technological schemes of his time and culture.

Almost a year later: August 23, 1954. The last contact. *Flying Saucers Have Landed* has now been published, and both Adamski and Desmond Leslie are in great demand. On this date, the visiting Desmond Leslie is away lecturing in Los Angeles. Adamski says that he tried to get Leslie aboard, but the space brothers wouldn't have him. What a disappointment for Leslie. He missed the farewell cake and the sexy dance, which made a wonderful change from impenetrable discussions about Universal Brotherhood, Holy Writ, and the Age of Aquarius. Unfortunately on this trip the master is back, and gives forth a blast about the "right path." If this is "enlightenment" then the Earth is in far greater danger than even Adamski ever thought.

Another perfect Bogart scene. Adamski finds himself back in his lonely hotel room in deep withdrawal. This time the fix hasn't worked so well. The pushers are holding back and increasing their prices. There is a monkey is on his back; it won't go away, and the new world he has found is starting to eat him alive. We can hardly blame him. He was on the edge of an emerging cosmos where all events and significances were to become disposable, "virtual," or "hyperreal." Some thirty years later, Baudrillard describes[102] well the Los Angeles to which Adamski travelled from his magic mountain to meet his space men and women:

"Los Angeles is a town whose mystery is precisely that it is nothing more than a network of endless unreal circulation—a town of fabulous proportions, but without space or dimensions. As much as electrical and nuclear power stations, as much as film studios, this town, which is nothing more than an immense script and a perpetual motion machine, needs this old imaginary makeup of childhood signals and faked phantasms for its sympathetic nervous system."

And so, as Adamski leaves his metaphysical city, the story of these trips comes to an end. However, in "An Unexpected Postscript" at the end of *Inside the Space Ships*, Adamski makes a move straight out of *Citizen Kane*. He describes dashing into his publishers "even as the presses are rolling on this book," possessed by yet another funny feeling.

April 25, 1955. The frame of reference "all day yesterday" gives this whole episode the feeling of a surreal time sequence in a science fiction novel. Unable to sleep, Adamski tells us he caught a coach to Los Angeles but this time he carried his own Polaroid camera, apparently with the space folk's prior permission. An unnamed "Brother" he has not seen before greets him at the hotel, but warns him that the magnetic fields inside the space ship might interfere drastically with the pictures. Once inside the ship, this Brother takes the Polaroid, saying that he will take the pictures while Adamski has a chat with Orthon, who has appeared almost on cue. Three of the pictures taken with this camera appear in the British Edition of *Inside the Spaceships,* published in 1956.

What a story. And it has not been done. The life, the vision, and the contacts—neither film nor television makers have touched the confusions and the tragedy. Writing in 1970, Desmond Leslie comments: "'George, dammit!' I once expostulated. Do you swear by all that's sacred that you are telling the truth?'

"'Desmond,' he answered quietly, 'You know my religious beliefs? One of these days I shall have to face my Maker. Do you think I'd dare face Him with a lie like that on my conscience?'

"There was no doubting the man's sincerity."

However, even telling Leslie that "Those guys were human just like you and me" on occasion Adamski would hedge his bets, if only to confuse, as was his way. When he last saw Leslie shortly before his death in 1965, he was still unwilling to admit anything other than a flesh and blood series of contacts. But Leslie does admit that on one occasion, Adamski said "no one of us could be taken to another planet in our system and see the home world of its inhabitants in his present bodily form or condition."

Much rich comedy has been provided over the years by many and varied attempts at constructing a single, elegant, unified solution to the UFO problem. Explanatory offerings have been as mad as anything Adamski had to offer. They range from "earthlights" resulting from geomagnetic strain and electromagnetic pollution to J. Allen Hynek's swamp gas explanation for the 1966 UFO sightings over Michigan. The very British "psycho-social" explanations (now fortunately howled off the international stage) have been particularly hilarious. If we reverse the psycho-social equations, then we have a much better focus. Laboratory rats may not be the only creatures within an experimental maze. Certainly contact with an alien Intelligence will rid us of all previous ideas of what intelligence is and how it works.

If we dismiss Adamski, it must be remembered that from his time onwards, the Western world became a huge doll's house, just like the inside of his space-ships, and gradually the entertainment-media complex becoming integrated with the military-industrial complex. Those who scoff at the idea of "fairy kingdoms" might well consider that our own Entertainment State is such a kingdom come about. Some cynics would say that the inside of the media-entertainment head is identical to the interiors of Adamski's space ships, both are doll's house machines with plenty of blood around if we happen to open the wrong door. If there was such an alien invasion, it was a long time ago now, and it was silent, overwhelming, completely effective. It is still striking deep inland from its beachheads, and building new dolls for new walk-on parts in cyberspace.[103] Through people like Adamski, invading agendas reached their targets, and the future was born.

We don't have to be Internet addicts to see "agendas" as pure disembodied information fields that are alien lifeforms in themselves. Adamski was in all likelihood seduced by a phenomenon that was pure manipulated suggestion, the kind of web-like information-field that will replace eventually all pulleys, levers, and even our beloved electronic pulsations. His achievement is that he was one of the first to introduce the world to levels of post-industrial power as pure suggestion, performance, mimicking and virtual products, which last not more than a minute of old crankshaft time. In the sense that he introduced ideas of power and control as cool things and not old-Hitler hot, he was a highly significant first modern.

The age was changing in Adamski's head, and one such head is enough. Time in that sense exists in very few individuals. Like Yali of Melanesia, he was to be left marooned and confused; time dropped him and he could not complete his stories. But perhaps initiation of the first stories is sufficient; after that, the mission of such a manic information-animal as Adamski is complete. His offspring were the eggs of a story-virus. Death comes only when the story cycle has lodged within the host. Then our teller of tales must go on to other story cycles beyond the sun and moon. Like Shakespeare, he leaves his fast-breeding stories behind as a form of immortality.

Adamski created a permanent pan-dimensional masterwork: his

books, his films, and his photographic collection. Seen as a whole, this complex is as good as any in the twentieth century artistic portfolio. Just like his distant mentor, Charles Fort, Adamski's images serve as modern protective talismans against all solutions, singular or final, partial or elegant. He is a major constituent of the strange power of the UFO. Even young skeptics of a very different generation jump up and down like natives round a beating drum and take extreme counter-ritualizing measures against his very name.

Meantime, contactees keep faith. They worship bits of very odd metal, unusual plastic, strange implants, and even a tasteless biscuit or two for similar protection against old industrial Fact. Against the Western twilight, they hold up these hosts and watch the sky.

CHAPTER 10

Entertainment State is Born

It can be seen by now that 1953 was a vintage year for Adamski. The American edition of *Flying Saucers Have Landed* appeared in late 1953, and it received as much popular acclaim as it had earlier in Britain. Adamski was certainly a busy man at this time. He was meeting his space folk and taking trips in flying saucers, and having trouble with the FBI, largely, it must be said, provoked by himself. He would return from outer space to his mountain home, and for light relief, he would have endless rows with his former worshippers.

There was no let-up. During this crowded year, Adamski was also privileged to receive a visit from none other than the renowned Captain Edward J. Ruppelt,[104] head of the U.S. Air Force Project Blue Book that investigated UFOs. Ruppelt's almost forgotten story of his visit to Palomar appears in the pages of the 1960 edition of his original 1956 book, *The Report on Unidentified Flying Objects.* Curiously, this new edition does not mention the date of its publication, but on page 270, Ruppelt mentions that Adamski met Queen Juliana of the Netherlands, "last week." Since this meeting occurred on May 18, 1959, we can assume that Ruppelt was in the middle of revisions of the new edition of *The Report on Unidentified Flying Objects,* which appeared finally in 1960, a very short time before he died of a heart attack at the early age of 37 years.

The Adamski story was not mentioned in the first edition of 1956, and therefore Ruppelt is looking back some seven years from 1959 to "one day in 1953" when he walked into the "four stool restaurant with a few tables" where he saw Adamski working as a "handyman" in the crowded restaurant "serving beer and picking up empty bottles." It is a very long focus pull, but Ruppelt gives us an invaluable cameo of Adamski at this time.

Ruppelt of course was visiting incognito, if only because he knew (and so did just about everybody else) what Adamski could do with just the smallest piece of story-protein. What he would have said and done had he known that he was serving beer to Captain Ruppelt of Project Blue Book can well be imagined. The visit would have been transformed immediately into some "full official admission" of a "final proof" etc., etc.

Ruppelt continues: "There was no doubt who he [Adamski] was because his fame had spread. To the dozen almost reverently spoken queries 'Are you Adamski?' he modestly nodded his head. Small questions about the flying saucer photos for sale from convenient racks led to more questions and before long the good 'professor' had taken a position in the middle of the room and was off and running."

Like many a stout heart before him, Ruppelt, of all people, falls for the charm: "To look at the man and to listen to his story you had an immediate urge to believe him. Maybe it was his appearance. He was dressed in well worn, but neat, overalls. He had slightly graying hair and the most honest pair of eyes I've ever seen. Or maybe it was the way he told his story. He spoke softly and naively, almost pathetically, giving the impression that 'most people think I'm crazy, but honestly, I'm really not.'"

As Adamski launches into his story of the desert contact, Ruppelt continues: "Now, even those in the crowded restaurant who had been smirking when he started his story had put down their beers and were listening. This is what they had come to hear. You could have heard the proverbial pin drop."

After the story comes a very precious and magic moment which Ruppelt must have remembered all his life: "At the urging of the crowd in the restaurant Adamski took an old shoe box from under the counter. One of his party [George Hunt Williamson], that day, had just happened to have some plaster of paris [bought previously by Jerrold Baker on the orders of Lucy McGinnis] and the shoe box contained plaster casts of shoe prints with strange, hieroglyphic-like symbols on the soles. Next he showed the sworn statements of the witnesses and the crowd moved in around him for a better look."

To think that Ruppelt saw all this for himself is amazing. But if he let the spirits of Twain and Melville into his head for a brief moment, he just as quickly threw them out. As mundane guilt fills him up, he rains on Adamski's parade: "As I left he was graciously filling people in on more details and the cash register was merrily ringing up saucer picture sales. I didn't write off the trip as a complete loss, the weather in California was beautiful."

The year 1953 also saw Helen and Bryant Reeve, a bright, good-humored professional couple from Detroit, becoming deeply impressed by *Flying Saucers Have Landed,* and its combination of personal and historical views. Bryant Reeve, an engineer, was on the verge of retirement, and had plenty of time to co-write with his wife Helen, *Flying Saucer Pilgrimage,* which appeared in 1957. This book casts light on the kind of life Adamski lived in the mid 1950s, and includes some interesting cameos of the visits to America of Desmond Leslie. It illustrates also the atmosphere in America when flying saucer fever raged in the years just before the legendary mass-sighting of lights over the Capitol building in Washington in 1952.

There had been some quite spectacular saucer sightings in Detroit in 1952, and in 1953, there was a sighting significant enough to be included in the 1968 *Scientific Study of Unidentified Flying Objects,* the much-criticized report commissioned by the University of Colorado and headed by physicist Edward U. Condon. In March, 1953, the pilot and radar operator of a USAF F-94B Starfire fighter were directed by Ground Control Intercept radar at Selfridge Air Force Base to intercept unknown targets over downtown Detroit. The crew reported "tiny specks in the sky, which appeared to look like a ragged formation of aircraft." The radar returns then showed the objects moving over the city's central section. The crew expressed great surprise when the objects did not resemble aircraft, and the pilot started his calculated interception run "without afterburner" at 500 mph. The ground radar had both the fighter and the objects "painted as good, strong targets" and the pilot reported that the objects "seemed to get a little larger all the time." The radar operator of the aircraft also began to get good returns and "thought he was picking up targets" when the objects disappeared both from view and the airborne radar.

Most surprisingly, the ground radar still continued to get "loud and clear" returns even when the aircraft itself was right in the center of the targets and turning in "every direction."

After three minutes the objects disappeared from the GCI radar and the fighter returned to base.

As one of the leading lights in a growing group of saucer enthusiasts, Bryant Reeve was interested in the kind of high-quality report the Detroit sighting represented. Enthused, he tried to telephone George Adamski at home in Palomar Gardens in November 1953, just after Adamski's second trip into space. He was most surprised to learn that the now famous man did not have a listed number there. Undaunted, the Reeves wrote to the Palomar address, and Adamski replied, accepting an invitation to lecture at the Detroit Institute of Arts, and insisted on receiving expenses only. The Reeves organized a group of some forty sponsors to finance a press conference and two lectures. The exciting day came when the group met the man himself: "There he was at the railroad station: tall, distinguished looking, gray-haired, wearing a beret that rivaled Field Marshal Montgomery's."

Thus did Adamski enter Detroit. The great industrial city in those days was the biggest and the best car-manufacturing center in the world. General Motors led the way in linking glamour and technology. The world licked its lips as the latest "flivver simply dripping in chrome" came off the production lines indeed looking a little like a space ship itself. In advertisements, early prototypes of Jane Mansfield and Marilyn Monroe draped themselves across Pontiacs and Chevrolets, making the citizens of other nations feel that they lived in dog kennels and picked their nose all day.

Like Dallas and Vegas, Detroit in the early 1950s was alive with new imagery and new money. Nobody bothered about what was later called the environment, and little interest was aroused by the growing problem the French were having with guerilla insurgents in Vietnam. Lee Harvey Oswald had just started shaving and the great American protest generations of the future still attended segregated schools. Those who watched *Creature from the Black Lagoon* in the cinemas and the Korean War film *Battle Taxi* at the drive-ins probably gave little notice to the Washington crusade of Republican Senator Joe McCarthy. But the young Lee Harvey

Oswald may well have paid more serious attention to the execution of the Rosenburgs in Sing Sing in 1953 for allegedly giving Soviet Russia some secrets of the atom bomb.

In an essay in *The Anomalist,* Karl T. Pflock[105] comments: "Even in the spreading shadow of the early Cold War. Things in America were rosy and optimistic. Anything seemed possible—for Everyman as never before in history. Everywhere one looked, it seemed a quick and big buck from War surplus, everything from boots to airplanes and ships. Uranium prospecting. And oil. And of course, flying saucers. It was a time ripe for confidence tricksters and slick operators, and there were many opportunities and angles for them to work, some a bit more exotic than others."[106]

Reporters from major Detroit newspapers were at the Adamski press conference, and a reporter from a newspaper in Windsor, Canada, had made the long journey. After cocktails and luncheon, the hard-boiled skeptics (as Bryant Reeve called the reporters), began their "inquisition." Reeve describes the scene, which had echoes of the kind of treatment Adamski was to receive on his European tour five years later in 1959: "The scene was unforgettable. George Adamski sat at the head of the table. Back of him were "blown up" pictures of his telescope and his saucers. The news hounds deserted their chairs, crowded round him, and literally rained questions on their unpretentious victim. Questions were fired so fast that they overlapped each other. From our viewpoint every approach, every ruse was being used to trip him up."

Adamski's public performances were not always good, but on this occasion he surpassed himself, impressing everyone by remaining perfectly calm, unruffled, and most courteous. This earned him good front-page coverage, and even the skeptical reports were mild. However, the good publicity did not impress the radio stations, which in those somewhat pre-TV days were still very important, having that popular community feel of early media that has almost vanished from the world. Bryant Reeves describes radio producers as saying the entire subject of flying saucers was "too incredible, apt to make us a laughing stock, can't risk it."

However, Ross Mulholland, a presenter of WWJ, a large Detroit radio station, was reluctantly persuaded by one Laura, a member of the Reeve's group, to grant Adamski a five-minute radio interview. Adamski's media performances always surpassed his public appearances in dynamism and power, and now given a live audience (how media time passes!), he took the entire place over. Here, as told by Bryant Reeves is a time capsule from the long-lost days of spit-and-sawdust American Radio. At "one P.M.": "Mr. Adamski went on the air with all the excitement of a premier performance. A thrill stole over the broadcast room. Technicians and helpers paused in their work to listen—almost in awe to this simple man who told of his contact on the Californian desert with a man from another world."

Ross Mulholland took questions from the floor and even from the on-duty radio technicians. The five minute dead line came and went almost unnoticed. Other scheduled programs were cancelled. Only station announcements and short commercials cut into the interview. The program ended one hour and twenty-five minutes after it started.

After this success, there was some disappointment at the first lecture, entitled "What Is The World Heading For?" When Adamski was off-color, he could be the most boring man in the world, dispensing his own brand of gnomic theosophical preaching, the mental level of which was barely above the advice column of a parish magazine. However, when he talked about science, astronomy, his photographing of flying saucers and his contact with men and women from other planets, he could be electrifying. Like Ray Palmer, the great science fiction editor of the 1940s and 1950s, Adamski, though he was getting on in age, was in touch with the burgeoning pop-mythology of that new and exciting technology that was going to be the making of America. If he did not communicate particularly well, that he communicated at all put him way ahead of dull scientists in an age when image, not fact, was becoming really important. When he spoke of contact with space beings, he was similarly inspired. This is just one of the reasons why some say that his experiences were authentic. When he dropped his religious spouting, there emerged a new energetic body language, a fresh urgency to his expression. It was observed to be a natural change, the kind of effect seen when a man speaks who has been almost moved out of his wits by some half-hidden event of the past. His language became brimful of those very images that were lacking in his religious expression. He went straight to the point with an incredible modern adventure story and audiences often came away deeply affected. In every sense, he extended new technological expectations to infinity, not as a science-fiction writer, but as someone who gave a new live dimension to what was becoming a worldwide phenomenon.

Adamski lectured to a new prosperous techno-industrial class with nothing of the doom and gloom that possessed Britain at this time. By comparison, Americans had few stifling class restrictions or the burdens of hereditary structures. In the 1950s, Americans were the world's winners, and they knew it. Adamski's audience was young, the Presley phenomenon was raging and fired by B-feature films (some of which have since become classics), and Americans enjoyed a new prosperity the like of which the world had not seen before. They were also stoked up by the books on saucers written by Frank Scully and Donald Keyhoe, published some three years before *Flying Saucers Have Landed*. Countless rumors of crashed saucers, recovered alien bodies, and military intrigue were also rife.

Fifty years later the debates still rage about all these things; like nothing else, their mythology is still quite intact. A few days before Princess Diana died, the *London Evening Standard* published a prophetic cartoon by illustrator "Jak" showing a landed Adamski-type saucer with a lowered entrance ramp. Elvis Presley stands on the ramp, welcoming Diana as she walks up to go inside. It is indeed strange that the folk of 1995 (the year of Diana's death) felt still so powerfully related to an image well nigh fifty years old!

There were many new agendas heading for the minds of Adamski's new young American audience, of which the newborn ufology was but one. The fledgling public relations firms that were later to become mighty corporations were flexing their muscles and starting to use what was then the new technology of broadcast television and high-definition widescreen Technicolor feature-films. The various new agendas stalked their way to this audience for all the world as if they were B-feature viral life forms themselves. Here was a first true "media" generation, and the forces that were to govern such a thing were historically unprecedented. Society was beginning to be stalked by ideas rather than old-fashioned enemies; clusters of show-business images angered, depressed, or frightened them rather than the physical threats of old. There was beginning to arise a cult of images, devices, and products in this new-born Entertainment State, which made all previous history look threadbare and depressing, with all its Wars, Leaders, Priests, and Serious Issues heading rapidly for the reject-edit can of history. The aims of what General Leslie Groves, who was in charge of the Manhattan Project, called "big science" had not yet been questioned; the Vietnamese war, the greatest disaster in American history, had not yet occurred, and the diseases of happiness had not yet been suspected, chartered, or experienced. As America looked to space, *Flying Saucers Have Landed* was just the kind of mad techno erotic fix that the young in particular identified with.

But somebody or something within quite a different process altogether was trying to divert this audience from certain kinds of imaginative contagion. At this time, many writers of UFO subjects, contactees or otherwise, detected attempts to control agendas, be they intellectual, consumer, or technological in nature. In a 1959 article entitled "Who is trying to Stop the Truth from Coming Out?" published in *Flying Saucer Review*, Adamski stated that after the publication of *Inside the Spaceships* there was a serious attempt in Detroit to bribe him into saying that the book was fiction. The offer was $35,000, a considerable increase on the first offer he had of $25,000. In this article he continues: "I was visiting the Scully home in Hollywood, when Frank [Scully] told me grimly that he had been offered $25,000 to sign a statement saying his book *Behind The Flying Saucers*[107] was fiction."

Both maverick anthropologist Carlos Castanada and writer Whitley Streiber, who wrote of his "visitor" experiences in *Communion* and other books at the end of the 20th century, had the same problems. Metaphors are in every way advertisements, and attempts to change metaphor are always surrounded by the kind of dangers no simple mechanical criminality could arouse. Forces beyond all belief are summoned.

Soon after the appearance of *Flying Saucers Have Landed,* the astute Leslie sent Adamski a letter in which he said: "I don't know what has happened, George, but all the mediums have suddenly disposed of their Indian guides, etc., and have replaced them with space people traveling in Vimanas."

This letter shows just how much both Adamski and Leslie were helping to change metaphor with their influential book; it was a kind of focus for a lot of subterranean thinking at this time. The material world itself cannot help but spring from change of metaphor, and later, as we shall see, just like the work of Mesmer, this virus was to enter much higher realms than that of the parlor psychic.

If Charles Lutwidge Dodgson had published his *Alice in Wonderland* as a "real" experience he would have found himself in exactly the same trouble as Adamski. As any good advertising expert knows, "fiction" itself is another name for that psychological management system intended to place the experience of imagining at a controllable distance. The technique is as old as humanity. To see the Garden of Eden story or the Odyssey as "unreal" not only serves as an understandable defensive technique, it also solves a lot of intellectual, religious, and cultural problems in one. But take such controlling fictional framework from a story, and within the very bedrock of Nature, deep alarm bells ring; some automated process tries to stop such an "escape" of stories from the prison house of their inked pages. Quite ordinary folk wake in the morning full of anger, determined to put a stop to what they consider to be a violation of decent moral and intellectual sense. As in the Lee Harvey Oswald story, back-bedroom cartoon figures step out of their frames and head for their targets trailing wires and smoke. They then press their paper-triggers and promptly disappear, like Oswald's many doubles.

A rich fantasy life is vital for product-success; it helps create the prototypes that barrel down American runways and not any other country's runways. Neither Marx nor Lenin ever recognized or understood postindustrial forces in which the UFO would play a considerable and lasting part. Their inability to see such things caused the collapse of America's greatest enemy without so much as a shot being fired, or almost. In this framework of high importance we can see that image making as powerful suggestion is just as politically important as profiteering, espionage, or economic planning.

Of course, there may be another explanation other than the crude idea of simple fabrication of stories and, indeed, hoaxes by individuals such as Adamski. He, and others like him may forever be the prey of a process that chooses them precisely because they will most willingly create new episodes to follow from the first "genuine" episoce. After they have become hopeless addicts, they become fast breeders of story-protein, which may be the whole object of the enterprise. The world is run by story-techonology, not facts, which are historically arriviste contraptions, doomed as reject footage of Mario Lanza, an episode of *I love Lucy,* or a physics text book of 1955. In this, Adamski's mythological engineering was identical to that inspired by still small voices in the head heard by the great world prophets of the past. By telling tales that competed with prime-time consciousness, he became just as valid as the Camelot target represented by President Kennedy. Plant a bomb, and the State knows how to deal with you without even thinking about it. Say you met a man from Venus and a far deeper State anger is aroused out of all proportion to your non-existent physical threat.

In this, thing have not changed since the death of Socrates.

Adamski's second Detroit lecture, entitled "My Experiences," was a great success. He changed from bleating obscure religio-philosophy to relating an external drama, and remained in control, even when the deep booming voice of a local Detroit character "Singapore Joe" Fisher came from the audience. Fisher was a British world-traveler and lecturer. He asked: "Mr. Adamski, what about sex on Venus?" To which Adamski replied like a character straight out of Herman Melville's *The Confidence Man:*" Well, sir, if you went to Venus, I do not believe you would have to learn any new tricks!"

A reception had been arranged by the Detroit sponsors at a nearby hotel, and at the request of many, Adamski was asked to speak impromptu. Here again he made the same old mistake, and talked almost exclusively about religion, to the disappointment of all present, according to Bryant Reeve. Adamski's bizarre evangelical ufology was a turn-off to most. He had the brilliantly mad child's junk-book approach of Frank Stranges, combined with the surreal comedy of Orpheo Angelluci, with more than a touch of the "techno" fairy tales of Howard Menger. A future time bored with, and suspicious of, complementary conscious descriptions of our time will look to the books of these authors as apocryphal texts. They will be regarded as the Dead Sea Scrolls of consumerism, along with Beatles' lyrics, and Presidential denials. Venusians apart, this is just one of the precious and vital things about the Adamski phenomenon; it tells how groups form, how beliefs are manufactured, and how a kind of possession occurs in terms of firm conviction. There is also pathos and tragedy; towards the end of his life, Adamski suffers a kind of mental decay yet captures on his last film, shot at Silver Spring, perhaps the most significant footage in all ufology.

Adamski's sponsors and his audiences were always most worried about the almost-believable experience being often just sentences away from unbelievably exact details of Venusian kitchen-practices, and ultrasonic dry-cleaning, no less. In this, he was a human simulacra of the UFO form itself: infuriating, refusing to be defined. He was one thing one minute, quite another the next; to raw audiences of those days he must have seemed something of an elemental sprite himself, just arrived from the very spaceships that looked a little like the shiny cars and toasters, or was it the other way around?.

Here again we are reminded of Melville's *The Confidence Man,* and Adamski at this time did indeed have something of the covered-wagon atmosphere about him, which appealed to a popular American audience. The effect of dispensing homemade potions was enhanced by him blithely including in talks bits and pieces from an encyclopedic "factual" knowledge culled in the main from the popular science journals of his day. When this exotic combination was mixed with a terribly mawkish Christianity, it formed a stream of cross-referenced mythologies that quite a few found hard to take. But then this is no more than a nice man in a clerical collar talking about bicycles and modulating quickly into miracles wrought by a man who walked on water and came back from the dead. If we don't like or accept the Venusian "etheric magnetism motor," then we certainly like the walking on water, or at least half the planetary population does. In this we manage mysteries rather than solve them.[108] The same scaling occurs generally through what we now call ufology. Daylight discs and nocturnal lights, yes, but abductions, no; humanoid forms, yes, lizard forms wielding scalpels, no.

CHAPTER 11

Management of Mysteries

It was possibly at meetings like the one in Detroit that Adamski began to form a solution to what was beginning to be a recurring problem. Why not try and integrate these things, combine them into one unified story? The publication of *Inside the Spaceships* in 1955 shows that he tried to solve the problem, but in a very awkward way. He put whole paragraphs of his bland and monotonous "Universal Law" philosophy into the mouth of the unnamed commander of the spaceship—so much so that this commander at one point, uses that exact phrase himself! To some critics, this sort of thing was the final proof that Adamski was a complete fake.

Carl Jung thought he had got to the bottom of it all when he remarked to Lou Zinstagg that he was inclined to think that Adamski's photographs were genuine, but that his "his story is an invention." But here Jung seems to have forgotten the principle of alchemy he so famously enunciated some year previous. In his essay on "Transubstantiation in the Catholic Mass" he stated that "the symbol becomes intercalated into the cycle of corporeal changes." Certainly any human group models, experiments, rejects, modifies, and comes into contact with other groups who are doing exactly the same things but in different directions and from different evolutionary standpoints. The mind reasons by the resulting mess of dirty noise, making experience anything but a singular united linear fabric. Rather is mind a multi-dimensional boiling cauldron, and almost anything may form out of such blending and choosing, such wishing and creating. In William Empson's paraphrase of Wittgenstein's philosophy, "anything that can be imagined can happen." Thus do we manage our wonders and our fantasies rather than "disprove" them.

But even the great Jung had difficulty in stepping out of some paradigms of limitation. He said to Lou Zinstagg that Adamski's Orthon had quite defeated him. Of the famous contact scene in *Flying Saucers Have Landed,* he observed: "When I got to the beautiful young man with the silken hair I could not go on reading. This sounds ridiculous to me—like a fairy tale." Since Jung's great gift to mankind was a deep analysis of the meaning, function, and psychoanalysis of the fairy-tale, this remark is surprising.

It is certain that Adamski re-structured his belief-system, as represented originally by his self-published fictional book *Pioneers in Space,* to try and make it work off the page into life itself. When this happens in the laboratory, men and women get the Nobel Prize. When it happens within the software of pure vision, they are usually vilified, accused of cheating, fraud and exploitation. It is the difference between someone writing about fairies and saying they saw one in a wood. Our culture has lost entirely Jung's idea of an intermediate state between the two. In this sense, Literature itself is all about a form of purely natural mind-control; as long as things don't spill out of the culture-dish, we can safely enjoy ourselves. It is likely that Adamski went from fiction to fact not in an attempt to deceive, so much as to create. The transparently honest Lucy McGinnis, Adamski's secretary for many years, saw this process in action. She told Timothy Good that, indeed, she was worried by the similarities between Adamski's earlier "fictional" work, *Pioneers of Space,* and the "factual" work *Inside the Space Ships.* She added, "It never bothered me to the extent that I made an issue of it, because, you see, I could have made an issue of it if I hadn't seen those ships."[109]

This triangulation between almost-fiction and almost-fact, with personal experience in between, makes up a rare moment regarding individual identity and cultural formation. On one hand, McGinnis is aware of a book that was cast as fiction. On the other hand, she is aware of another later book in which that fiction has been edited as fact. The two sides of this equation would cancel themselves out *if she had not seen the ships with her own eyes.* It is as if the ships were made of the very flow of information from the first book to the second. If Jung had been more patient and looked more closely, he of all people would have detected that process within the whole Adamski affair. Lucy McGinnis was privileged to see such a complete triangulation between almost-fact, almost-fiction and uncompromising personal visionary experience.

The British writer Nick Pope, who was in charge of UFO Investigations for the Ministry of Defense, is a more recent author[110] who has experienced such a triangulation. He went from being a "hard" Ministry of Defense man into a kind of no-man's land, then on to pure fiction, with rumors of his own "abduction" in-between. Thus fifty years later, Pope, like Adamski, traveled through all three information-dimensions with the bonus of a claim as equally fantastic as that of Adamski.[111]

After a few weeks, Adamski was invited back to Detroit. This time, despite bad weather, he filled 4,700 seats of the 5000-seat Masonic Temple, which was festooned with banners bearing his name. But again, his performance was disappointing. He had never had any training in this business of proper public presentation as the PR man had yet to arrive properly on the historical stage. Also, the halls in those days were just halls. They had practically nothing of today's modern sound systems, and even fewer audio-visual presentation aids. America at this time was still very much a hailing-distance culture, and Adamski appeared nervous and ill-prepared. As was not uncommon in those days, the single complicated projector was nowhere near powerful enough to properly present films and slides to a mass audience. Things were not improved by Adamski's lack of knowledge about how to present himself and his material to such a large public audience. At this stage in his life, he had no proper assistant in attendance, no manager, and no personal presentation advisor.

According to Bryant Reeve, Adamski's insistence on reading out in full a long and complicated letter nearly brought things to a complete halt. Even an amateur con-man would have done far better this. By far the most reasonable assumption is that Adamski was being his fumbling self and telling the truth as he saw it. Bryant Reeve observes that Adamski was somewhat relieved when he caught his train to New York.

In mid-1954, Desmond Leslie came to California to meet his co-author for the first time. In October he traveled to Detroit to meet the Reeve's group. Bryant Reeve was impressed immediately by this "fine, tall, cultured young Irishman." Leslie was grabbed quickly by radio station WWJ's Ross Mulholland, and again an electrifying live broadcast was made, some tapes of which still exist. Leslie then packed 1,200 folk into the largest auditorium of the Detroit Institute of Arts, and amused everyone with his witty tales of encounters with stiff British astronomers. He also raised smiles with his equally amusing tales about even stiffer English skeptics, whose essentially Victorian minds were still with Kitchener at Kartoum, as most of them still are.[112] Amusing as all true Irishmen are when speaking of the English, he described them as viewing anomalies as if they were hordes of the great unwashed about to break into the front parlor. Apparently he was also inspiring when he talked about how the English had no concept for the mysterious.

All this of course required brilliant wit and sophisticated skill. Compared with Adamski's fumbling efforts, Leslie performed with a brilliant wit and sophistication that satisfied many doubters of the authenticity of the saucer phenomenon. In the course of this same lecture, the "Saucerer Royal" (as the Reeves dubbed Leslie), talked about saucers being photographed during contemporary nuclear weapons tests, and he touched also upon areas of contemporary saucer interest, including topics which the definitely non-discursive Adamski rarely broached. In this sense Adamski lost out. He already had his Theosophical-Christian "solution" to the saucer phenomenon, and therefore talking about what went on in Hangar No. 27 of Muroc Air Base in any detailed modern analytic sense would have been as irrelevant to him as asking Jesus about the back of his left earlobe.

Leslie was to meet the Reeves again a year later, when he lectured in Colombus, Ohio on October 26th, 1955. There he gave the audience the latest saucer reports from Britain, including one very English account of a gardener being knocked off his bicycle by a saucer. Again, in the Leslie manner, he put the saucer "problem" in an historical perspective quite new to most American audiences. Says Bryant Reeve of Leslie: "…he brought out the point that if he had talked about television one hundred years ago he probably would have been put in a straitjacket; two hundred years ago he would have been burned at the stake for witchcraft!"

CHAPTER 12

The Sub Plot: *Flying Saucer Pilgrimage*

In October 1954, Bryant Reeve took full retirement, and he set out with his wife Helen for Mexico. This was to be the first part of their "Flying Saucer Pilgrimage" which was eventually to produce their book of that name. They contacted groups in the Mexico City area that had a saucer interest, and within a short time they became well known, appearing in newspapers, and on television. They even appeared for two minutes in a Luis Bunuel film of all things, *Ensayo de un Crime (Rehearsal for a Crime)*. They were also elected charter members of the newly formed Mexican Society of Interplanetary Investigation.

All this made them "celebrities" in Mexican eyes, aided by their known friendship with George Adamski and the publication of the Spanish translation of *Flying Saucers Have Landed*. The Reeves appeared on a television program "Mesa de Celebridades" (The Table of the Celebrities), to be questioned about "platillos voladores" (flying saucers). This was presented from the roof-garden restaurant on top of the Continental Hotel in downtown Mexico City, and it was a prime-time program watched by the cognoscenti and "smart set" of all Mexico. The astute Helen herself scored particularly well when asked about the possibility of the whole saucer business being a mass hallucination. She replied saying that if such a thing could happen, then would be a bigger mystery than the saucer business itself.

Thus all was going well for the Reeves in Mexico until one day they picked up their mail and found a letter from none other than George Adamski himself. He said that he would be coming to Mexico for a vacation and rest on March 21st, 1955, most probably because he had just completed *Inside the Spaceships*.

The "saucerers" of the Mexican and English Speaking Group duly met Adamski at the airport. Bryant Reeve says that Adamski's arrival was the beginning of: "...a series of bizarre events that proved the old adage—'anything can happen in Mexico.' Some of these happenings so nearly resembled a fantastic light opera plot that even while they were occurring they seemed to us more like fiction than reality. As we all seemed to be playing parts in this amazing drama, we had to pinch ourselves at times to make sure we were really awake."

On top of this Mexico effect, the Reeves also received in full the "Adamski effect" often observed by those who entered his orbit. Desmond Leslie was himself quite familiar with this effect. During Leslie's stay at Palomar, for example, there was hardly a dull moment, with many incidents straight from the pages of John Fowles' novel, *The Magus*. In the summer of 1954, Desmond Leslie visited Adamski and stayed at his house in Rincon Springs on Palomar Mountain. One evening, while walking nearby, Leslie says, "I noticed a very bright ball of light rising from Adamski's roof, about a quarter of a mile away. It rose rapidly, rather like a silvery gold Very Light, and continued to rise until it disappeared from sight."

The following evening Leslie saw a similar effect while sitting on the patio with Adamski and Alice Wells. He felt at the time a "curious cold feeling" come over him, and he felt also that someone was behind him, and watching him closely: "I swung round in time to see a small golden disk between us and the Live Oaks fifty feet away. Almost instantly it shot up in the air with an imperceptible swish, leaving a faint trail behind it, then vanished. George grinned solemnly. 'I was wondering when you were going to notice that!' I was amazed."

Leslie has the same problem as Nicholas Urfe in *The Magus*. The time-space equations do not quite fit the movement of ideas and materials, people and events. But then neither do normal space-time equations fit the physical schemes of the major American assassinations. Seeing such things, as he did with Adamski sitting beside him, Leslie, like Urfe, might well have asked who was pulling the strings? Is Leslie a liar, or had Adamski himself rigged all the stage machinery required for these strange effects? Or are we on a kind of modern Prospero's island, with the mechanical explanations far more fantastic then that they would seek to explain? Or are the explanations themselves a function of the deception?

Lou Zinsstag, wrote of meeting Adamski in 1959: "...the few days I had spent with George had given me the insight that I was dealing with an extraordinary person. I already knew that there was another side to this man, a mystical one perhaps, and that there was probably another story to his story."

We can understand what Zinstagg is taking about when her Dutch friend Rey d'Aquila received in clear a telepathic test-message sent by Adamski himself to all members of his "Get Acquainted Group." Apparently, in the Adamski style, the message was banal, and Zinstagg is dismissive, but she does not seem at all impressed that it got there at all.

This kind of "definitely provable" event was to dog Adamski all his life, baffling all but his most severe critics, who often got out of an embarrassing predicament by denying everything and anything. But just one of the problems in dealing with Adamski was the sheer number of high quality reports coming in quite independently. The following statement by astronaut James McDivitt made in *Omni* magazine in 1980, is particularly significant. While a USAF jet pilot in 1951, he said that for "..several days in a row we sighted groups of metallic, saucer-shaped vehicles at great altitudes over the base, and we tried to get closer to them, but they were able to change direction faster than our fighters. I do believe that UFOs exist and that the truly unexplained ones are from some other technologically advanced civilization."

The Mexican and English Speaking Group planned the inevitable press conference, but made the mistake of using the Reeve's apartment for this. Adamski was besieged, the apartment overflowed with reporters and photographers, and the event looked as if it was going to be a total success. However it had been noticed by some members of the Group that a certain number of reporters were not sympathetic at all. Fears were justified when the event got hardly any press coverage.

While Bryant Reeve was organizing a *conferencia* for Adamski, he experienced the comedy of being mistaken for the great man himself. Helen Reeve had her own comic episode when she observed a group of influential Mexicans trying to get into a lift. They were anxious to meet Adamski, but the social and professional pecking order of entrance into the lift had to be carefully organized. While this was being sorted out, the lift, of course, kept going up and down. The group of rather provincial Mexicans could not understand this motion, and they would be there to this day had not Helen ushered them all inside regardless.

Similar Mexican practices prevailed at the *conferencia*. Apparently in Mexico, no speaker was ever allowed to continue for more than a few minutes. The result was a haze of quite impromptu comments and questions in both Mexican and English. Some of these interruptions were instantly translated into one or the other language, often by several over-enthusiastic members of the audience at once. Any apparent inaccuracies of translation became immediately points of loud multi-lingual contention.

Adamski himself virtually disappeared in what became a mass of internecine controversy, but he had better luck a short time later when he appeared at the Insurgenta Theatre. A world-famous mosaic mural created by the artist Diego Rivera adorned the front of the theatre, and astonishingly, Rivera himself actually turned up for the event, which shows the kind of people Adamski managed to attract at this time. The pair had a conversation, and Adamski expressed his admiration of the mural.

In the foyer was hung a long banner: "Conferencia Los Platillos Voladores Por George Adamski," and despite a lack of press coverage again, the Group filled the large theatre by word of mouth. They charged five pesos (then 40 cents in American money) for entrance to defray expenses, an action which would cause them much trouble later. Again, Adamski's lecture was interrupted when a television crew turned up and tried to film the event. They caused so much noise and disruption they were asked to leave, which by Mexican standards, must have been some noise and disruption.

Next came a grand reception at the American Club. Bryant Reeve describes the scene, and again demonstrates Adamski's pulling power "all in the interest of saucers": "Lights, photographers, caviar, cocktails, reception lines, introductions, music! Distinguished men in fine attire and beautiful ladies in colorful dress. A sprinkling of diplomats and military personnel. And waiters really doing their stuff."

But all was not well. A member of the Group reported that an uninvited guest was inquiring about how much Adamski charged for his lectures.

Though he was told that no one had been charged, subsequently another man appeared who served a subpoena on Adamski. This concerned the paltry fee charged for entrance to the Insurgentes Theatre, which apparently violated Mexican law since Adamski did not have a work permit. It was obvious that though he talked only of flying saucers, he had by this time quite a powerful apparatus following him and trying to discredit and restrict his activities. Such quite tangible action was the source of much early conspiracy theory regarding Adamski and many other contactees. If Authority thoroughly despised and dismissed the phenomenon, it nevertheless paid it a great deal of secret and semi-secret attention.

Worrying about whether he was going to be deported or even jailed, Adamski found yet another writ waiting for him when he arrived back at his hotel that night. This one summoned him to a Court Hearing the next morning. At the hearing, his papers were taken away, which made him *persona non grata* in Mexico. The Reeves tried to get the American Embassy to help, but such machinery moves slowly, and the next few days were spent trying to keep Adamski out of jail, a move that would have had serious consequences with regard to any future passport application.

Because of this business, Adamski received adverse publicity that resulted in the cancellation of some television programs. Cancelled also was an important lecture to La Asociacion Nacional de Tecnicos Mexicanos (the National Association of Mexican Technical Men).

The whole drama headed towards a whirlwind finish. A few days after the Hearing, a Senõr Hero (sic) called on the Reeves. He was obviously a powerful and influential man, and he took notes as the Reeves described what had happened to Adamski. He assured the Reeves that all would be straightened out the next morning, and took his leave. In Mexican fashion, at midnight, he rang again and invited the Reeves and Adamski to a midnight feast at his house.

They collected Adamski and a Mexican friend, who had a powerful car. They had hardly started the journey to Señor Hero's house some miles away in Coyoacan, when they were stopped by two grim-looking traffic policemen on motorcycles. Their Mexican friend had the wit to mention Senor Hero's name to the policemen whereupon their entire attitude changed. The baffled party were then escorted with screaming sirens, and the pale-faced Reeves noticed that at times the speedometer read 100 miles per hour.

They arrived finally at a beautiful mansion and were greeted by Señor Hero and his wife. Hero said that all the wrongs of the Adamski affair would be put right, and indeed they were, the very next day. Hero also managed to re-schedule Adamski's lecture to the Mexican Technical Men.

Before Adamski left Mexico the beaver-like Reeves arranged a meeting between himself and the "Mexican Adamski," one Salvador Villanueva Medina, a chauffeur by profession. Helen and Bryant Reeves were present, together with an interpreter and a friend, Señor Gebes, in whose house the meeting took place. The session took the form of Adamski asking questions about saucers that no-one could have answered without having being inside one. Medina passed the test, and the Reeves found the experience a fittingly awe-inspiring end to their days in Mexico, a place as hot, dramatic, and as full of vibrant hues as Adamski's stories themselves.

The splendid Reeves now leave the George Adamski story, as on April 10th, 1955, they cross the border at El Paso passing through country where the young Adamski might well have hunted bandits, illegal immigrants, and smugglers when he served with the US Cavalry. We leave them as they head for the next part of their magical Californian journey. They will meet George Hunt Williamson one of the original members of the Adamski desert contact group, go to Van Tassel's Giant Rock UFO Airport, and many other points of enchanted America.

Adamski was to return to Mexico in late 1956, where he spent some months on vacation in Chalapa, Jalisco, Mexico. There he shot a 16-mm color motion film of a huge, domed spacecraft hovering over a highway. He also made a short film about an incident that had occurred in Guadalajara some three years before. Apparently a huge spaceship had landed near a banana plantation. Two "men" from this ship were invited by the farmer of the plantation into his home where they stayed for two hours, during which the farmer gave them fruits, flowers, and seeds apparently at their request. They took off, but returned four days later and took the farmer for a ride in their ship. After four more days, the farmer returned and went straight to the Mexican government with his story.

The government formed an investigation committee that studied the case for three years. Two hundred witnesses were interviewed and soil samples taken. In his film (shown later in Europe in 1959), Adamski shows the farm and its surroundings, and also many of the people directly involved, such as officials and policemen. The affair ended on a disturbing note with the disappearance of the farmer and his family.

Adamski returned to Palomar Terraces in early 1957 at the urgent request of Lucy McGinnis, his dreadfully overworked secretary. McGinnis, one of the witnesses of the original desert contact, feared financial problems might cause the collapse of Adamski's fragile organization.

During the latter part of the following year, in order to raise funds, Adamski traveled with Carol Honey on a 4,000-mile lecture tour reaching as far north as Bellingham, Washington State. In 1960, Honey, writing in the Introduction to Adamski's last book, *Behind the Flying Saucer Mystery,* gives an example of the kind of informal contact many serving American officers made with Adamski. Then, as now, the UFO is made of countless such whispers. During the intermission of a lecture given at Everett, Washington, a public information officer from Paine Air Force Base complimented Adamski on his "scientific down-to-earth and physical approach to the subject." He said that: "when the psychics were kicked out of the UFO situation the Air Force would be able to release its information."

But then, as now, there was a lot of confusion about what is meant by "psychic." The confusion stems from the admission that we do not know what electricity or magnetism are exactly, and therefore the whole structure of physics is an act of faith. Being acts of faith, magnetism and electricity both are as much "psychic" structures as anything else. The concept of "lines of force" is an element of the metaphorical structure by means of which we manage such things rather than "know" of their inner nature. Again, we have our concept of "wonder management" as distinct from fact versus fiction. Those things we tend not to call "psychic" are those things that have been best advertised and sold most avidly within the culture. In a "factual" world the metaphors are tuned and coherent, ready to build any number of subsequent consequential worlds whose appearance is equally convincingly "real." Of course, this structure is never ever completely stable. Perhaps as many "paranormal" events occur as micromete-orites striking the earth in an hour. "Unreality" begins with increasing dis-order within this structure, almost as if the metaphors are fighting one another rather than agreeing.

With Adamski the metaphors were certainly fighting one another. Though he insisted always that he did not like "psychics" or "mysticism" at all, such were certainly present in his simple-minded Christian evan-gelism, his early "Gaia" view, and also in his ideas of telepathy.

There were certainly many instances when Adamski demonstrated beyond a shadow of a doubt that he had psychic ability. On the morning of the 16th of August, 1958, he was traveling towards Grants Pass, Oregon, on a speaking tour. Carol Honey, the man who had replaced Lucy McGinnis, was traveling with him. Adamski said he had a "tele-pathic hunch" and asked Honey to drive back to a small café they had just passed.

"As we entered the door," Honey would later write in *Flying Saucer Review,*[113] "a very small blond girl approached, and George acted as if someone had hit him on the head with a hammer. In fact he acted so strange about her that it caused me to get suspicious. After she showed me that she was reading my every thought, it finally dawned on me that she was probably a space person. She looked from a distance as if she was about 12 years old. Close up, however, she looked much older and I remarked to Adamski that I thought she was about 45 years old...she did-n't identify herself in any way and...we left and continued on our trip."

We are left to wonder what the previously quoted Air Force officer would have had to say to such a down-to-earth and "scientific" approach to the UFO phenomenon. But the clincher took place the following day, when Adamski took a call at the motel in Seattle where he and Honey were staying. According to Honey, a man said: "I called to tell you that you and the young man were both wrong. The girl you met in the cafe was not 45 years old and she wasn't the one you thought. She is her sister." Adamski told Honey that the girl looked identical to "Kalna," as described in *Inside the Space Ships.* Honey concluded by saying: "This was absolute proof to me...no-one knew we were at this motel. No-one knew the route we had come over and no-one could possibly have known my thoughts as to the girl's age."

Perhaps, as it were, Adamski and Honey glimpsed the equivalent of a four-master pass by their island at a great distance. As islanders, little did they know that they will have to wait five hundred years perhaps for another sail. But by that time Kalna's sister will have changed, and the sail will take the form of a smoking funnel.

We are left as Nicholas Urfe is left with a feel of Proustian infinity at the end of *The Magus:* "She is silent, she will never speak, never forgive, never reach a hand, never leave this frozen present tense. All waits, suspended. Suspend the autumn trees, the autumn sky, anonymous people. A blackbird, poor fool, sings out of season from the willows by the lake. A flight of pigeons over the houses; fragments of freedom, hazard, an anagram made flesh. And somewhere the stinging smell of burning leaves."

CHAPTER 13

America Mystica: 1958

Though an immigrant Pole with an accent, Adamski had America young and old written all over him. He had one of those tub-thumping semi-educated minds one meets in Twain or Melville, Hemingway, or Whitman. Certainly he was mentally hyperactive. He quotes Emerson and John Ruskin in the same breath as Air Force UFO investigator Captain Edward Ruppelt and the Gospels. In his last book, *Behind the Flying Saucer Mystery,* he gives the names, characteristics and functions of the launched satellites of his day almost at the same time as he talks of telepathy and travelling on Venusian spaceships. This constant cross-referencing of fantasy, imagination, and substance is, of course, often the hallmark of genius; but though he had the mental courage to take a thorny path, he lacked disciplined reading and study. His channel-surfing soap-box mind never stopped its endless bough-chatter; but nevertheless with this ability, he certainly drew some of the great mythological cartoons of his time.

When we look at Adamski, we look at a part of the very inside of the American mind, pregnant with experimental structures, machines and ideas, all interwoven with the mysteries of Jayne Mansfield, Marilyn Monroe, and the assassinations. No other mind on the planet is like this. If we laugh at that, we might bear in mind that Star Trek, Uncle Sam's national flagship, would not have been possible without taking on something of Adamski's original vision. This alone puts him on the level of Fritz Lang and the creators of the Flash Gordon films, with the supercharged bonus of a reality-claim. In Adamski's mind is the source of American triumph and dread: designs slot into other designs, and the gimmickry works, but is all this a cargo-like deception buried deep like a charge of dynamite with the heart of the mystery of machines?

America is a device culture. Its cities look like circuit boards; its two computer programs control the entire planet. There is no alternative to being American, no more than there is an alternative to watching television, even lacking a set. At times Adamski's doll-folk in flying saucers act as if they were the attendant spirits of both America's genius and tragedy. Though he was of a very different generation than Jack Keruouac, Adamski was similarly an American figure standing at the dawn of a new world when Europe was waiting to be reborn. Perhaps such figures disturb Authority because, as advanced prototypes, such folk represent disturbing changes to come. Before 1945, in Britain and Europe, almost all such figures had been murdered by socialism, both national and international.

Odd folk trouble Authority if only because it doesn't understand them. Weird views are not directly criminal, yet they subvert society in a much more subtle way. Since it is not possible to prosecute, shots are put across personal bows in hidden ways, and covert pressures applied. The odd person is made to feel that no matter how small they may be, no matter how mad or ridiculous, they have nevertheless been noticed. Conformists are left alone; they are effectively dead matter to systems of Authority, and actual criminals are finite, their actions and motives fully comprehensible.

But that living cauldron of experiments with shapes and colors, surreal directions, and outright denials of received truth is the *outsider.* In imagining and communicating, the outsider is vital to the process of changing metaphor. Change of metaphor is in turn vital to that physical change which the majority of humanity equate to "reality." Knowing that vital new images can change society just as can "fact," Authority therefore watches image-makers (such as John Lennon, Timothy Leary, and Wilhelm Reich, for example) just as it watches the more obvious banks and property of the so-called "real" world. Authority knows that imagination can change the cultural bedrock in subtle ways. It is usually not the apparently nonsensical substance of the act of imagination that is the center of interest as much as the act of imagining itself. Adamski certainly made seemingly nonsensical statements, such as saying that Venus is inhabited by human-like forms. Though this might indeed appear to be nonsense, it certainly brings the picture of such an absurdity into a mind, though momentarily. Though the mind may reject immediately such rubbish, nevertheless, for a fleeting instant, it has created a picture of an inhabited Venus, if only to reject the image immediately. This fleeting act of imagination is the very first minute building block of a possible universe in which Venus might indeed be populated in the manner described by Adamski.

Authority, of course, must never be underestimated. It knows that the deviant thought, once reinforced by some powerful means of suggestion, may start to mutate. The end of this process could well be the manufacture (or part manufacture) of a universe containing such a possibility as an inhabited Venus. The introduction of this thin sliver of a suggestion into the half-formed programmatic "real" is the practice and object of classical occultism. Reinforcement follows by whatever means. Boil a cauldron full of advertising, suggestion, propaganda, and collective will to believe and Adamaki's Orthon appears on cue, rather like Faust's Satan, promising our heart's desire. We thought these old cultural umbilicals had gone from us, but they are indestructible. They still serve to make up the kind of half-forgotten dialogue with Nature that conjures up the half-forms glimpsed in John Keel's *The Mothman Prophecies,* or Patrick Huyghe's *The Field Guide to Extraterrestrials.*

Of course, deviant thoughts require outsiders, and if ever there was an outsider, it was George Adamski. He almost certainly didn't know it, but he was a prototype media-head. If he was chosen for some alien experiment, then this was the most likely reason. Mentally hyperactive, he moved in many dimensions simultaneously. He was also one of those inspired people who have no problem with Wonder. When faced with utterly fantastic claims, many are inspired, while others feel angry and insulted, guilty and ashamed; still others feel intellectually violated and/or morally outraged. Fantastic claims can arouse just as much hatred as can "real" murderous actions. Perhaps domains of thoughts defend themselves and go to war just as do nations.

But there are those who have no problem with fairies or UFOs. They see such things as natural elements within an order of nature; these are obscure or distant mysteries just as are the better-managed mysteries of electricity and magnetism. Somewhere within the vast interiors of the outsider, there has been a failure of the sort of cultural colonization that is supposed to convince that one thing is "unreal" while another thing is "real." Leslie's chapters in *Flying Saucers Have Landed* are Adamski's unconscious: there the deep past is still ticking away, subverting the future and ridiculing the transient present. Behind all frenetic energies such as his, there is this higher disturbance of History. Hearing such a voice is to hear sounds from old mine workings long since thought abandoned. With this energy and the growing range of accusations against him, Adamski was bound sooner or later to hit trouble.

And when he did, many bells began to ring.

In May 1952 the Special Agent of the San Diego Office of the FBI wrote a memo to J. Edgar Hoover. It was about Adamski. In conversations and letters Adamski had made some mildly pro-Russian and anti-American remarks. But it wasn't this so much as he had accumulated a large following through broadcasts and public appearances. Even before the "desert contact" of late 1952, Adamski was a veritable living website of his day. He had always complained about American nuclear tests; he gathered information, he spread fantastic rumors concerning conspiracies, secret technologies, government cover-ups, and environmental policy; he libeled, he accused, and he played tricks, if only in self-defense. Though common now, such multi-faceted raw energy feeding on horizons just born was new for his time. Many were attracted to him also because he integrated vision and technology with a New Age Christianity. In the early 1950s, the body of Christian belief had hardly got past the Industrial Revolution. Christian theology was still looking askance at the changes wrought by the railway engine; at that rate, rockets and space were going to take a long time to enter its horizon, if ever. No matter how mad Adamski's rumors were, to make Christianity to any degree sexy, techno-logical, and mysterious at the same was an achievement of genius, no less.

Adamski's defense against official surveillance was no less brilliant. He got in touch with police, military, defense, and intelligence organs at the drop of a hat. He was never one for a fixed defense. Like a good tank commander, like indeed the flying saucer itself, he was always mobile, unpredictable, and fought close up, showering almost-libels and asking many leading questions in one sentence. These methods were the shock tactics of a deep-penetration panzer attack that often threw the vast, slow-er-thinking intelligence organizations into chaos.

Adamski often quoted one agency to another, and often cross-corresponded, thus causing referential confusion in what were essentially bureaucratic organizations. He played the role of a concerned American citizen approaching Authority with whole armfuls of gifts. By doing this, he disarmed those who would make predictable accusations of disloyalty or subversion. To say that his gifts were unwanted was to stand on the slippery slope of the argument.

On the 13th of March 1953, a Riverside, California newspaper, the *Enterprise,* reported that Adamski had claimed that all his material had been cleared with the FBI and USAF Intelligence. This followed a speech Adamski made to the Lions Club of Corona, California the previous evening. As a result of this newspaper story, investigating officers from both the FBI and USAF visited him. They forced him to mail a letter to the *Enterprise* correcting this report. They also got a written statement from him that he would not make such a claim again. But the agents made the mistake of putting their own signatures to this document as witnesses

On the 10th of December 1953, an investigator for the Los Angeles Better Business Bureau[114] wrote a report and submitted it to the FBI.[115] He said that his organization was considering prosecuting Adamski for fraud with regard to his claimed "real" encounters published in *Flying Saucers Have Landed* (which had by then just been put on sale in Los Angeles bookshops, hence the interest). This investigator revealed during an interview that "Adamski produced a document having a blue seal in the lower left corner, at the top of which appeared three names of Government agents."

As a result of this report, on the 17th of December, an FBI and an OSI agent went back to "Palomar Gardens Cafe" again and threatened Adamski with arrest on the grounds of having forged an official document. The text of this FBI report of the 17th reveals that he was "emphatically admonished to cease and desist in referring to the FBI or the OSI as having given him approval to speak on Flying Saucers."

Adamski, with yet more promises of good behavior, backed down, but then turned the tables by spreading rumors that he had been "silenced" by the FBI. Some of his tactics of clogging the machine in this way were certainly echoed much later in the two-stapled hippie manuals of people such as Jerry Rubin and Abbie Hoffman during the Vietnam protest era. Anyone who knows anything at all about government departments will know that such procedures are a surprisingly effective way of ensuring internal confusion. When such confusion starts to feed back upon itself, there results a kind of microphonic howl-round frequently encountered in UFO investigations. When this happens, we see the edifying spectacle of the bee-dance of incorrigibly skeptical enquirers and their manic-depressive conclusion that there is nothing left mysterious beneath the visiting moon.

So instead of a liar, a fraudster, or con-man, the much-misunderstood Adamski can be seen as essentially a shaman-like prankster, an early equivalent to Britain's Ken Campbell or Ireland's Doc. Shiels. To those of a mechanical and industrial age (whose only alternatives are the yes/no and false/true paradigms), such an ancient cultural figure is difficult to get into focus. For skeptics in particular the activity and function of such clown-figures is even more difficult to understand. It is rather like trying to imagine some modern version of King Lear's fool.

Like the shaman and the fool, Adamski could be, on occasion, a magnificent performer. He effectively produced a blinding stream of images, symbols, metaphors, strange juxtapositions, weird connections, a whole living theatre which annoyed, baffled, outraged, yet inspired. Like Charles Fort, another deeply disturbed anarchist American, Adamski used this kind of rolling barrage to turn Authority round to question its own innards, and not George Adamski. He loved also to goad Authority into unsubtle, awkward, and rather brutish actions against him, so that all resistance looked cloddish and childish. When we look upon all this as truth by performance-theater, then we avoid the depressing skeptical merry-go-round of tiny little skeptical minds (of which the British are the worst), trying to decide whether his experiences were "real" or "false." For the shaman, that concept which we call the Objective Real is a box of tricks and illusions in any case. Far superior cultures to our own have had little commerce with Fact. Even for Shakespeare, the Objective Real would have been a meaningless concept.

All modern problems with the UFO stem from this single consideration alone. Our culture lacks an effective language to describe something that exists outside the old industrial colonization of yes and no.

The outsider, living in this intermediate state, is an amusing yet frightening figure, and serves to remind folk that the rules of the reality-game are never ever fully settled. This is the oldest fear in the world. The "threat" to Authority is that the outsider (perhaps despite himself or herself), may walk through the walls just once. In the case of all the major American assassinations, once was enough.

Like Andy Warhol, Adamski, if he did anything at all, made junk culture live in an unforgettable and even a profound way. He also had other qualities of the American Hero. He was a true soldier, he took the heat and came through. He had flair, he had style, but above all the old cavalryman had magic. By stopping the world from taking all this away from him, he showed that he was a piece of the Right Stuff, as much as Chuck Yeager or anyone else.

CHAPTER 14

George Adamski's 1959 World Tour

George Adamski's legendary world tour began with a flight to Hawaii on January 19th, 1959. He could not have had a better start, for Werner von Braun had made an astonishing statement in *Neues Europa* of January 1, 1959. Speaking of the strange deflection of an American rocket from its orbit, he said: "Far stronger powers face us than we had thought originally, operating from an unknown base. I can say nothing more at present. We are coming in closer contact with these powers. In six to nine month's time we may be able to say more."[116]

Adamski could not have had a better send off than that. In addition, daily reports of flying saucer sightings were emerging from all over the world, showing a disturbing pattern of intelligently controlled daylight disks, nocturnal lights, and even stories of close encounters. On the very first day of the year, an object hovered over Newport Beach, California, witnessed by three policemen and three lifeguards. After fifteen minutes, the object broke up into four parts, each of which departed in different directions at high speed. On January 8th, two USAF pilots witnessed a brilliant blue-green teardrop over Phillipsburg, Pasadena, and on that same day two Swedes, Hans Gustavsson and Stig Rydburg signed "sanity testimonials" regarding what is considered to be the first Swedish contact case.

At this time, the jet-age itself was just getting into its stride. By the spring of 1959, Boeing's Renton plant was a hive of activity, with model 707 deliveries for Pan American, TWA, Continental, BOAC, Braniff, Sebena, and Lufthansa. This was a time of almost sexual heat in technology and industry, and the world thrilled as many strange and beautiful new shapes roared and screamed off runways. For the first time since 1945, it was possible to forget the horrors of World War II; the sleek new airplanes recovered in every way of a sense of celebration, and were symbolic of a renewed faith in human possibilities. The first small satellites were bleeping away, and in the year before Adamski set off around the world, the Russians launched Laika the dog into space.[117] With the first high-quality Technicolor feature films getting planet-wide distribution, and color television and indeed computers and space rockets on the horizon, the atmosphere in 1959 was pregnant with cosmic excitements that would come to fulfillment in the next decade.

On the 9th of April 1959 the names of the seven foundation-member astronauts were announced. In September, the Russian Lunik II satellite hit the moon and sent back data about magnetic fields. The following month, Lunik III orbited both the earth and the moon, and obtained photographs of the moon's far side. Entering training in this same year was the Russian cosmonaut Alexsei Leonov, who would be the first man to walk in space in 1965. In Yaroslavl, a young blond blue-eyed 22-year-old Valentina Tereshkova had just joined the Air Sports Club as a parachute instructor. She was to become the first woman astronaut, going into orbit on June 14th, 1963.

It was indeed dreamtime in space, with some 500 man-made objects in orbit, as well as dogs, monkeys, frogs, and germ cultures. Therefore, it is not surprising that, as Adamski tells us in *Behind the Flying Saucer Mystery,* whether in Australia, Thailand, Calcutta, Pakistan, Egypt, Greece, or Rome, everywhere there were readers of his best-selling books.

There were of course some ominous shadows gathering at this time— 1959. This was the year of the Nixon versus John F. Kennedy election battle, and in this same year, a despairing Lee Harvey Oswald slashed his wrists, had his life saved by his Intourist Guide, Rima, and woke up to find himself in the insane ward of the Botkin hospital in Moscow.[118] Some two and a half weeks before Adamski commenced his tour, the dictator Fulgencio Batista had fled Cuba and Fidel Castro had seized power, scooping up $8 million in Mafiosi casino receipts.[119] That year also saw strong U.S. Army Green Beret units with rapidly expanding air and sea support already in action in South Vietnam, fighting against guerilla incursions from the North. The North Vietnamese People's Army was led by two men whose names were almost unknown to the American public: Ho

Che Minh and Vo Nguyen Giap. But perhaps the crowning event late in the year, as far as the general public was concerned, was the visit of Nikita Krushchev to America, where he met Marilyn Monroe, who commented "Krushchev looked at me like a man looks at a woman."[120]

Almost half century later, these stories and dream structures of 1959 dominate still. In 2001 we have hardly a battery of power-images that can compare with these names, which still command vital energies in young and old. They are magic names in the fullest sense, and like the UFO, they are things wonderfully preserved from the corrosion of time. Within an instant any one of these images from long ago can still banish all the grown-up "factual" games of industrial, technological, financial, and social-democratic discussions. They are the equivalent to the mediaeval Orders of Angels and Devils. As such, despite ourselves, we still "reason" by means of these myths and legends, and in this they are essential components of the contemporary Western mind, going far deeper into the unconscious than "fact." Whole generations of people young and old now give up a good part of their conscious identities to the countless soap structures that have mutated from such elemental names.

As early as 1959, there were rumors of the connection of both John F. Kennedy and Marilyn Monroe to UFO conspiracies.[121] In this same year, ex-SS officer Wernher von Braun (who would have destroyed the United States of America without a single thought if his rockets had been powerful enough) worked[122] for both Walt Disney's TV show and NASA. Here was indeed our own Entertainment State in embryo. With quite other plots emerging that were even in 1959 judged to be beyond all human contrivance or control, the structure of the so-called "real" was beginning to deteriorate like a newspaper under heavy rain.

Each night we are reprogrammed by such stories as the rains of time cannot wash out. Each night they abduct us, and each day we are required to act out some portion of these tales that make up the machinery of Western time, space, and consciousness.

For this mythological screen there is no OFF switch.

On his world tour, Adamski threaded the UFO through many of these names and plots, making it a dream journey through dimensions of time and consciousness, dreams and ideas. At the time the tour started, there was significant US government activity regarding the rapidly increasing number of flying saucer reports. On the 31st of January, 1959, the John McClellan Sub-Committee of the Senate of the United States received a briefing on what were then beginning to be called Unidentified Flying Objects. In February there were various USAF policy meetings to review the situation and possible approaches to it; these discussions led eventually to the 1965 USAF Scientific Advisory Board Ad Hoc Committee to Review Project Blue Book.

The McClellan Sub-Committee deliberations did little to frighten off the UFOs. Neither did Ruppelt's suspiciously revised new last chapter of his book, *The Report on Unidentified Flying Objects,* which now contained negative conclusions about UFOs. On February 24th, passengers on a commercial flight over Pasadena witnessed three disk-like unidentified flying objects, whose color varied from yellow-to-orange. In Britain, on the evening of the 26th of February, a very clearly defined object was seen over what was then called London Airport. This disk, yellow in color, hovered over runways for twenty minutes at an altitude of only two hundred feet. It did not registered on the airport radar, but according to Air Ministry officials, four reliable witnesses, including the traffic control officer who observed it through binoculars, spotted the object. An official Air Ministry statement given to Reuters said the same object was detected at the same time from the RAF base at Stanmore. The thing itself later casually wandered off, disappearing into mist and rain. It was doubly vanished by the kind of explanation that in later years would become a modern folk-ritual: the Air Ministry said it was the "nose cone of a civilian plane," and the airport itself decided that it was the planet Venus seen through a layer of clouds.

Inevitably there were the associated conspiratorial matters. In 1959 an elderly woman dying of cancer confessed to researcher Charles Wilhem that in her working life she had held a Top Security Clearance while at Wright-Patterson Field and had seen two saucer-like craft in a secret hangar. One craft was intact, the other damaged. She said she knew also of two "small creatures" preserved inside another secret building, and had handled personally the paperwork on their autopsy report.[123] This rumor joined other apocryphal stories, like the one about the Roswell incident in 1947, which still persist to this day.

By 1959, the body of what we now call ufology was complete. Its cloud-form had entered the major aspects of human culture: military, technological, psychological, social, and religious. For an insubstantiality based on little more than rumor, it managed to show considerable power in penetrating the equally important and influential domains of the erotic, the esoteric, the conspiratorial, and the then rapidly expanding world of media and entertainment.

Adamski was received first in Honolulu as the world-famous author he was certainly in 1959. He was greeted by the traditional "aloha," bedecked with leis, and in *Behind the Flying Saucer Mystery,* he talks of the monkey-pod tree, whose uniquely-grained wood makes "dishes, novelties, and souvenirs." In New Zealand the flower-decorated clocks (which "keep accurate time") impressed him, as did craftwork rugs, and hand-carved crossbeams. Wide-eyed before other tourist gems, he includes, in typical Adamski manner, a detailed description of the Kiwi bird, all this perhaps not exactly what is required in a book which is supposed to be about the mystery of flying saucers, but Adamski, inside and out, was always prime advertising fodder. He is attracted by all and everything, and acts rather like a deprived child grabbing candy for all he is worth. In this sense he was a man who doubted very little, and he was satisfied very easily. He beams gleefully yet again as he is taken on picnics and excursions; he describes hot-water pools and steam-wells; as his camera whirls, he praises folk who are kind, respectful, and pleasant. In turn, he impresses Sister Heeni and the rest of his Maori escort when half a dozen streaks of light appear overhead in the sky as he photographs the palace of the old Maori kings at Ngaruawahia.

His reputation is further enhanced when, after he has just left the township of Taupo and is on his way to Napier, several UFOs are seen. The local paper reported them as observed "high above the township of Taupo in bright sunlight," adding that in addition to these sightings, "it is rumored in Rotorua that many people, including more than 100 Maoris, saw two spacecraft flying in formation between Ngaruawahia and Hamilton last Sunday."[124]

This is the trouble with Adamski: just when we are ready to consider both his life and art as prototype pieces of extremely advanced factional entertainment, he has the infernal cheek to pull it off. In this, he has to be watched very carefully. Like the championship boxer Mike Tyson, there were some massive contradictions within him, but he was a champion, and if true champions have anything to teach us, it is that time is not always distance divided by velocity. As things appear to fly from both Adamski's mind and his page into the sky and back again, he is a reminder of those saints of history who were deeply embarrassed because they could not help levitating in full public view. Of these, Desmond Leslie, in *Flying Saucers Have Landed,* mentions Saint Teresa of Avila, Saint Joseph of Copertino, and those two-hundred saints registered in the Calendar of the Saints as being more or less adept at this amazing form of alternative transport.

Adamski's progress was triumphal. To overflow audiences in Napier, Wellington, Wangnui, and New Plymouth, he lectured about his trips in flying saucers and his conversations with the humanoid crews. By comparison, mere Earth-folk (particularly females), are far less impressive. Adamski gives a dusty answer and shows a rather abrupt and ungallant attitude toward a "French actress" who introduces herself to him. Just when we think that here he has a suitable opportunity to truly celebrate his triumphs, his candy-hunt collapses, momentarily. Acting almost like contactee Howard Menger, his apocryphal counterpart, he greets this woman with a coy near-blush. It is almost as if she were one of his flying saucer child-women who is being a little too forward. "I told her the interest lay not in me, but in the subject I was presenting," he snaps. Some might say that when a man does that to a French actress, it is time to die.

There are few visionaries who can move immediately almost from a snubbed French actress to such a definitive multiplication of entities as the following: "It is an established fact that a scientific approach to a controversial topic will draw more people. Intelligent people will realize that the spacemen are in no way related to psychics and mysticism. This logical thinking on the part of the public has been the major factor responsible for the success of my books and lectures."[125]

Not a bad statement for a man who dedicated his life to teaching a Christian form of Occult Theosophy. Here is his calling card:

Prof. G. Adamski
Speaker and Teacher of Universal Laws
and the Founder of Universal Progressive
Christianity, Royal Order of Tibet
and the monastery at
Laguna Beach

Those who are rendered speechless by this typically wondrous presumption of Adamski that he has anything like a "scientific" approach, are however, set up for the left hook that follows. As people begin gathering in New Plymouth's hall on the evening of the lecture, it appears that Adamski had done it yet again: "A minister and members of his congregation had seen a large space ship cruise over the city. This caused much excitement and as I arrived, people were eagerly wondering if the space ship would return."[126]

If we look at these first stages of the world tour as being merely entertainment fun and games, then that certainly was not how some areas of Intelligence were looking at them. Nicholas Redfern in *A Covert Agenda* shows a declassified FBI report[127] written in 1959 by Leon Crutcher, First Secretary of the US Embassy in New Zealand. Crutcher comments that Adamski filled all the 2,200 seats in the Wellington Town Hall, and he takes particular notice that Adamski made references to security restrictions, and saying the US authorities "know a lot more than they will tell."

Copies of this document were forwarded to the CIA, the US Army, and the US Navy.

Adamski leaves New Zealand after saying (mercifully) that he is "unable to relate fully the scenic beauties," and arrives in Australia, where after having typical troubles with work-permits, accommodation, and the workings of what both himself and Donald Keyhoe called the "silence group," he pulls it off again: "In Adelaide, after my second successful lecture in that city, a group of us were standing in the hall waiting for transportation. One of the ladies sighted several ships. Some of the ladies in the group observed the craft in detail before the ships passed out of sight."[128]

One should ideally go into a gym and have boxing lessons before reading *Behind the Flying Saucer Mystery.* Again, after such an amorphous statement, loosely written as it is with an air of an almost casual lack of concentration, he lands this time a right hook. The *Sunday Mail* report of March 28th, 1959 reported a sighting from Purnong, 91 miles Northeast of Adelaide: "WE SAW A SPACE SHIP—Eerie Object Puzzles Town. By Staff Reporter John Pinkney.

"In recent weeks, multi-colored objects have streaked across Purnong's skies, frightening the townsfolk. Two local men swear that on March 13th, they saw a huge dome-shaped craft take off from a field. The men are Mr. Percy Briggs, Purnong Landing carrier, and Mr. Carl Towill, postmaster at Claypans. Mr. Towill said: 'The thing was bigger than an airliner. Mr. Briggs and I are convinced that it was intelligently controlled.' The two men said they saw an enormous dome-shaped craft glowing in the dark and as they walked towards the mysterious object it rose silently into the air, hovered, then shot away at immense speed."[129]

But after reporting this, instead of giving us some meat and potatoes, Adamski gives us a description of his visit to the Lone Pine Kola Bear Sanctuary! But again, we must be wary, for even after he had left the Far East, he trailed many UFO sightings and incidents, and it would have been too much to ask certain sectors of the public not to associate at least some of these with his trail-blazing visit. Just one of the more spectacular sightings was that of a shuttlecock-shaped UFO seen by hundreds of staff and technicians at the Woomera rocket range on July 20th, where the doomed British Blue Streak space rocket was being tested. This was one case within an emerging pattern of apparent surveillance of scientific and military establishments, which still continues to our own day.

While Adamski was still in Australia, there were utterly fantastic reports coming out of remote areas of New Guinea, but most being unverified, went almost unnoticed. However, a couple of months after Adamski's departure, there occurred one of the most well-described and witnessed UFO descriptions on record, and one moreover whose comical absurdity was straight out of the Adamski book of waking dreams, with additional material by Jules Verne. If in this case the witnesses had not been so numerous and so impeccable, one would not even bother including this case in a book and asking readers to pay for the doubtful privilege of reading such nonsense.

At about 6.45 p.m. on the evening of 26th June, the Reverend Father

Gill of the Anglican Mission at Boinai, New Guinea saw a large object like an inverted saucer hovering over the Mission house. He observed human-like figures on top of this shape, moving perfectly normally, as if carrying out some kind of routine task. They glowed, like the ship itself, and a thin blue spotlight projected up into the heavy cloud cover, which stood at about 2000 feet. Other similar shapes appeared, moving in and out of cloud. Using the height of a mountain as comparison, Gill reckoned the altitude was some 500 feet. At 9:10 p.m. the shape on which the humanoid figures had been seen showed a red light and disappeared into the clouds.

At 6 p.m. the following night of the 27th, even more fantastic things happened. According to Coral and Jim Lorenzen's account in their book *UFOs: The Whole Story,* the same object appeared, and this time many watchers below could see some kind of rail on it (what a wonderful Verne-like touch!). One "man" appeared to be standing at this rail and looking down at the group of people on the ground below. Gill, in a marvelously English and very Anglican moment, waved to this "man," as did many of the earnest bible students observing with him. There must have been not a few sleepless nights after seeing the result of this action, which moves back from the age of Verne to the pages of Sterne's *Tristram Shandy:* "To the surprise of all the observers, the figure which appeared to be watching did the same. One of the Papuan teachers waved both arms over his head and two of the figures responded in kind. Both Gill and the teacher then repeated the waves, and all four figures on the object did the same."

These "men" disappeared after a while, and the watchers below left the thing in the sky to wander off by itself, while they went to a church service. There, they doubtless pondered on the difficult theological problems posed by what they had seen.

On Saturday, April 19th Adamski arrived in London with the press still speculating about an air crash in America on April 1st. The Captain of a C118 transport out from McChord Field AFB at Tacoma, Washington had given a Mayday signal, saying that the aircraft had "hit something." A little later the big aircraft smashed into the side of a mountain between Sumner and Orting. There were no survivors, but investigators for the Aerial Phenomena Research Organization were able to find witnesses describing two yellowish objects following close behind the plane. Troops were brought in to cordon off the area, and military staff interviewed residents near the scene of the crash and advised them not to talk about it to anyone.

Adamski registered at the Hyde Park Hotel, had dinner with Desmond Leslie, and was interviewed on the popular BBC Radio program, "In Town Tonight." With the help of his co-worker in Britain, John Lade (later to become director of *Flying Saucer Review*), he rapidly established a court, and such influential British writers as the Earl of Clancarty (Brinsley Le Poer Trench) were to call on him there. Trench wrote later that he was "struck by Adamski's tremendous vitality and his undoubted charm," and Trench's book *The Sky People* was published by Neville Spearman in the year following Adamski's visit. In 1962, this same enterprising publisher issued Trench's powerful and scholarly *Men Among Mankind*.[130] This book was an original development of many of Desmond Leslie's revolutionary ideas on cosmology and architecture as discussed in *Flying Saucers Have Landed*. By comparison, Trench's book puts those who later ransacked Leslie's work, such as Erich von Daniken, to shame. In subsequent years, Trench was to publish several popular and influential books on UFOs, such as *Operation Earth* (1969), and *Mysterious Visitors* (1973). Though his views were often just as controversial as those of Leslie and Adamski, his books were very well written and contained strong and informed arguments. In 1979, as a measure of his influence in Britain, Trench initiated a three-hour debate on UFOs in the House of Lords,[131] and he was able to found the House of Lords All Party UFO Study Group.

Others had prepared the way for Adamski. In 1958, George Hunt Williamson, one of the original witnesses to Adamski's desert contact, had made a successful tour of Britain and had appeared on BBC television. He was a highly regarded scholar, and he caused considerable interest by saying that he had a gift from Peru for the Queen, and would like to present it to her personally. While in London, Desmond Leslie introduced Adamski to George King, whose Aetherius Society had similar views to his own. King, a London taxi-driver, had marched to Whitehall in 1958 with members of his Society. They carried placards demanding that Harold

Macmillan's government tell the public the truth about flying saucers. This Society aroused Intelligence interest in Britain. Nicholas Redfern in his excellent book *A Covert Agenda*[132] shows that between 1962 and 1963, Secretariat 6 of the Air Ministry had obtained a variety of papers[133] from the Aetherius Society for study.

Adamski and King got on well. King even claimed that he had met similar beings to those Adamski had met, and both agreed that their beliefs had nothing to do with psychic phenomena. This separation was emphasized often by Adamski, but throughout their lives both these men tended confuse their terms of reference regarding matter and spirit. In 1960 King arranged spiritualist meetings in California and in the late 1950s Adamski referred to his space contacts more as "psychic guides" than flesh and blood folk. After a lifetime of pouring scorn on such things, such changes caused him to lose many of his followers.

This situation is typical of the confusions that still characterize the debates between the objective school of ufology and those groups who take a mystical, religious, or metaphysical view of the phenomenon. This problem is a particularly modern one; for Shakespeare (who would hardly have understand the idea of "objectivity"), Nature and Mind were a seamless robe.

In recovering from World War II, the 1950s were a time vulnerable to mass-suggestion of all kinds. The major belief systems of the world political, religious, social, were in ashes: try as they may, they could not account for the limitless horrors of the two world wars. In a tired Europe at least, religion in particular had been choked into a terrified silence. It no longer had any effective explanations, and had retreated from the broad stream of intellectual debate, despite the success of the British tours around this time of the Christian evangelist Billy Graham, an early Nixon intimate. It is interesting to note that exactly at the time Adamski arrived in Britain, another much-abused American, L. Ron Hubbard, the founder of Scientology had arrived to establish his headquarters in East Grinstead, where Scientology remains active to this day.

There were other common factors. The FBI was particularly interested in many of these high-profile visionaries. All were getting near social and political power-centers, and all were minting new metaphors as fast as they could. If only some of these radiating metaphors were to have more than a half-life, it is possibly by a hair's breadth that these men avoided the fate of Jack Parsons and Wilhelm Reich, and many more to come after, such as Timothy Leary and John Lennon. Ideological systems as emerging moral geometries ring the deepest alarms.

The great physicist James Jeans once said that Nature does not like being observed too closely, and those few thinkers who have a concentration far in excess of the average are often dealt with by a process that has absolutely nothing to do with normal mechanics of conscious social-democratic justice. This process of detection appears to have two elements, an explicit and an implicit. The first is purely conventional police interest, which explains itself. The second is much more interesting. It seems that in their unusual seeing, such people as Adamski come near to those forces that are running the show. Authority rarely has any problem with physical attack; it is prepared for it, and usually knows the directions from which it will come. There is no mystery about grenades.

Subversion by changing metaphor is more difficult to counter. Metaphor, unlike a bullet, gets everywhere. Whether he or she prospers or dies unpublished in a gutter depends on what stories the prevailing paradigm intends to run, and no hard feelings. The storyteller, with his age-old technology, is still political dynamite. Stories as complex expanded metaphor enter and mutate the very interstices of matter/symbol/spirit formulation. Like radiation again, they pass through brains as fertilizing signals whether we like it or not. Mere bullets cannot do that. Just like TV, stories have no OFF switch. Stories are present, root and branch, both in equations and literature. In the development of Newton's calculus, we can read the history of the emerging social need for a grasp of flow and acceleration, and the idea of *radiation* is one of the 20th century's great binding metaphors; most things moral and political are *transmitted* and *broadcast*.

In this sense, Adamski was received by many in Europe like some magician from a dream-future. He was the first powerful shot of 1960s vibes. He was delightfully anarcho-eccentric, like L. Ron Hubbard, and indeed Howard Hughes. There was also the perceptible smell of sulfur about him that made him stand out from other visiting American gurus, such as the rather plastic Billy Graham. Adamski was a likeable rogue, suggesting that neither Truth nor Reality were necessarily about good behavior. In a dour and gray British culture, this was a revelation before which most breathed a sigh of belief.

As far as most of the British upper classes in particular were concerned, Adamski had another attractive feature. He had neither intellectual ability nor education, both of which are still regarded by the British ruling class as a terrible threat from the clever bourgeoisie, who are always trying get above themselves. Adamski merely described. He related a parable. He didn't push particularly hard. Like the rest of the early contactees, he whet appetites that were already in formation. He was a master magician for whom cleverness was a mere affectation. As a teacher of Theosophy for many years, he was bound to know that the merest scrap of effective description at the right time and place acts like some science-fiction creature. It can rapidly clone itself, and like the joke, there is no possibility of escape from its clutches.

Like George King of the Atherius society, Adamski knew also that certain kinds of stories arouse powerful, often-dangerous forces from slumber. That is perhaps not quite as obvious as it sounds. As ink on paper, or merely verbal recollections, stories have almost no physical existence; they are almost pure software. They are almost entirely symbolic, yet often societies allocate considerable energies to the destruction of those programmatic states called belief systems, energies that are quite out of proportion to the non-physical threat of pure belief.

The most ardent UFO skeptic must admit that Adamski and his kind were changing metaphor. We can conceive here of what the State might term a Higher Criminality in which the stakes were not going to be the possession of territory, but the possession and dissemination of information. In 1959, Western society was beginning an almost exponential rate of change. There was also the beginning of the realization that as we grew such multiple antennae as had never been seen before, we were going to bump into things beyond all previous conception.

It is not surprising therefore that in Britain, as elsewhere in Europe, many influential folk, some high in the state apparatus, were looking forward to Adamski's visit, although perhaps many such did not quite know why. At this time British culture was profoundly uninspired; its leading figures were as grey as any in the Eastern Bloc, and its single black-and-white 405-line channel was a marvel of nervous lower-middle-class dullness. The arrival of a man who said he had met extraterrestrial beings and traveled to outer space in a flying saucer may not have been well understood by a first-generation paranoid and hesitant mass-culture, but the upper crust were reacting to it as the arrival of some court magician.

The year 1959 saw the publication of Carl Jung's influential book, *Flying Saucers: A Modern Myth of Things Seen in the Sky*. In this same year, a direct contrast to Jung;s book, *Rumor, Fear, and the Madness of Crowds* was published in America by Ballantine, written by J.P. Chaplin. This was a far lesser book by a far lesser psychologist, but it was more popular than Jung's book, reaching a mass-market audience. In his chapter entitled "Celestial Crockery," Chaplin solves every single problem by saying that like such things as the airship wave of 1897, and visions of flying saucers were the result of collective hysteria. It must be said, however, that for a book of the 1959 era, he explains very clearly the view of the flying saucer as a psychosocial construct. This is a view of the UFO phenomenon is still held by many today and it is interesting that Chaplin is one of the first to talk in a modern sense about the connections between mass media, ufology, and the possibility of a fractured sense of popular perceptions. "One can only speculate on the effect of a Sputnik launching during the peak of the saucer scare," he says, adding that "the Believers at any rate, would have seen the most ominous portents in such an event."

Chaplin puts the fear and tensions of 1959 very well, his view is typical of many academics of the late 1950s, and he reminds us of the scientists Donald Menzel who was satirized by Leslie in *Flying Saucers Have Landed*. Chaplin says: "Aside from the atomic anxiety characteristic of our time, but related to it, is the factor of the incredible scientific and military discoveries made during the past twenty years. These too, must be taken into account in any explanation of the saucer hysteria. With the invention of the Bomb, the breaking of the sound barrier, the formulation of plans for a space missile, and the like, almost anything was believable. Moreover, the volume of science fiction produced during the two decades before the saucers must not be forgotten. It threatens to catch up with the detective story as the most popular genre of escape literature."

Again, the subtlety of Jung's "the symbol becomes intercalated into the cycle of corporeal changes" eludes Chaplin, and he falls into the subjective/objective trap, throwing the baby out with the bath water as he continues: "The fact that it is fictional makes no difference. As the proponents of this kind of literature themselves point out, today's fiction is tomorrow's science. The end result of adding together all this scientific fact and fiction was to create an atmosphere saturated with mind-shaking accomplishments besides which flying saucers did not seem beyond the bounds of possibility. Putting this environmental factor with the first —the age of anxiety—we find that once again, as was true in every other instance of mass hysteria discussed in these studies, the Zeitgeist was partly to blame. In this case it was undoubtedly the major factor."[136]

But can the "psycho-social" idea (a mystical thing in itself) create the wonders that have been seen in the skies of the earth over the past fifty years? If it can, then this idea is a wonder that puts the humble flying saucer very much in second place.

Such powerful scientific men as R.V. Jones[137] and "Prof" Lindemann,[138] Churchill's scientific advisor during World War II, were equally dismissive as Chaplin, and very much for the same reasons. In 1952 Churchill was an elderly man in his last administration, but he had at least made an effort. In July 1952, probably in response to the worldwide news coverage of the dramatic wave of UFO sightings over the White House, he demanded that he be enlightened about "all this stuff about flying saucers." The Air Ministry told him that there was nothing of significance in the matter.

Others, however, thought very differently. In March 1954, HRH Prince Philip had invited young Stephen Darbishire[139] to Buckingham Palace to ask him about some photographs he had taken. In February of that year, Darbishire, together with his cousin Adrian Myers had taken two photographs of a flying saucer near Coniston, Cumbria. Both photographs were of a craft astonishingly like the Adamski bottle-cooler design. The important point with respect to Adamski is that Good publishes for the first time in *George Adamski: The Untold Story* the second Darbishire photograph which shows a shape-deformation almost exactly equal to that shown in stills of Adamski's later Silver Spring film, shot in early 1965. Again, any laughter against Adamski is stilled: he could not possibly have seen this second photograph, which had been in private hands for some years before that date.

Prince Philip entered the UFO picture yet again in the 1950s, according to Air Marshall Sir Peter Horsley, who claimed in his book *Sounds from Another Room* that he had met an alien in 1954 who requested an audience with the Prince.[140] At that time, Peter Horsley was Equerry to Prince Philip. His ability was such that in 1969 he became Assistant Chief of Air Staff (Operations). We therefore listen most carefully when Horsley says that he reported the incident to Lieutenant-General Sir Frederick 'Boy' Browning,[141] who at the time was Treasurer to Prince Philip, and who was also deeply interested in UFOs. Attempts were made to trace the original contact, but in an episode reminiscent of many later films, and the books of John Keel, the trail ran cold.

Several other leading personalities of the day made significant statements. Desmond Leslie in a 1963 article, "Politicians and the UFO," quotes Earl Alexander of Tunis, as once saying to him: "This problem has intrigued me for a long time...There are of course many phenomena in this world which are not explained, and the orthodox scientist is the last person to accept that something new (or old) may exist which cannot be explained in accordance with his understanding of natural laws."

In the *Sunday Dispatch* of 11th July, 1954, Lord Dowding had written: "More than 10,000 sightings have been reported, the majority of which cannot be accounted for by any 'scientific' explanation, e.g. that they are hallucinations, the effects of light refraction, meteors, wheels falling from aeroplanes and the like...They have been tracked on radar screens...and the observed speeds have been as great as 9000 miles an hour...I am convinced that these objects do exist and that they are not manufactured by any nation on earth. I can therefore see no alternative to accepting the theory that they come from an extraterrestrial source..."

Earl Mountbatten was Chief of the Defence Staff from 1958 to 1965, and had himself been as close to a "close encounter" as he probably wished to get. Desmond Leslie, in the article "Did Flying Saucers Land at Broadlands?"[142] tells of how bricklayer, Frederick Briggs, working on Mountbatten's Broadlands estate near Romsey, observed a landed saucer, complete with occupant. This occurred on the morning of Wednesday, the 23rd of February 1955, and Briggs immediately told his colleague Ronald Heath, an electrician also working on the estate. Heath and Briggs reported to their foreman, a Mr. Hudson. He in turn informed Lord Mountbatten, who then inspected the site of the landing, but due to a heavy snowfall, no physical ground traces were evident. A statement was then drawn up by Mountbatten and signed by him personally.

According to Maurice Barbanell, the editor of *Psychic News*, Mountbatten had expressed his belief in reincarnation many times both publicly and privately. In *Mountbatten: The Official Biography*,[143] Philip Zeigler says that the Defence Chief was sympathetic also to the views of the Theosophical Society, a body of spiritualist and occult law, aspects of which Adamski had taught almost all his life. John Dale, author of *The Prince and the Paranormal*,[144] gives another implicit Adamski connection.[145] Dale quotes from a letter Mountbatten wrote in 1950 to Peter Murphy, his close personal friend, concerning flying saucers. For the most senior British military man of that time, Mountbatten shows talent as a science-fiction visionary, and also sounds astonishingly like Adamski himself: "Why should life in another planet with entirely different conditions in any way resemble life on our planet? Their inhabitants may be 'gaseous' or circular or very large. They certainly don't breathe, they may not have to eat and I doubt if they have babies—bits of their great discs may break away and grow into a new creature.

"The fact that they can hover and accelerate away from earth's gravity again and even revolve round a V2 in America[146] shows that they are far ahead of us. If they really come over in a big way that may settle the capitalist-communist war. If the human race wishes to survive, they may have to band together."[147]

These experiences and statements by the leading figures of the day show the atmosphere in the early and late 1950s with regards to the flying saucer phenomenon. They also explain the tremendous reception of *Flying Saucers Have Landed*.

At the time of Adamski's arrival in Britain, Major General Donald J. Keirn was Chief of the USAF nuclear engine programs.[148] He said that although the Air Force had no proof that intelligent beings existed elsewhere, the UFO reports had "emphasized our innate curiosity...It is entirely possible that some of them may have passed through our stage of evolution, and may have already achieved a higher level of social and technological culture than our own."[149]

In this same month, Dino Kraspedon's book *My Contact With Flying Saucers* was published in Britain,[150] and an article by Desmond Leslie appeared in *Flying Saucer Review*[151] entitled "Mexican Taxi Driver Meets Saucer Crew?" If we think that is funny, on 24th December, 1959, a few months after Adamski had returned to America, the following warning was issued by the Inspector General of the USAF to every air base commander in the continental United States: "Unidentified flying objects — sometimes treated lightly by the press and referred to as 'flying saucers'— must be rapidly and accurately identified as serious USAF business...Technical and Defense considerations will continue to exist in this area....(UFO) investigators should be equipped with binoculars, camera, Geiger counter, magnifying glass, and containers in which to store samples."[152]

While in the Pacific and Mediterranean areas, Adamski was in a good mood. He was a happy man, at one with the people and the culture. Both the physical and cultural environment in Australia and New Zealand was after all not that far removed from his own native California. Also, populations not conditioned by a European post-war acid skepticism far more easily accepted him. As in California, the sense of wonder was miraculously still intact. Though, yes, there had been a terrible war against the Japanese, that corrosive existential pessimism (Samuel Beckett, Sartre, et al) caused by unimaginable horrors of Nazism was not present.

In that pre-sixties time, therefore, Europe was very much the other side of the coin as far as Adamski was concerned. Old-fashioned class structures were still intact, one-channel black-and-white TV had only just arrived, and there was a fair amount of anti-Americanism about. Although it was acknowledged that Britain could not have won the war without American help, the fact that America had become very much the top dog, and the British Empire was falling apart, did not help Anglo-American relations on any level. Although he was not a young man at the time of the tour, Adamski was essentially a Sixties Californian person. He had been there generations before the beatniks and the hippies appeared, and all his life he had lived in early self-help communities that were the forerunners of the communes that would follow.

Though Adamski triumphed in Britain, we get the feeling that he was glad to leave. It went against his fundamentally good nature to constantly have to prove himself. He wanted converts, and he knew that he was going to get even less of those in his coming visit to Europe than in Britain. His poor performance as a public lecturer in Europe was made worse because he was not at all as relaxed as he had been in the Far East. In 1959, Europe was not the place for a visionary American. Billy Graham, perhaps, but Adamski, no. A handful of the top folk (mad as ever) might like him. The population at large might just love him, but it looked like the new power group of young middle-class intellectuals and media pundits (hardly present in other parts of the still war-torn world at that time), were going to eat him alive on principle. In the later 1960s, Britain was to recover its sense of humor, and to become largely a new society, but all that was too late for Adamski.

It was raining on Monday the 20th of April 1959 as Adamski made his way to the BBC television studios at Alexander Palace, traveling through a London that had more high cranes in the air than buildings. He was going to be interviewed by Patrick Moore for one of the early "Panorama" programs. This legendary program boasted an audience of nine million, which was high for those days. Moore himself represented the first of a new generation of television presenters who asked tough questions instead of the yes-men of the early years of television innocence.

Certainly Adamski was a little tense in a Britain only just beginning to recover both economically and socially; there was as yet little warmth and gaiety. After sunny climes, it must have been psychologically difficult for him on his first visit to Europe, where there were are no koala bears in sight, no rolling-eyed natives, no garlands around his neck, and this time, not a single sensational UFO sighting to help him. He must have known that the whole tone of his endeavor had to change to fit a very different cultural environment. He gives the impression of knowing that his usual brochure language and coy remarks on scenery, decor, and folk-art will not do him any good. He knows also that any gushing description of tight-trousered male sylphs with choir-boy voices selling cut-price phony "spirituality" from flying saucers will see him slaughtered. Europe will be much amused and beguiled by his photographs and films, and a few might listen twice to his technological fantasies, but he expected little else. The glow of the warmth and enthusiasm of the people of other continents has gone, and the atmosphere has everyone expecting Patrick Moore to knock off Adamski's head before the whole British nation.

We can imagine this Californian not feeling all that comfortable in an Anglo-Saxon nation which has always had a traditional dislike of both physics and metaphysics, though in Isaac Newton and Faraday, England had certainly created the former almost single-handed. Above all nations, Britain hated mystics, romantics, fantasists, and intellectuals all, with intensity only rivaled by a hatred of clever people on principle. To many it must have seemed that if this strange American George Adamski was to come apart at the seams, it would be in Britain, where the corrosively mundane culture of the late 1950s would utterly vanish any crazy Californian sunshine within him. It must be remembered that in 1959, the ghost of the 1956 Suez failure still haunted an iron-age Britain, where steam trains still ran to Victorian time-tables, and millions of coal fires still poured thick black smoke over London as they had done since the time of Charles Dickens. It was to be two or three years before half-naked young men and women with dyed hair danced in circles before Glastonbury Tor, with copies of *Flying Saucers Have Landed* in their last war-surplus rucksacks.

But a champion should never be underestimated or written off. One of Adamski's major assets was a magnificent address. Though 67 years old, he looked as good as always. He had polish, and also a calm confidence rare in a man of almost no formal education. Compared with the then very young Patrick Moore, the grizzled Adamski had been through the university of life, and Moore didn't know that such street fighters don't play by the rules. Adamski measured up to the situation and reversed the terrible odds against him; quite disappointing his enemies, critics, and detractors, he calmly reduced Moore to dust. It was a feat that has probably never been equaled in the forty years that have passed since that time. The overconfident Moore, a regular tough-nut, was outfaced, and outclassed. He fumbled, and immediately fell victim to the Adamski charm. Moore liked him, and that was fatal. He just couldn't bear to hit him hard.

Adamski, with the aristocratic cheek of a true champion, had the nerve to offer his condolences: "As the show started, he tried to disqualify my knowledge of astronomy, but his attempts were unsuccessful. The program was entirely too short, and unfortunately, public opinion went against him. Even the most hardened critic stated in the next day's press that I had won the debate by 'sheer dignity.' Public reaction was very great and Moore was given two months leave of absence from the show."[153]

To make Patrick Moore take some time off is a feat almost as great as leaving a worldwide trail of flying saucer sightings. It is to be noted that Moore, a somewhat shallow and superficial entertainer-cum-"personality" more than anything else, does not discuss this interview in his typically facetious 1972 book, *Do You Speak Venusian?* saying merely that he had "met" Adamski.

As if calmly looking for bigger game, Adamski leaves the lollipop world of media, and flies almost immediately into far higher realms. He runs straight into a row with no less a person than the formidable Air Marshal Lord Dowding, RAF Fighter Command Chief in the first part of World War II. Dowding, a devout spiritualist, had been fascinated by *Flying Saucers Have Landed,* and he had arranged for Adamski to give a lecture in Tunbridge Wells on the 21st of April 1959.

Here, it is as well to be aware of the kind of man Dowding was. Like Mountbatten or Earl Alexander, Hugh Dowding was a very great Briton of truly mythological status. It can be said that without his brains and energy, Spitfire and Hurricane fighters would never have had the radar environment to operate in. Without that new-technology, in all probability, the Luftwaffe would have held an air-umbrella over the British beaches, and Operation Sealion (the invasion of Britain), could have gone ahead with the destruction of the British nation as a consequence. If Churchill had been in charge overall, operationally speaking, Dowding was the one man in late summer 1940 on whom everything depended. The miraculously rescued British Army had no weapons after Dunkirk, and the Royal Navy was almost impossibly overstretched. It is an insight into the British character that the nation which produced the Industrial Revolution hated brains and technology so much that this situation had come about.[154] Unbelievably, Britain was prepared to run the risk of disaster at both the Somme and Dunkirk rather than come to terms with technology that was, after all, largely the fruit of the nation's loins.

That Dowding had brains and brilliance made him ripe for a typical British crucifixion. In this respect, when the so-called "fantasies" of George Adamski are talked about, here is an even greater fantasy: after

1940, the RAF got rid of Dowding, preferring the (mistaken, as it turned out) "big wing" theories of Leigh-Mallory and Sholto Douglas. Compared with that decision, Adamski's strange views could be judged as sane by comparison. Dowding, indeed, saved the nation, but that he had more brains than Douglas and Leigh-Mallory combined, and was undoubtedly a warrior of genius (though he didn't look like one), condemned him in British eyes. Just as were cursed T.E. Lawrence, Alan Turing, and Barnes-Wallace. That Dowding was also a dedicated spiritualist helped finally to seal his fate.

What does Adamski do before this Lion of British history? He refuses to lecture because a work-permit had not been arranged. He was paranoid about this matter, because he was convinced that he had enemies out to exploit every opportunity to damage him. In a very short time Adamski has an agitated Lord Dowding running round like an harassed store-manager, something that Goering's mighty Luftwaffe had not been able to do. As Dowding phones a lawyer for advice, we have a scene from a Marx Brothers film as Adamski describes it: "All tickets had been sold, and Lord Dowding was very perturbed. He called his attorney, who told him it was quite all right to proceed with the lecture. Another friend talked with the attorney, and was told the same. Then I was asked to speak with the attorney. When he said everything was in order, I asked him if he would put that in writing. When he said, "No, it is not necessary," I stood my ground."[155]

After an intense donnish discussion, which would have done a 1940 Fighter Command Control Room credit, a plan was formed. Lord Dowding would preside on the platform with Adamski, who however, would only answer questions from the floor. To have heard "Stuffy" Dowding carefully explaining all this to a well-heeled audience, and to hear him say also, like a disappointed local cinema manager, that arrangements for refunds had been made, if so required, must have been to experience the essence of a superb English moment. To follow this with a two-hour discussion about good-looking men from the planet Venus must have made it a night to remember in the annals of Tunbridge-Wells.

As if this were not achievement enough, Adamski produces next what might be called an interlude before his next big change of scene. Yes, he meets a "spaceman" on a British train. It could only happen on the way to

Weston-super-Mare, a center of that ritual scourging the British call holidays. On April 23rd, Desmond Leslie sees him off on the train, which in those days still had compartments with no connecting corridor. Despite this being a reserved compartment, there is another passenger, a man, who starts immediately a conversation with Adamski, who comments: "To my amazement, he was a spaceman working as a scientist on projects for the British government! He, and countless others like him, are working in various scientific projects for every government in the world. In his way space people can help us reach out into space, with our own science and our own ships, bringing us nearer to the understanding that abundant life exists throughout the Cosmos. This is the only way the people of Earth can be awakened from the state of lethargy and apathy, into the realization that a far greater destiny than they ever imagined awaits them."[156]

Having not allowed the spaceman to speak for himself, and having past off what could have been the greatest event in history in a few bland sentences, Adamski continues immediately with a description of Western-super-Mare as a "pretty coastal town" etc. Since modern science has wasted land, sea, air, and earth and every day tortures to death billions of live animals, we look askance at the idea of aliens "helping out." But perhaps again Adamski is not "wrong" or "right," it is just that his mental processes act like a custard-pie slapstick clown and the pratfalls of Chaplin. If this is the "fuzzy" view of human mentality, then researchers in Artificial Intelligence are going to have a hell of a job imitating its sense of a "reality," which nearly always turns out to be a bit of a cultural paste-up in any case.

Like the psychic spoonbender Uri Geller in studios and laboratories a decade later, Adamski ducks and weaves, shifting the scene, the reference base, the focus all the time, never getting cornered, charming experienced interviewers, turning their brains to ice-cream, at least momentarily. As with Oswald and Mike Tyson again, with Adamski, no one ever knew what was going to happen next. In Britain, he overcome almost all opposition, and became an overnight hit.

Such a view of such a process may well include the option of Adamski having us on for a while, if only to reinforce what was a significant experience in the first place. If he was, it really doesn't matter nearly as much as some of his detractors think it does. Deception and invention mixed with more convincing elements are part of the UFO syndrome in any case. Considering *Behind the Flying Saucer Mystery* as a text, the conjunctions and levels of many different atmospheres, tones, and fabrics, work very well in giving us an idea of the UFO phenomenon as a partly objective manifestation. Being such, the phenomenon works on the "real" and "unreal" levels simultaneously, eliminating them altogether as categories of experience and knowledge. When we talk so blithely about "alien technology," one thing is certain: it is not going to consist of improved juice-blenders.

Taking a tip from the Melanesian experience, if we see alien "mechanism" it is more than likely that we are being fooled.

In this respect, even though nearly a half-century old now, Adamski's books are still superior to a thousand or more works that have appeared since that time and that have taken a linear approach, arguing "factually" from case to case in a strictly logical fashion. Though this approach is effective in demonstrating the case, it gets nowhere in analytical terms.

Throughout Adamski's three books, personal and textual dimensions stretch quite beyond the page, to make up examples of the very first pop-art "faction" genre, accomplished when Andy Warhol was still at college, and the creators of such "faction" classics as *Alternative 3* [157] were not even twinkles in the eye. The style is the equivalent to what was called in those early days of the 1960s "action painting" or "collage" rather than "literary," for Adamski (unlike the accomplished Desmond Leslie) didn't pretend to be a writer proper in any sense. In this respect he was successful in that by breaking all the rules he got to the target area of this particular subject, which of all subjects demands that the rules be broken.

These early books on flying saucers represent a new genre, which quite defeats the old ideas of assessing literature in terms of the polished styles of no doubt very clever and accomplished folk. Like Howard Menger's *From Outer Space to You* (1959), Adamski's books are examples of "bad" art that is of very high value by inverse virtue of gross default rather than by practiced professional application. This untutored expression leads to some delightful cliff-hanging moments: a much more convincing passage comes immediately after the spaceman encounter, with the short brochure description of Western-super-Mare sandwiched in between. Such a style as this there never was. But it worked well enough to get an invitation to Scotland, where he was quite well received by some very non-metaphysical folk.

On the 29th of April 1959, Adamski lectured at the Midlands Institute in Birmingham. Writer Christopher Allan was present[158], and in a letter to this author, he described how the Institute was packed and the audience overflowed to another hall to hear the lecture on the sound system. "I do not consider that Adamski gave a good performance," writes Allan, "and his films were very poor."

In an interview with Adamski the day after, the Air Correspondent of the *Birmingham Post* was a bit more positive. He described Adamski's photos as showing up "against the blue sky as moving specks of light." A report in the *Birmingham Mail* of the 30th of April described heated discussions breaking out in the audience, and said sniggers were heard throughout the hall when Adamski talked about his contact with Venusians. This same report contained typical examples of the facetious attitudes of the time towards this subject. The *Birmingham Mail* reporter describes the behavior of a woman in front of him whom he thought for a moment was ill. However: "She was merely being racked by great gusts of helpless, silent, and irrepressible laughter."

We can understand her feeling. On January 21, 1955 Desmond Leslie, on his return from staying with Adamski in California, gave a talk in Tunbridge Wells to the local Flying Saucer Club. Introduced by the indefatigable Lord Dowding, he said in his talk that Adamski had also communicated in Polish as well as English to the space folk. He added that they had learned the languages of Earth "by picking up our radio signals for the past 60 years." Surely our sympathies must go out to those particular aliens who monitored Polish radio for sixty years. They must have been in the state of Melville's character, Bartleby, who had spent all his life sorting through mail sent to addresses that could not be found. No wonder that a week after this event the *Tunbridge Wells Advertiser* commented that "A Venusian would make a profitable return for Bertram Mills' Circus."

From astonishments in Tunbridge Wells, and meeting strange friendly space men on trains, we find Adamski on the 5th of May in Scotland at the Central Halls Tollcross, with tickets at three shillings each.

He then met with Leonard G. Cramp, a most brilliant British nuts-

and-bolts engineer of that time. The inclusion of Cramp introduces quite another turn in Adamski's definitive modern mythological journey; future times will look on his books and adventures both as a kind of Pilgrim's Progress through the tricky scaffolding, dangerous cat-walks, and shaky flooring of 20th century explanatory apparatus.

Cramp was a solid British engineer who used some solid British mathematics and physics to take a fresh and original look at the flying saucer business. He wrote two brilliant books on UFOs: *Space, Gravity, and the Flying Saucer,* and *Piece for a Jigsaw.*[159] Both books have become much sought-after classics, though they are long out of print.[160] As far as Adamski himself is concerned, Cramp's achievement was in obtaining a kind of objective verification of the "bottle-cooler" saucer that Adamski claimed he had taken photographs of in Palomar Gardens on the 13th of November 1952.

In February 1954, a schoolboy, Stephen Darbishire, mentioned earlier, had taken a photograph of a flying saucer at Coniston, using his crude "Brownie" camera. Using orthographic projection, Cramp showed that Adamski's saucer had the same *ratio of dimensions* as that of the Coniston saucer. Adamski, comments: "Cramp proved that it would be impossible for someone to copy my photographs and make a model of a space ship that would have exactly the same ratios of dimension when photographed from a different angle. The scales of measurement, from porthole to flange, cabin height and diameter, and top to bottom, were all identical in both the English and American photographs!"[161]

With such a confirmation that what he had photographed was a "real" object, lesser authors than Adamski would have brought such a book as *Behind the Flying Saucer Mystery* to a triumphant conclusion, but like the UFO phenomenon, Adamski has not yet finished with us. There is only one level left for him to utterly charm with his hypnotizing rays of wonderfully crazy Californian sunshine, acting like a magical love-potion on a Europe just coming alive after unspeakable horror, and that level is Royalty.

Towards the end of April 1959, Adamski had finished his British tour, and was staying at the home of Desmond Leslie, when the phone rang. On the line was a reporter from the *Daily Herald* asking Adamski if he would verify the report about a rumored meeting with Queen Juliana. Here, Adamski, possibly exhausted, and eternally paranoid, hesitated, and told the reporter that the story about the interview was indeed just a rumor. He did this because originally he received his invitation to meet Queen Juliana and Prince Bernhardt[162] of the Netherlands when he was lecturing in Brisbane, Australia, some months before. Miss Rey d'Aquila of The Hague had arranged an interview for May 18, 1959, and Adamski had accepted promptly, but with Royalty involved, Adamski didn't want to confirm or deny anything.

The *Daily Herald* got in touch immediately with the Hague office, which promptly confirmed the interview, and all hell broke loose. The edition of the *Herald* of April 29, 1959 carried the heading: "Juliana's New Joy—Flying Saucers." The Hague added that the talks would be "confidential" and "between the two of them alone," but this only served to fuel the ensuing fire. In our own day, we can imagine the press reaction if the late Princess Diana had invited a leading UFO expert to talk with her. The reaction to the deep friendship between Prince Charles and the mystical writer Laurens van der Post comes to mind as an example of the "HRH talks to plants" attitude of the tabloids of our own time.

The American press did not support its native son. In an article on May 19th, entitled "Dutch in Saucer Discussion," the *Los Angeles Examiner* thundered: "The press has given Adamski, from Los Angeles, a chilly reception. The Catholic People's Party newspaper *De Volkskrant* said, for example: 'We are not opposed to a court jester on the green lawns of the Royal Palace, provided he is not taken for an astronomical philosopher.' "

Adamski had been interviewed by Dutch Television on May 16th, and some of his saucer footage had been broadcast. This had caused great debate in Holland, most of it not in Adamski's favor, if only because his films were not of the very best quality.[163] Matters were made worse because The Hague, in turn, had made a mistake. The European press, smelling that something was not all that it seemed to be (as usual with George Adamski), discovered that the "two of them alone" statement was simply not true. First, Prince Bernhardt[164] was going to be there, as were quite a few other important people, most of whom had, significantly, military and scientific status rather than social. It was a story too good to be missed as the following crew assembled, giving more the atmosphere of a conference than a conversation.

One of the Dutch newspapers reported: "Those who were present at the conversation included Mr. C. Kolff, President of the Royal Netherlands Society for Aviation, Lieutenant-General H, Schaper, Chief of the Royal Netherlands Air Staff. Also present were Professor Jongbloed, of Utrecht University, an expert on medical science dealing with aviation, and Professor Rooy, of Amsterdam University, who gave lectures on mass communication."

It is obvious from the power of this assembly that just the bemused curiosity of Queen Juliana, or Prince Bernhardt's amateur interest in all aviation matters, did not sponsor it. The talk lasted for well over an hour, longer than was anticipated, and as it proceeded, it became, according to Adamski, more in the nature of a debriefing than a tea party as he was closely questioned about his books and his experiences.

There was of course some opposition, but according to Adamski's report in *Behind the Flying Saucer Mystery*, it came in the curious form of an attempt to "discredit" the space visitors rather than deny their existence. His typical attacking response was to accuse all and sundry of not disclosing information: "I have known of no major officials of our Air Force and few astronomers, who have told what they actually know about the visitors from space. It is a known fact that the secret files and confidential reports of the Air Force have never been released to the public, or even to high officers in the government. I am inclined to believe that this applies to all governments."[165]

Adamski admits that this outburst was "a little rude" in front of the Queen of the Netherlands and her government officials, but once more the Adamski charm carries the day: "I think Her Majesty knew exactly what I meant, for she gave a tiny smile of acknowledgement."

Leaving the Palace grounds and being rushed to a lecture at the Hague, Adamski passes saluting crowds, showing that anyone who had any kind of contact with the Queen in Holland was no ordinary mortal. After he had delivered his lecture to more salutes and applause, he was asked about the details of the royal conversation. He would not say, of course, and this led to more bad relations with the press, and in the ensuing days, he had to put up with reading dozens of made-up accounts, examples of which in our own time we are more than familiar. *Paris Match* for example, carried a reconstructed "Interview with the Queen," complete with made-up questions and answers. Adamski complained about this, but since as a fallible human being, he certainly tarted-up at least some of his own experiences, perhaps he allowed himself a private smile before sleep at these part-fictions feeding off part-fictions and the chain-reactions of both matter and spirit which ensue from such alchemical conditions.

It is difficult to believe that Adamski did not know that to a post-war world, surrounded by the ruins of both mechanism and rationalism, it was all going to be quite irresistible. According to Carol Honey (a friend and associate of Adamski for many years after Lucy McGinnis departed) enthusiasms were further enhanced in 1959 by leaked reports of Adamski saying outright "certain heads of government informed him that they were also contactees." As John Keel's book *The Mothman Prophecies* shows, the Contactee Syndrome consists of very strange fractal-like geometry. Long before he met George Adamski, Carol Honey serviced the radios in the Callair light plane from which Kenneth Arnold saw the original "flying saucers" in 1947.

After the meeting with Queen Juliana, there were rumors that Adamski would come back to Britain and meet members of the Royal Family. The British *Daily Mail* on the 21st of May quoted Adamski as saying that "Some people high up in British society are trying to arrange a meeting." In the same report, however, the *Daily Mail* reported that a Buckingham Palace spokesman had denied that there were plans to receive Adamski.

Adamski left Holland in style, trailing praise and congratulations. Miss Rey d'Aquila, in a letter to her co-workers, dated June 13th, 1959, quotes the concluding words of Professor E.L Seeliger, physicist and former Delft Professor (and close friend of Queen Juliana), at the end of the Amsterdam lecture: "The things that we have heard may sound strange to most of us, if not to all, but strange things happen every day, if out eyes are open. I hope that we will be open-minded and benefit from the things we have heard today."

True to form, personality, and mission, Adamski had once more arrived in a foreign country in style, and to maximum publicity. It must be remembered that this was not the reaction to a mere media star. In those days (as distinct from our own), such simple-minded folk could not possibly have attracted some of the leading lights of the high-powered spectrum. No, Adamski sponsored debate on the deepest and most interesting levels concerning the most important contemporary matters. In 1959, debates which interfaced technological and esoteric matters were almost non-existent, and whether we believe in their claims or not, we are deeply indebted both to Desmond Leslie and Adamski for having initiated such discussions. It must be remembered that this era still considered the most fundamental human concerns and activities to be very solid and somewhat separate matters; the blurring, overlapping, and confusions of a mass-media and consumer age were yet to come.

In this, Adamski and similar authors were unwitting post-modern thinkers in that they (though, of course, mostly by default) initiated the first post-war discussions about the staging and advertising of cultures such as that scientific philosophy which of course so strongly opposed their views. Today many important thinkers see the advertising of science as the true objectives and products of science and not its so-called "real" products, many of which are somewhat trivial and irrelevant. Such a change of view is partly due to people like Adamski, whose name has survived when many of the names of the thousands of scientists who opposed him have been forgotten. In this, he was amongst the first to hint at the full-blown mid-life crisis science is now experiencing nearly fifty years later.

Like the UFO phenomenon itself, Adamski penetrates to the heart of the military-industrial-*mythological* complex, and introduces a virus of fundamental questions. At the Soestdijk Palace in Utrecht were all the divisions of elemental power and symbolism: Royalty (essentially mystical) interfaced with both Science and the Academic world, and all interfaced in turn with both the military and (we can be sure) the Intelligence services. Seen from our own point of view four decades later, this unique moment emerges as a rich semiotic nutrient consisting not of "objective" or separate "factual" elements or states, but the kind of culture dish in which many things were later to form.

Adamski at the Court of Queen Juliana was a modern Cagliostro, and for a very brief time, the Dutch Court became that microcosm from which our present society was formed. The Internet itself is rather like that Court, and is giving a new view to what was previously seen as historical "causation." We may have to accept that we engineer our way out of cultural traps and dead-ends using the most devious and under-handed means in which fantasy and dream are the fundamental catalysts, such things being far more important than, say, traditional economic or "factual" views. This impulse may eventually make up the substance of our experience of technological *time* itself.

The Dutch press raged with questions. What does the government know about flying saucers? Are they keeping something from us? Are there such things as alien visitations? Again, it must be remembered that in 1959, these questions were relatively new, particularly in Europe. And, of course, the snowball was unstoppable once it joined both rumor, and the growing number of disturbing sightings by pilots, policemen, housewives, taxi drivers, and fishermen from all over Europe, never mind anywhere else.

This is the main strength of the UFO phenomenon: if ufology was to vanish tomorrow, and the memory of such folk as Adamski be erased completely, we can be sure that the hundreds of sightings per week from all over the world would continue. This gives all opposing philosophers their biggest problem concerning the UFO: unlike spiritualism of the 19th century, there is an almost daily supply of dramatic evidence for their existence, cross-referencing country, race, class, gender, political view, social and financial status, education, profession, and IQ. Today, the UFO has reached the stage where it has become a "virtual" construct whose "reality" varies from the almost solid to the almost vaporous. Talking about a recent controversy concerning confusion about the claimed reception of alien signals, Peter Gersten commented: "EQ Pegasi was a signal, whether it actually occurred or not. Remember we are dealing with messages where truth or falsity is irrelevant."[166]

Of such stuff is our own Entertainment State made.

For Adamski, Holland was the top of the curve. On May 23rd, 1959, he arrived in Switzerland exhausted, with some lung congestion. He was the guest of writer Lou Zinsstag, whose sanity and kindness and her sincere belief at that time helped Adamski to live through what was not a particularly happy period for him. Like Lucy McGinnis, Adamski's secretary for many years, she would later modify her views somewhat.

As a good organizer, Zinsstag also advised on Adamski's presentational difficulties. As Desmond Leslie has pointed out, Adamski was not a practical man at all, adding that he was "just about able to drive a nail in straight," and the late 1950s was a time before Public Relations and Personal Presentation Management had been invented. While privately Adamski's well-mannered charm carried all before him, on a public stage, strangely, he was a disaster. He was one of those people who are tailor-made for television, but who on stage cannot help looking and sounding like an awkward amateur.

Lecturing in a non-English speaking country presented Adamski with some other problems he had not encountered before. He had never been the most well organized of men, and in the past he had experienced some difficulty with the inconvenience of carrying around some hundred slides or more, a number of which had been broken and even stolen. He had prepared therefore a single reel of film that expressed the core of his work and beliefs, interspersed with still and motion footage of flying saucers shot by him. Since in those pre-video days of 1959, it wasn't easy for not very mechanical folk such as Adamski to stop and start film footage without horrendous complications, his comments between running frames were far too fast for the translators. While this situation was improved somewhat by Zinsstag's German introduction, Adamski's actual lectures were another problem.

He had never been a good public lecturer under the best of circumstances. Desmond Leslie said that when on the lecture platform "his mind seemed to tangle in knots, and many who queued avidly to hear him came away disillusioned and disappointed." He stumbled over words, and did not speak evenly. In Europe, he had been worried constantly about whether the translator was able to follow what he was saying. According to Zinsstag's account, he had tried to remedy this by making a crude "one-sentence, over-simplified version, which sometimes sounded like a dictation exercise in a sixth-grade class." To be fair to Adamski, we must remember that he had no formal education or professional journalistic training, no teaching or lecturing experience, and spoke his Native American with quite a strong Polish accent. Unfortunately, the first lecture he gave in Switzerland was translated by what Zinsstag describes as "an elderly gentleman who, though he spoke English well, failed to understand Adamski's American pronunciation and Polish accent."

Bearing these practical problems in mind, matters were not improved by deliberate and determined attempts by organized groups to sabotage his somewhat fumbling public presentations. The first lecture, by Adamski standards, went quite well, apart from a single troublesome interruption. A man jumped onto the stage and accused him of being an impostor, but the man was soon ejected.

Adamski says that on the morning (Zinsstag says it was the afternoon) of his second lecture in Zurich on May 29th, he was interviewed for "more than two hours" (Zinsstag says it was three hours), by two reporters from the main German weekly newsmagazine, *Der Speigal*. As an example of how Adamski masks things in his own mind, in *Behind the Flying Saucer Mystery,* he describes his reaction to the article when eventually he claims he saw it in print: "They did leave out some rather important links, and thus impart an ever so slight 'leg pulling' slant to it." Since *Der Speigal* didn't have an English language edition at that time, this appears to be the height of optimism when we compare Zinsstag's (a German speaker, of course, as distinct from Adamski), description of the magazine article in her own book: "...the title of the ensuing article ran *'Auf der Venus gibt es Kyhe'* (On Venus there are Cows). The content of the lengthy article was correspondingly shattering, and ridiculed him from A to Z. I never sent it to Adamski, and neither did anyone else."[167]

And here is Adamski making the best of all possible worlds: "Considering everything, the magazine displayed a high amount of courage and independence."[168]

A hint of yet more impending difficulties came when the Chief of Police in Zurich called on Adamski and asked to be given a personal showing of the film. The policeman appeared astonished by sequences of the film, which showed a large metallic spaceship and not just lights in the sky. The atmosphere was pleasant enough, and the policeman was friendly, but Adamski was disturbed somewhat when he added that he would be present at the second Zurich lecture with "some of his officers."

His intuition served him well. A photograph taken at the start of the meeting on May 29th in the vast Congress Hall, shows him on stage sitting next to Lou Zinsstag, and for once, he looks anything but happy. The police did indeed attend, but they were all in civilian clothes, and could not be distinguished from some 300 rowdy students amidst the 700 people present. Screaming and clapping, shouting, stamping, and singing, this student group, mostly from the Technische Hochschule, reduced the event to ruins, throwing on to the stage whatever they could lay their hands on. The plain-clothes police present took no action apart from one of them mounting the stage and asking for calm in a weak voice, which could hardly be heard. According to a *Daily Express* report of the 31st of May, the students threw hundreds of cardboard saucers at the stage. One student waved a banner with a quote in German from Schiller: "With stupidity the gods themselves struggle in vain," though it is doubtful if this got to Adamski as he was pulled away from the microphone by brawling students.

The whole event was quite obviously a set-up, but it quieted down for a while and Lou Zinsstag was able to talk about the contents of the film, which was about to be shown. As soon as the hall was darkened, however, the students set off firecrackers, blew trumpets, and threw fruit and beer-bottles. Strong beams of light ruined the film show, evidence that the whole thing had been prepared. These lights came from car headlamps fixed to the balcony and powered by the hall's main electrical supply.

Finally the police acted and closed the hall, but Adamski, whose cough was now worse, decided to end his European tour on this sad note of conspiracy and paranoia. He said to the *Daily Express* that he would not lecture in Switzerland again.

There were more pleasant moments than this. One evening Lou Zinstagg accompanied Adamski to a very formal dinner party given by Mr. Vorster, an immensely rich man who lived in a great manor house above Basle. Vorster was a member of Lou Zinstagg's Get Acquainted group. Adamski, like the man he was, astonished the Vorsters by displaying immaculate table manners. Without hesitation, he handled the complicated (and uniquely Swiss) cutlery layout in a princely fashion. The Vorsters and their guests were equally impressed when shown Adamski's film and heard his accounts of fantastic events.

A German woman, Mrs. Wissler, sent her notes of this occasion to Lou Zinstagg. Mrs. Wissler recalls a particularly fascinating story told by Adamski, which is related by Zinstagg in *George Adamski: The Untold Story*. Adamski claimed that that a USAF pilot (unnamed) came to Palomar to see him and told him that his plane was once stopped in midair by an "enormous cigar-shaped spaceship." A hangar door opened, and the plane was "sucked in." The men in the craft—who spoke "perfect" English,[169] said they were from Venus, showed the pilot around and were very friendly. They gave the pilot a message written in strange hieroglyphics, and asked him to deliver a message to a certain person in the Pentagon (whose name Adamski withheld). The pilot (released together with his plane) eventually delivered this message. He was given four copies by the aliens. One he kept for himself, one he sent to President Eisenhower, one he sent to the Pope (Pius XII), and the other he delivered to Adamski personally, having he said, read his books.

The guests at the dinner party sat astonished as they passed around a copy of this message. The message was indecipherable, but before we scoff, we should appreciate that according to Zinstagg, the artwork in its construction was frighteningly complex.[170] Zinstagg does not reproduce this particular message in her book, and warns us not to confuse it with the message illustrated elsewhere in *George Adamski: The Untold Story*. This is another message allegedly written by one of Adamski's extraterrestrial contacts. If the letter handed round at the dinner party was anything like this one, then its complexity rivals that of the Voynich[171] coded manuscript, which quite defeated William Friedman,[172] the great American cryptological genius who cracked the Japanese Purple Code used in World War II.

If Adamski was a con-man, then as well as being one of the world's best trick photographers, he was also a cryptographer who could challenge and beat William Friedman, as well as being a graphic calligrapher of unsurpassed genius. It could certainly be said of Adamski that none of his tricks were cheap.

Adamski's tour of Europe ended in the spring of 1959, for which he was thankful, since he was both sick and exhausted. Just like a character from Thomas Mann's novel, *The Magic Mountain,* he sits on hotel balcony in Locarno. He could feel perhaps the first rays of 1960s sunshine falling on a still war-weary Europe where the last bits of Heinkels and Lancasters were still being dug out from the acres of new building sites. He has what for were for him were unusually dangerous thoughts. His paranoia becomes intense. Like many before him, he is now fully convinced that Switzerland, "where the world's gold is buried," is the central headquarters of a world conspiracy which includes the "Silence Group" he fears: "The invisible reins of financial influence extend from Zurich to puppet organizations in every nation! Has it ever occurred to the reader that every nation is financially linked to the Bank of Switzerland, in the country which has enjoyed complete neutrality during every world conflict...."[173]

In this, though Adamski does not have the courage to be openly racist, he gets as near as he can to it without naming names.[174] Just as with Herr Castorp in Mann's novel, the place oppresses him deeply; he is just as exhausted as is the sick Castorp, and we can imagine Adamski craving Californian sunshine, away from a Europe still digging countless wargraves, and re-arming rapidly for possibly another even more horrendous conflict. He is drained, and an uncharacteristic and ill-concealed spleen is active: "Geneva is a gigantic chessboard where the nations of the world are played against one another, according to the dictates of what the Swiss themselves term "The Colossal Financiers." All of this is accomplished under the cloak of neutrality, in Switzerland, where wars are not permitted to happen."[175]

Adamski's mental level has collapsed. Momentarily, old Europe has reclaimed him. We sense the onset of those titanic confusions, which were eventually to destroy him: "I sat on the balcony and thought again of the widespread mysticism that has been falsely applied to the visitors from other planets. The fraudulent mystic groups, professing to be in 'psychic' contact with the space people, have aided the 'Silence Group' immensely. They have caused confusion and kept the entire space program in a state of ridicule."

Something has happened to Adamski. Perhaps at the hotel bar, an old soldier, on hearing his thick Polish accent, asked him about the War, then only fifteen years gone. Certainly something has dimmed the American sunlight inside his head. For a moment he is a Californian no longer. His darker Polish unconscious is active. Looking East from his balcony in Locarno, a line from Berlin to Moscow via Warsaw would run through a thousand places of 20th century death, any one of which might well have consumed him had he stayed where he was born.

Being of Polish Romany[176] stock, he is a Survivor. In a moment of remembering, the countless dead hosts along the Vistula and the Don might have come near, an old ancestral host to darken the sun of the New World.

The Swiss hotel becomes Thomas Mann's Berghoff Sanatorium in his novel *The Magic Mountain*. Adamski becomes at one with an evolving literary landscape; no longer do we have an isolated "study" in ufology. We have a figure moving across a landscape of time and endeavor against which any accusation of imposture becomes as meaningless as it became for Arthur Koestler's Rubashov in *Darkness at Noon*. For a moment, George Adamski doesn't know who he is.

Voices are gathering. Perhaps the souls of the 30 million corpses of World War II alone are near. The accents of Gdansk, Vilna, and Kracow culture crowd upon him. He senses the mass arrests, the sealed trains passing through in the night leaving blood on the tracks, the screams of children from the walled-up ghettos, and the machine-gun fire from the Russian massacre of a major portion of the Polish intelligentsia in Katyn wood in 1943. And, of course, not all that far from Warsaw, there was an old Polish cavalry barracks called Auschwitz. As a homosexual with Romany blood, Adamski had missed that place by a mere fraction of an historical second. When a man misses death by that almost imperceptible thinness of time, an ill-concealed part of him plays it out time and time again.

As an American, all this he has lived through as shadow play. But for a moment, his American identity has fled. Like scores of millions of his original nation, in the last years of his life, he still feels the chill: he must flee, he must go, leave at once, tear himself away. Escape, run, run for your life! These were the last words heard from the father of another tortured American Pole: the film director Roman Polansky. He, too, was to live suspended in a world between images and substance, a world lit by flashes of intrigue, vision, conspiracy, and world-fame.

Yet another haunted Pole is near: the novelist Joseph Conrad (born

Josef Konrad Korzeniowski). Adamski on this balcony in Locarno has come near evil. The most remote contact with evil changes a man. He can pass through twenty of the toughest of jails, have the most painful of experiences, yet not necessarily contact evil. Evil has nothing to do necessarily with the dramas of violence or temper, or cliff-face differences in character, opinion, or background. Evil may have nothing to do with hatred or dislike. Evil is Conrad's Heart of Darkness, and Adamski in Zurich is right in the middle of it, for a moment a figure sculptured by the ghosts of Mann and Conrad.

It is rare that vital symbolic change can be located and defined in such a man. Like Polanski, Adamski was one of the first virtual citizens who would have seen the "X Files" TV series as one long documentary. This alone makes him a study in how the 20th century has created and controlled Time and Imagination, against a background of evolving Technology and media, with not a little archetypal terror along the way.

The young Samuel Taylor Coleridge wrote in a world in which the word *fiction* was beginning to mean something quite different to what it had meant to Dr. Samuel Johnson. One hundred and fifty years later, George Adamski was to live his last few years in a world in which the idea of *fiction* was to change once more. Like Coleridge again, Adamski had little time left as his mental visions had reached a peak.

But his old Romany psyche was great at sensing change of all kinds. The new power in the land was going to be Media. Later, of course, Roman Polanski was to learn this the hard way. Within a decade of Adamski's death, this new Estate would quite overwhelm almost all other systems of reference. Two decades on again, Media would have succeeded in transforming the world into one big cartoon in which cultural advertising was to be the new measure of truth and reality. This was the perfect environment for Adamski's personality, his books ,and photographic and film portfolio as performance art, if nothing else. Like the haunted Polanski again, everything about him was prototypal.

It is highly probable that this moment on the hotel balcony in Locarno was the very time when he decided to create his own cartoons. He would watch the system absorb them as later it would absorb countless other programmatic radiations, from the first James Bond films to the "X Files" television series and the creation of the Internet itself. As Marshall Mcluhan has pointed out, after Adamski's death in 1965, meaningful thinking uncontaminated by media was no longer possible.

In the early 1960s, this was a Copernican change noticed by few; the world looked as it always did: traditional politics, economics, and sociology no different than in the past. In the cultural undertow, however, the equations of "objective fact" were beginning to look like industrial relics, "acts" from a previous age, if only because nobody trusted the Official Reality any more than they would trust a cornered rat.

The input=output structures of old industrial Authority no longer described adequately the characteristics of an emerging media culture. The influence or "output" of media "products" was far in excess of what went in to "make" a particular media construct. This new world-structure consisted of shows and advertisements, all of which had Andy Warhol's mere fifteen minutes of performing time, and very little else, before being dragged off into the wings.

Mentally hyperactive, Adamski was always ultra sensitive to such changes in time and era. He was one man who did not want to grow old in his mind. He sacrificed everything for this. Perhaps with that alchemist's intuition that the false stage in reasoning is a vital stage in creation, he decided to create worlds in the way that the media all around him was creating them.

Adamski leaves Locarno for a short visit to Rome with Lou Zinsstag, prior to departing for America. Just as for Carl Jung, Rome looms like a beckoning figure of death and retribution. As vast European shadows deepen around him yet again in the Roman Coliseum, again he felt Polish rather American. But one thing about him has perhaps not changed. The only time he lifts his head up in Rome is at a dinner with friends, where he pays attention to the "style of clothing worn by the waiters" and their "manner of serving."

On June 17, 1959, Adamski left Rome by plane for Denmark, where he changed at Copenhagen for the long Polar flight to Los Angeles. A group from the Danish "Get Acquainted" program said goodbye before he commenced the grueling flight home. By modern standards these flights were made at a fairly low altitude, and window blinds were drawn down in the noisy aircraft to avoid the glare of ice and snow. After refueling stops at Greenland and Winnipeg, the sick and exhausted Adamski must have been glad when he finally arrived back in the sunshine of San Diego.

CHAPTER 15

Winter on the Magic Mountain

A damski, looking back at his world tour, wrote: "Many times since then I have reviewed the events of those six months. I believe the truth was brought to many people of the world, as requested by our space brothers. Yet to this day I am deeply concerned that the 'Silence Group' and other selfish interests might continue to hinder our progress."

And a year after leaving Europe, he wrote: "The spring of 1960 dawning upon the scene of economic, political and social dissemination found also the minds of the world inhabitants filled with vague wanderings. The air was filled with talk of strikes, war and want. Every man was concerned with the ever-increasing civil and international complications."

Thus he returned to America. There, like Toad from *Wind in the Willows,* he makes a remarkable recovery to carry his wrecking mission to higher and higher levels, sandwiching a visit to the Pope in between meeting members of the United Nations and, so he claimed, President Kennedy.

Adamski would return to Europe, but by then the thrill had gone. He had seen something from another world, but in the traditional fairy manner, like Coleridge after the composition of *Kubla Khan,* his visit to this domain had left him broken. After 1959, his enchanted kingdom was collapsing in suspicion and fear, in mistrust and accusation.

While preparing the second edition of his *The Report on Unidentified Flying Objects* in 1959, Ruppelt gives a very good idea of how thin was the ice on which Adamski was skating when he returned to America from his world tour: "...the old maestro George Adamski is still head and shoulders above the rest. The hamburger stand is boarded up and he lives in a big ranch house. He vacations in Mexico and has his own clerical staff. His two books *Flying Saucers Have Landed* and *Inside the Spaceships* have sold something in the order of 200,000 copies and have been translated into nearly every language except Russian.

"Only a few months ago, while on one of his numerous nationwide lecture tours, a saucer unexpectedly picked Adamski up in Kansa City and took him on a galactic cruise before depositing at Ft. Madison, Iowa, where he had a lecture date. He 'wowed' the packed auditorium with his 'proof'—an unused Kansas City to Ft. Madison train ticket.

"Last week in the Netherlands he repeated his exploits to Queen Juliana. But at Buckingham Palace, Mr. Barnum, all he saw was the changing of the guard."

Despite such sneers from those who should have known better, Adamski had certainly seen something from another world, but in the traditional fairy manner; like Coleridge after the composition of Kubla Khan, his visit to this domain had left him broken. His enchanted kingdom was collapsing in suspicion and fear, in mistrust and accusation. Further evidence of sad decline was the deteriorating quality of the newsletters to Adamski's Get Acquainted groups. It was obvious that he was now making it all up as he went along. One example from a newsletter issued by Adamski in 1962 will suffice to show the state of his mind at this time. In June 1962, Lou Zinstagg received Admski's "Report on my Trip to the Twelve Counsellors' Meeting of our Solar System that took place on March 27th through 30th." Zinstagg was not surprisingly taken aback by the first paragraph:

"On March 26th, I left on a spacecraft for the journey. The ship had come in on the 24th to one of our (U.S.) Air Bases where a high official of the U.S. Government had a conference with the crew. After the conference, the craft was returning to its home planet Saturn. The trip took nine hours, at a speed greater than 200 million m.p.h."[177]

The situation with Adamski recalls what the writer Laurens van der Post said of his friend, the writer Roy Campbell, in the *London Evening Standard* on Sept. 24, 2001: "People accused him of lying about himself. I do not think it could be called lying. I think he was so deeply absorbed in the images that kept pouring into him from his own dreaming unconscious, his own need of a personal mythology so kept him on the path of poetic meaning which was a constant hunger in him, that he could not help it."

These observations describe the state of mind of many who have a stroke of genius. Such deep confusions often break up social and personal relations. But out of his shattered life, Adamski could still exercise what Charles Fort called a "wild talent." A few fragments of the enchanted domain still clung to him. Lou Zinstagg, the very epitome of bourgeois sanity, was quite astonished when on May 31, 1963, she, together with co-worker May Morlet, saw Adamski enter a sidedoor of the Vatican building while the group were on a visit to Rome. He was let in by a man dressed in black, although seemingly not a priest. This man wore a kind of breastplate, and Adamski himself carried a small package that he said was a gift to the Pope. Adamski said that this package had been given to him by a spaceman in Copenhagen, two weeks previous, when he was lecturing in Copenhagen and was the guest of Hans Peterson, an organizer of the "Get Acquainted" group. Pope John XXIII had but two days to live, and Adamski later said to Lou Zinstagg that the Pope thanked him personally and said that he knew that such a package was coming to him.

Of course, we shall never know what the mysterious package contained, but whatever it was, someone in the Vatican was grateful. A short while later, Adamski showed Zinstagg an Ecumenical Council medallion of between 18-22 carat gold, worth 300-400 Swiss francs at that time. Though Zinstagg does not say that Adamski said that the Pope himself had given this to him, he proudly pointed out the date of the coin: May 31, 1963. This coin was not available at the time; the Ecumenical Council, which was to issue it, had been suspended because of the Pope's illness.

After the Pope died, Adamski said that though space people were present at his bedside, sadly, they were unable to do anything to prevent his death.

Nearing his mid-seventies, Adamski's magic was becoming fickle. All he seemed able to manage was a kind of blown-up circus that compromised his personal worth and dignity. He told Lou Zinstagg that he had been entrusted by the space folk to give a message to President Kennedy. This was an invitation to visit one of the huge mother ships at an air base in Hot Springs, California. Again, a spaceman allowed Adamski into the White House, and allegedly Kennedy made the visit to the ship.

With such stories, many thought that the magus had become a con man, fallen from magic to trickery. Carol Honey, Lucy McGinnis, Rey d'Aquila, Lou Zinstagg, and most of the rest of the sorcerer's apprentices were to leave him, abandon him on his mountain where the gods no longer spoke to him. Or if they did speak, they told him stories that would put a tomcat into stitches.

Though, like Carol Honey, Lucy McGinnis remained forever convinced of the truth of Adamski's first desert contact, she decided finally to desert him. For her there had been too many indications that not only was Adamski now writing space-episodes himself, he was at the same time practicing a form of self-hypnotism. He was also immersing himself in occultism, a practice which previously he always said he abhorred. In particular, it appeared to both Lucy and Carol Honey that the meetings with the space folk, which Adamski talked about so freely, were now taking place inside his head. Since Lucy was the great organizing hub of his world, without her the organization began to fall apart.

With Lucy gone, Adamski announced that he would now concentrate on theosophical teaching and hand over practical control of his affairs and organization to Carol Honey, his close associate for many years. Unfortunately, Honey now found himself in direct conflict with the kind of things Adamski was saying in the Newsletter.[178] As editor, he claimed that some of Adamski's articles now concerned full-fledged accusations of witchcraft and he refused to publish them.

Also disturbing was the manner in which Adamski now referred to what he termed the Cosmic Brothers in localized terms, talking about them in a completely familiar way, as if they were close neighbors who lived nearby. In direct contrast to this folksy simplicity, he would describe the agendas and intrigues of such beings. These were not only Byzantine plots involving world leaders and organizations; they were intrigues between groups of space-beings themselves. Adamski said that the group of Cosmic Brothers with whom he was in contact were here to teach us all how to live a better life, both physically and spiritually. But in a 1963 meeting with Orthon, he was told that there were enemy aliens who were out to confuse people "either through impressions or direct contact." These were not Cosmic Brothers, but were very different space folk out to exploit humanity.

This latter group had been responsible for many of his difficulties in the past, and he claimed that it was these folk who had taken Lucy McGinnis away from him. Finally, he accused Honey of being in league with the opposing groups of space beings, adding: "The way to know the true space people whose purpose is to help us is: they do not create trouble between peoples or friends. Nor do they find fault with any of our religions. They are not here to expose our ignorance. Any that do contrary to this as Mr. Honey's group is doing are not here for a good purpose. And all space people are not benevolent. Many have weaknesses like we have and especially the majority of the Martians."[179]

We are left to wonder what Cosmic Brother Firkon thought of this last remark since he was a Martian.

Predictably, this kind of talk alarmed those who received the Newsletter, and support for Adamski dwindled. Honey tried to right the situation by inferring that Adamski was temporarily out of his mind. But any hope that the sane Honey would put the situation right were dashed when he in turn advertised his own work on telepathy. His treatment just happened to be a mirror-reflection of Adamski's views, developed by him over some forty years.

Thus the great adventure ended with accusation and counter-accusation from all quarters of the sun and moon. Of course, when two telepathic metaphysicians throw vitriol at one another, it takes the form of the complete spectrum of conscious manifestations. The accusations and counter-accusations within the Adamski-Honey debate concerned what was "psychic" and what was not, and all this was pursued to a "scientific" fault, if you please.[180] One party claimed a near-substance, the other party an almost-shadow materiality; into this they mixed in mutual charges of mysticism and gangsterism. Thus they raged at one another as in a Vincent Price movie, with metaphysics becoming physics and vice versa, all in one wink of a quantum-raven's eye.

Nearing his mid-seventies, Adamski's magic mountain was preparing for winter. The season was on the wane in Prospero's cell, and sets of "new boys" were in town who were not kind sprites like Orthon and Kalna. By 1965, all Adamski could manage was a kind of blown-up circus that compromised his personal worth and dignity. He told Lou Zinstagg that he had been entrusted by the space folk to give a message to President Kennedy. This was an invitation to visit one of the huge mother ships at an air base in Hot Springs, California. Again, a spaceman allowed Adamski into the White House, and, allegedly, Kennedy made the visit to the ship.

With such stories, many people thought that the magus had become a con man, fallen from magic to trickery, and even his much-hated "psychic" activity. Carol Honey, Lucy McGinnis, Rey d'Aquila, Lou Zinstagg, and most of the rest of the sorcerer's apprentices were to leave him, abandon him on his mountain where the gods no longer spoke to him. Or if they did speak, they told him stories that would put a tomcat in stitches.

Though Adamski continued to lecture and broadcast up to the end of his days, his worldwide support collapsed after 1963. Doubt had triumphed. From claims of "teleportation" at "200 million m.p.h." it was an easy victory. But these were days before mass media culture questioned the advertisements of Rationalism. The idea of both truth and the physical world as "solid" things was still very much in vogue. The Star had not yet taken over from the Scientist, who was still a class act at the top of the bill. Our own full-fledged Entertainment State had not yet arrived. In those pre-assassination, pre-Vietnam days, there was still a little cultural time left in which to think that fact could be readily separated from fiction, and that science and democracy both would save humanity.

Adamski mixed Christ and technology, myth and the concrete, cool and pleasant sanity and the utterly fantastic claim, and he lived in the battleground between all these mixed metaphors. In doing so, he fell into the ruthlessly selective machinery of the Western mind and was crushed.

But some like Alice K. Wells, kept faith, and in his early seventies, George Adamski was to meet a guardian angel who would protect and sustain him in his last days. With the young Madeleine Rodeffer as his companion, the 74-year-old cavalryman was to make his last charge and astonish the world before he left it for good.

Or almost for good.

CHAPTER 16

Miracles Must Be Small, and Not Happen Very Often

Our psychology defines itself not so much by what it includes, so much as by what it leaves out. Long ago, Charles Fort provided a theory of fuzzy perceptions, which applies not only to the Adamski story but to Roswell and other UFO stories. Fort illustrated this theory by relating the uproarious example in *Lo!* of what happened at the Swanton Novers Rectory in 1919. He shows many metaphors coming from different directions and getting into a kind of traffic jam.

In August, 1919, a housemaid, Mabel Louisa Philippo, worked in this Rectory, in which paraffin, petrol, methylated spirits, and even sandalwood oil poured from various points in the house, some fifty gallons of the stuff being caught in drums! The Rector, in response to a request from the *Daily Express,* reported as follows: "Expert engineer arriving Monday. Drippings ascribed to exudations, on August 8th, of petrol, methylated spirits, and paraffin. House evacuated; vapor dangerous; every room affected; downpour rather than dripping."[182]

The *London Daily News* gave reports from an architect, a geologist, and a chemist, who told of the enormous quantities of liquids flowing. A Norwich newspaper gave an account from the foreman of an oil company, who had caught more than two gallons of oil, which had dripped in four hours from a particular appearing-point. Conditions had become so bad that the Rector, the Reverend Hugh Guy, had been driven out and had moved his furniture to another house.

Ceilings were bored through, indeed even taken apart; photographs were taken, but still the flow continued. At this point, a pair of professional stage illusionists, Mr. and Mrs. Williams, were brought in to watch the girl (in conditions which remind us of today's skeptical magician, The Amazing Randi). They placed a glass of salted water (thus being detectable) in the kitchen, and stated they saw the girl throw this glass of water at the ceiling. They also said that the girl "admitted she had done it, and finally she broke down, and made a clean breast of it."[183] A few days later, however, in an interview with a local newspaper, the 15-year-old girl denied that she had "confessed," adding that she had been beaten by Mr. and Mrs. Williams! Yet another stage-magician, a Mr. N. Maskelyne, then appeared, presumably to watch both the girl and the Williams. He found no evidence of trickery, reporting to the *Daily Mail* of September 10th, that "barrels" of oil had appeared during the time of his observations. As concerns the "confession," the *London Daily News* reported, also on September 10th: "According to the little girl's statement, she was at no time alone in the kitchen...she insists that she was the victim of a trick, and that great pressure was put upon her to admit that she had thrown salted water to the ceiling. 'I was told' she said, 'that I would be given one minute to say I had done it, or go to prison. I said that I didn't do it.'"

There then occurred another bewildering double take: The Rev. Guy himself made a kind of "confession." He wrote to the *Times* saying that although he thought the girl had thrown the water, she had, in his opinion, confessed to nothing. Therefore the Williams were suspect. As for the quantities, the Rev. Guy shrinks those, just as he shrank the pseudo-confession of the girl. He says in this same letter: "It would have taken only a small quantity to create the mess." Fort comments: "The meaning of this statement is that, whereas gallons, or barrels, of oils, at a cost of hundreds of dollars, could not be attributed to a mischievous girl, 'only a small quantity' could be."[184]

Thus small miracles are allowed to peep over the knife-edge of acceptance, but even when they do appear, because they are small, they are not accepted. This attitude is summed by novelist Anatole France's remark, upon seeing the cast-away walking sticks and crutches hung up at Lourdes: this sage asked: "but where are the wooden legs?" These "small" miracles have also another restriction placed upon them: They must not happen very often. Thus "fact" is really a matter of size and frequency rather than being absolute in itself. And so we have miracle-management rather than any simple-minded idea of "concrete objective reality."

This truly marvelous mess of double-takes, both human, ideological, spiritual, and mechanical, plus many different levels of dumb-fake-fakery, is not only the ideal model of a Fortean world, it is the world of George Adamski. It serves also as an entrance into the bewildering tangle of the crop-circle controversy.[185]

Just as we might ask Adamski about the madcap chase to interpret the marks on the soles of an alien's boots, we might ask what on earth has salted water to do with the various kinds of "oil" detected by impeccable witnesses? And what about the quantities? Was Mabel Louisa Philippo upstairs, pouring all this stuff down through the ceiling? Seventy-five years later, was Lieutenant Colonel Philip Corso crazy when he talked about alien autopsies at Walter Reed and Bethesda hospitals as casually as if he were talking about admission for a broken ankle?[186]

Whether poltergeists in 1919, or aliens in 1953, it all smacks of those marvelous Victorian intellectual comedies of "seances" reported by the Society for Psychical Research in this period, where international philosophers tied down a medium's hands, eminent professors held her feet, and accomplished academicians tied her blindfold. Louis Pauwels tells of a report in the minutes of the Paris Academy of Sciences, concerning the examination of the first phonograph. Apparently, as soon as a voice was heard from the machine, the permanent secretary threw himself upon the man who was demonstrating it, and seized him by the throat, thinking he was some kind of ventriloquist. But to the stupefaction of everyone there, the machine continued to "speak."[187]

It seems there is an element in all these cases of the vast confusions within both the present-day Cold Fusion controversy. When an "era" does not want something for whatever reason, or when there are investigations which affect vital definitions which might effect major scientific assumptions, experimenters are faced with plots which lead right to the center of the main operational ideas of their Age. These ideas, acting in every way as concrete personae, put the human players in a kind of whirling Swanton Novers cum Adamski drama. It is as if many kinds of cultural advertising (in the sense of persuasion) are trying to get through a narrow bottleneck of "acceptance" at the same time. The object of these different systems (and that includes systems of rational explanation) is to enter that prime time which is usually taken as "reality."

There are created situations where a simple line between truth and falsehood cannot be drawn. The whole game-play exists in what we might term an "intermediate state,"[188] where there is nothing "real" in the proper sense: people and ideas, situations and metaphors, all are in various states of complex Fortean transition. Some situations crystallize out, their "objectivity" almost achieved, such as the splitting of the atom, or the finding of the DNA structure. But others, whose "objectivity" is less securely achieved, are stillborn. They suffer various degrees of part-acceptance, to finish up in a kind of museum of twilight forms of semi-materialized matter and ideology. Examples are Ron Hubbard's auditing meter, and other almost-theres such as the ("no molecules at all") Jacques Benveniste experiments on homeopathy.[189] We might include also the many "fuel-less" engines whose inventors tend to disappear in mysterious circumstances.

CHAPTER 17

Things that Haunt the Outer Edge

In February, 1965, a few months before his death, Adamski was staying with his friends Madeleine Rodeffer, and her husband Nelson, in Silver Spring, Maryland. On the afternoon of the 26th, with Nelson away at work at Walter Reed Hospital, Madeleine and Adamski shot some film of UFOs seen near the house. In the second part of *George Adamski: The Untold Story,* Timothy Good gives a detailed account of the content of this film, the peculiar circumstances in which it was made, and the even more bizarre things that happened to it before he saw its final version in Brussels in December, 1965.

The 12-still photo sequence Good himself chose to publish in *George Adamski: The Untold Story,* is of quite decent quality. Included also are no less than five enlargements of which show that the UFO itself is a typical Adamski "bottle cooler" type, complete with a dome above a base which has the shape of an upturned saucer. The object is itself in motion, the right-hand side only is becoming hump-backed, and the three-sphere undercarriage is shown retracting and lowering. The motion takes place against a background of trees, and the UFO is seen coming in from a distance, until it is near enough to the camera for details of the structure to be seen. The shape changing alone is frighteningly convincing, and both Leonard Cramp and optical physicist William Sherwood testified to the authenticity of this film.[190]

But as with many pieces of UFO "evidence," the film that Good saw in Brussels in 1965 had a somewhat checkered history. After shooting the original film earlier in the year, Adamski and Madeleine were astonished to find that it had been grossly interfered with after they had given the raw footage to a firm to be processed. Good comments: "...the original film had been stolen and replaced with a copy, with many important frames missing and even some fake footage added by person or persons unknown."

Stolen from whom, exactly? The processing firm in Alexandria, Virginia, recommended by Adamski's friend Bill Sherwood, a Kodak technician? If so, didn't anyone complain, sue, or go dashing to the processing house armed with hard questions? Theft and Misappropriation are criminal offences. Did the firm get in touch with the police, or at least undertake an internal investigation? Were they insured against loss of customer's property? Did they write a blushing apology to Adamski? Apparently there was some kind of communication with the firm, since otherwise it would not have been known that the original had been stolen.

The total absence of such questions, never mind answers, has a familiar feel to students of conspiracies. It is all far beyond finite lying or blushing skullduggery. The absence of such simple rationalizations always indicates that we are approaching those worlds so well described by John Keel in *The Mothman Prophecies,* Jacques Valee in *Passport to Magonia* and Patrick Harpur in *Demonic Reality*. This confused atmosphere almost always surrounds the characters of the contactee world; this may be called the Lee Harvey Oswald atmosphere, though they are shorn fortunately, of Oswald's confused politics and violent nature. But no matter how pathetic, incompetent, unintelligent, comical, or plain stupid and ridiculous, they somehow put their backsides on the line in a similar way to Oswald; their lop-sided commitments and their equally lop-sided characters allow them to step in and out of similar cartoon-frames, and press similar toy-triggers. Rather than dealing with death, the contactees produce pieces of unredeemed Nature which astound, suggesting to us that the world operates not by "factual objectivities," but by a process which keeps perception permanently off-balance, and makes received experience that mess of imprecision that so infuriates researchers in Artificial Intelligence. In this sense, the pieces—whether films, photographs, alleged implants, burns, radar traces, or even unconscious memories— exist in a kind of snowflake time in which they might well masquerade as something else, disappear completely, or become fragmented, rather like a newspaper under a heavy rainfall.

"Following the death of Adamski," Good comments, "Madeleine

Rodeffer experienced a great deal of ridicule and embarrassment, and nearly all copies of the "faked" film have been stolen—in the United States and elsewhere." Good, in *Beyond Top Secret*[191] tells us that Stephen Darbishire had the same problems, and quotes a personal letter to him from Stephen himself: " When I said that I had seen a UFO I was laughed at, attacked, and surrounded by strange people…in desperation I remember I refuted the statement and said it was a fake. I was counter-attacked, accused of working with the 'Dark Powers'…or patronizingly 'understood' for following orders from some secret government department. There was something. It happened a long time ago, and I do not wish to be drawn into the labyrinth again. Unfortunately the negatives were stolen and all the prints gone…"

In this, we must assume that all these things have slipped down one of those rabbit-holes of the twentieth century landscape in which were lost UFO gun-camera films of the 1950s, certain Lee Harvey Oswald documentation, and the total life records of Bob Lazar, who blew the whistle on Area 51 where he claimed to have seen back-engineered UFOs and the dead bodies of aliens.

We might well bear these things in mind as we take a another draught from Good's offered bottle, shrink to the size of the small door, pass through, and join a modern mad hatter's tea-party.

One jolly name-dropping spaceman calling before breakfast is one thing, but three more equally jolly after lunch, is getting near "Alf" territory. The spaceman who called at the Rodeffer house before breakfast is one White Rabbit enough when he says that he was on his way to meet no less a person than the Vice President of the United States: "Madeleine got up between 8.30 and 9am, and as she went downstairs she was greeted by Adamski with some fantastic news. Shortly after Nelson left, he said, one of the 'boys' had come up to the house on his way into town to see no less a person than Vice-President Hubert Humphrey."

Though probably no one has checked Hubert Humphrey's diary for that day, it is unlikely that anyone will ever bother. Any more White Rabbits like this, we think, and we will throw the book away and go and watch the morning kiddy-cartoons. But something tells us to have patience, for as this particular day goes on, while it might not tell us much about flying saucers and aliens, it will certainly show that what we call "reality" may reveal dimensions that beggar belief. Lon Milo Duquette, author of *Angels, Demons & Gods of the New Millennium* remarked that "very few of us ever realize quite how profoundly gigantic and ubiquitous our heads really are."

Sometime between three and four in the afternoon, after Adamski has helped Madeleine Rodeffer load her Christmas-present 8mm Bell and Howell movie camera, the pair look through the dining room window. They noticed a "small craft" moving over some trees (*moving* is surely preferable to Good's "hovering back and forth"). At exactly the same time, a gray car draws up in the road at the bottom of the drive, and three men (no physical descriptions given) come to the front door, exclaiming enthusiastically: "'They're here. Get your cameras. They're here,' Madeleine claims the visitors announced. The 'boys' had arrived—in more ways than one apparently!"

We enter then a scene from the mid-sixties which since has spawned a thousand space-operas With her leg in plaster from an accident, Madeleine Rodeffer (who in 1965, had a totally astonishing likeness to the young Queen Elizabeth the Second), stomps onto the porch followed by the sick and aging Adamski. She has her hubby's gift-camera in her hands, loaded with cheap Dynacolor film from a local Sears Roebuck store. But she fumbles and cannot operate the camera. She gives it to Adamski, who shoots some film with it, having most carelessly left his own 16mm Kodak camera behind somewhere.

At this point Good loses momentarily his famed objectivity and starts to slip down the tunnel past the jars of orange marmalade: "It will quite naturally be asked what the three alleged extraterrestrials were doing during this time, and why they did not offer any assistance. It is my assumption that they were acting in liaison with their colleagues in the craft. One of the tasks was perhaps to ensure, by mental means, that no-one else in the immediate neighborhood was aware of what was going on, thus guaranteeing privacy while the craft was being filmed. To have assisted in this would have defeated the object of the exercise."[192]

The localized, almost nonchalant familiarity here is as amazing as anything else. Everything here is leveled off to localizations, as if someone were to say that they met King Henry VIII between buying cat-food and going to the launderette, but they didn't speak to the King for very long, because he appeared to be in a very bad mood. Like King Henry, the "boys" here act as thousand-place decimals inserted between two systems that are only first place decimals. It's a matter of psychic scaling. In automatically assuming that the aliens have a mission, entities multiply themselves most unnecessarily at a great rate by applying such a fine rational focus to an experience that was an absurd blur more than anything else.

The saucer disappears and Adamski and Madeleine try to get back into the house as the temperature outside is below freezing. But Madeleine has slammed the door to on the latch, and the pair stomp round to the patio, where the saucer is seen again. This time it is so close that "human" faces are seen through portholes.

Good continues his interview with Madeleine: "What happened after the craft disappeared, I asked? 'The space people said, "Well, that's all. I hope we never have to do this again because it is too dangerous." They said it's too dangerous because of our military. And that is all I remember. There was very little conversation. They were here only minutes, then they left.'"

That is a pity, because if these people were aliens, whatever "little" conversation there was, could well have changed the entire course of human history in a morning. Note again the lack of concentration revealed by both Madeleine and Adamski.

In re-examining these Ur-texts of the 1960s, we discover the mother of all modern American UFO conspiracies as Good asks Madeleine how bad the "fraudulent" frames looked when they returned from processing: "'It looked like an old gray hat at one point,' George said. 'It was all faked stuff that they had taken,' she explained. They took the original film from us, and what I think they did was re-photograph portions of the original onto a screen and then take camera equipment and fake some stuff." Madeleine continues, with yet another amazing idea: "Perhaps they actually came out here and did some filming on their own, and then re-filmed a whole roll and somehow took out good portions and inserted fake portions. The film I got back is not the original film at all. It's a copy."

One has to point out here that such a conspiracy on behalf of the processing company would have required it to be fast on its feet. The firm was located not by Bill Sherwood himself, but by a neighbor of his. As a random toss, that would satisfy some pretty rigid test-conditions. We assume that it did not occur to anyone in the Adamski group to preserve the "fraudulent" footage since (if aliens had interfered it with), it would have proved undoubtedly as interesting as the "good" footage, just as would the discovery of a "bad" quarto of Shakespeare. As with "bad" quartos, there are more questions than answers, and the Adamski group appears to be limp about what has happened to their property. In contrast, we can be sure that the aforementioned Reeve couple would, of all people, have barnstormed down to reception, and God help the firm if they'd tried the same thing on say, the physically impressive Aetherian, George King, who was a dead ringer for Christopher Lee playing Dracula. Did the firm have a log of its operators, we ask? Was there any paperwork, or logs of who was processing what and where? Were any technical staff asked questions? Was the "bad" film shown to the firm's boss, or supervisors? Was there a check to see if this was not merely a mistake in quality control? Was there a refund?

The lack of answers to these questions points out a major characteristic of the group: their local mechanical rationale is not strong. Perhaps that is how the whole thing works. Their very ineptness is a screen against normality. Madeleine was herself, by most accounts, a bit of an Alice, and of course Adamski, like Oswald and Uri Geller again, had been a super-Alice almost all his life. As in John Fowles' novel *The Magus,* a willing suspension of disbelief is part of the ritual initiation into the god-game. Once the game has been launched, they must at least try and play by its almost-incomprehensible rules. This same process happened to Geller and Andrija Puharich in turn, as described in the book, *Briefing for the Landing on Planet Earth* by Stuart Holroyd,[193] and on occasion, even Timothy Good as narrator gets drawn in deeper and deeper, sometimes losing his focus, along with his characters. But perhaps that is why he is one of the world's best investigators. In becoming almost a part of the process, he takes risks, most which come off

This lack of a disciplined response is telling of the characters involved. In all charity, it must be concluded here that with the exception of Good himself, we are not dealing with people, bless them, who are of the clearest and sharpest mentality Compare their commitment and enthusiasm to their lack of concentration. They fumble with the cheapest and most simple of equipment. Madeleine did not know her camera needed an orange filter for daylight shots, and Adamski left behind his much better camera. But then as Lou Zinsstag points out, Adamski was so bad at common-sense arrangements and mechanical things, she had to take over the practical management of his European tour herself.

In this, the phenomenon is certainly a part-function of individual and group personalities. The inexcusable fumbling of Adamski and Madeleine, the drunken rages of the psychic "thoughtphotographer" Ted Serios, the extremely superficial mind of disco-child Uri Geller, indicate that such people are *playing,* rather than thinking. Thinking, as we know it, is a very late arrival on the historical scene. For hundreds of thousands of years we reasoned as only young children now still reason. Researches into Artificial Intelligence have now come up against the play barrier. The chief characteristic of all play is the waste of time involved in it as an activity. Its free associations and mobility thoroughly disturb intellectuals all; they want the roundabout to stay still, and it will not; it continues to generate very large numbers of noisy and redundant connections. One cannot help the feeling that prior to fetching fire from heaven, as it were, the lives of many of the contactees, were, in any bourgeois sense at least, complete wastes of time in themselves.

With Adamski and Geller in particular, the impression is given of eager minds actively ransacking the power-metaphors of their age. They do this rather in the manner of a child eagerly sorting through a big box of toys. In becoming children somewhat they forget the rules of a guilt-ridden consciousness that insist that the world is essentially mundane. Here is how Madeleine describes Adamski's reaction after both spacemen and the UFO have gone away. Good asked Madeleine what happened after the craft disappeared. She responded: "I was very pleased of course, to say the least! George was even more excited, I guess. He was just like a child at Christmas receiving all the toys he wanted. He said no-one should ask for more proof than that."[194]

Even Lou Zinsstag, a discreet woman of impeccable manners, feels that she must mention the infantile sexuality of some of Adamski's jokes. Rather like Geller and indeed Oswald again, Adamski had one of those minds that hardly sees "fact" at all; rather he saw color-combinations of ideas. In this, factual mistakes hardly mattered to him, and being over-enthusiastic in almost everything he ever did, he made plenty of them.

Like his metaphor-surfing life, the drama of the "bad" film continued, indeed like the progress of some fragmented film in itself, in which there were some almost-real parts, some almost-forged parts.

Adamski left Silver Spring in the final week of March, and went to Rochester to edit the film, assisted by his friends, Fred Steckling and Bill Sherwood, who at that time was a project manager for Kodak. They marked carefully the good parts to be copied, and the bad parts that were to be left out. One of the good sections that remained of the original "bad" film was a sequence in which the craft hung motionless above the patio for a short time. But according to Good, when Adamski returned from Rochester to Silver Spring with his copies, this particular section had promptly disappeared, as if some agency were still capable of exercising an option through any stage of the process.

When Bill Sherwood talked to Good in later years, he said that he had no recollection of these patio shots, even though he himself had "counted every single frame with a special viewing device." Good reports[195] also that Fred Steckling told him many years later, in 1976, that Adamski had told him at the time that the "space people" had taken back this section because it revealed details of their craft they did not want known. Steckling added that Adamski told him that the missing section was "…in good hands, and those who've got it have a right to have it."

At this point, Good, rather like Geller and Puharich, becomes seduced totally by the game itself, becoming one of the group and asking the group's questions rather than his own; he applies also a metaphor of distance to something that is somewhat distant (to say the least), in the first place: "This seems rather far-fetched, implying incompetence on the space people's part in permitting the film shown in this section to be taken in the first place. Madeleine believes that they would hardly go to all that trouble and then censor the film, and he has a point, but if their (sic) judgment is not always perfect, I think their (sic) action was justifiable. If Adamski was right, one can be forgiven for wondering if the entire film was 'rearranged' by the aliens. Madeleine, at any rate, thinks that only terrestrial agents were responsible for the faked portions."

So here we are back to the Swanton Novers Rectory confusions again. According to Good, the aliens are not only engaged in deception, but they could be incompetent in that deception. Momentarily, the phenomenon has consumed Good; he has fallen victim to the many levels of perception and convention, methodology and reference-planes, view-points, prejudices, and innocent mystifications and not-so innocent demystifications inherent in the situations as he sees it.

In order to get out of the confusion, he has given the aliens solidity: he gives them a moral and personal identity; they have social needs and exhibit operational uncertainty. According to Good, they can therefore be argued for and against in a manner rather like a barrister presenting a case. This is classic creation of a social construct moving rapidly towards those acceptance limitations that constitute the programmatic "real."

In reasoning that the alien's judgment may not always be perfect, and that their action was therefore justifiable in order to protect their interest, the space folk are becoming conceptually localized. Their actions may therefore be spoken of as clearly and logically as if they were apprentice shop assistants involved in an investigation of alleged theft of the tea-money.

This, of course, is a dangerous moment. Angels and the tips of pins are near. This is a perfect picture of entities taking over a group. The dangers increase when Madeleine dashes to quite another point of the fuzzy scale of entity-multiplication: "Madeleine, at any rate, thinks that only terrestrial agents were responsible for the faked portions." The existence of the shadowy human agents referred to here is so ephemeral that it equals the almost-existence of the space-folk. Thus in this world of the half substance of almost-created folk-lore, the human agents are becoming identical with aliens. And, of course, the human agents will make mistakes, too. How many quadruple-takes are there in this possible overlap of human mistakes and alien mistakes, mixed with Adamski's juvenile naiveté, and Madeleine's gushing and energetic enthusiasms?

If we proceed in this manner, and reason that another alien level may well have *their* own triumphs and disasters and degree of incompetence and so on, we have the comforting Fortean though that the entire universe might consist of endless versions of the Swanton Novers Rectory debacle!

With that in mind, and just a little patience, we can almost hear the beating heart of the UFO mystery.

As if that were not enough, we must assume that, like human beings, aliens also have their vastly different cultural and social levels. One level may indeed be in awe of another, higher level, who being doubtless fallible in turn, will make mistakes, and have prejudices, and be again in awe of a yet higher level. When these cross-references are summed to infinity, any "experience" becomes, no matter how brief, no matter how mysterious or otherwise, an ancient wall-painting weathered by sun and storm, penetrated by ivy and lichen, and alive with the forms of peculiar life experienced before breakfast by Adamski and Madeleine.

One of the things that the UFO phenomenon may be teaching us is that we may well have to replace the "real" versus the "unreal" or the "paranormal" versus the "normal" by an array of warring information-systems, any one of which may command the high historical frontier at any one time. In order to come to terms with the veritable mass of ever-increasing UFO evidence and reports, we may have to take apart every single assumption of the connection between mind and nature as inherited and as currently perceived.

A child might remind us that in such a welter of grown-up thoughts, we must not forget that at times it sounds very much as if more than something is having us on. If we can do it to the Melanesians, it sure as hell can be done to us. Perhaps that assumption is the only thing that can really "explain" both the Swanton Novers Rectory debacle and the Silver Spring film.

All human groups have their own myths. They use these to mentally navigate and form metaphors, without which no "thinking" would be possible in any meaningful sense. All myths, rational or utterly fantastic, are rain dances before sun and moon. UFO contactees live with aliens as many still live with Princess Diana, Elvis Presley and John Lennon, all of whom, like Christ, have been "seen" on Earth after their deaths, and all of whom now have a fledgling spiritual and social function. Skeptics and rationalists too live with their own myths of fact, objectivity, and experimental evaluation as equally mythological measures of experience. The difference between Adamski's claims and the almost-belief of men and women that they are almost-like James Bond or Marilyn Monroe, is that the crews of the flying saucers seen by Adamski have jumped out of the culture-dish. They have jumped out unrestrained by arts, religious, or media conventions, and have appeared on film emulsion, radar screens and in the skies of the world.

A function of the UFO phenomenon may be to teach us that given certain conditions, this baffling process works. Out of doubt, uncertainty, absent-mindedness, lack of concentration, Adamski and Madeleine teased out a unicorn-event: a quite clear sequence showing a UFO moving over nearby trees and *changing its shape* as it does so. It is a wonderful moment equivalent to when Geller bends a spoon, or Ted Serios got a picture of a London bus on closed virgin film while surrounded by a round dozen doubting scientists who have used every methodological trick (including fraud!) to prevent fraud.

The anomalous event is an alchemical thing, the deepest action of cultural defiance, whose politics are born out of every conscious and unconscious desire to tip the apple cart over, if only to smash its mechanical impostures, the claustrophobic oppression of its too-triumphant rationalism. Adamski's refusal to disbelieve, with all its confusions and double takes, has triumphed. In this, like Charles Fort, he is as much an American Hero as Thomas Edison or Alexander Graham Bell, who did it the easier way.

For a brief moment, Adamski silenced the voices declaiming Thou Shalt Not. Through that willing suspension of belief, that gap in cultural time and space, pour Charles Fort's "damned" events; what better picture of the political prisoners of the 20th century and what better epitaph for Adamski and his kind than this: "Battalions of the accursed, captained by pallid data that I have exhumed, will march. Some of them livid and some of them fiery and some of them rotten. Some of them are corpses, skeletons, mummies, twitching, tottering, animated by companions that have been damned alive. There are giants that walk by, though sound asleep. There are things that are theorems and things that are rags: they'll go by like Euclid arm in arm with the spirit of anarchy. Here and there will flit little harlots. Many are clowns. But many are of the highest respectability. Some are assassins. There are pale stenches and gaunt superstitions. and mere shadows and lively malices: whims and amiabilities. The naive and the pedantic amid the bizarre and the grotesque and the sincere and the insincere, the profound and the puerile."[196]

It has to be said that Adamski's deep confusions, sexual and otherwise, were always marvelously creative. He used them to entertain and frighten, to amuse and disturb, to mystify and annoy. Science raged at Adamski, yet Power listened, and the popular press were as baffled as ever by the unusual and bizarre nature of his beliefs and experiences. All expressed a common fear: that truth and reality may not be worthy or profound, or even purposeful, and that what is termed "reality" may turn out eventually to be scandalous beyond all conception.

Adamski moved through mid-20th century psychic dimensions as an action painter throwing onto canvas colors no one had ever seen before. Always living between page and fable, experience and text, technological vision and religious faith, it must be admitted that he had some genius. If he asked unwittingly for laughter, we must remember that he had also that level of Faustian nerve and cheek to outface the world's grin and take the consequences.

Those who criticize George Adamski might well compare their own achievement with his. Our world would have been a much more comfortable place had Adamski been proved to be an imposter. But perhaps, as Charles Fort suggested, there is no such thing as a complete imposter. To call a Fool an imposter is to misjudge the rich and complex relationship between Fools and Kings, with ordinary mortals living, or partially living, on the battleground between them.

Perhaps Nature does not experiment socially, choosing instead to concentrate upon certain individuals, such as Adamski. The rest, like the animals, go on happily flapping and hooting, snorting and grunting, to infinity. Perhaps that is why certain people lead shattered lives. To be "chosen" is to be the subject of some illimitable cosmic experiment. Just as we are about to award the Reeves, Frank Stranges, Howard Menger, and Adamski very low marks out of ten, we must remember that soon after their pan-dimensional texts were published, flower power hit California, Adamski's home territory. After that, the world was never the same again, and blond space folk were seen everywhere. Adamski's life-long obsession with Theosophy, which in some way links almost every single one of these early saucer visionaries, had reached social meltdown. If we do not think that is at all important, it should be borne in mind that partly because of this development, America later suffered a humiliating defeat in Vietnam.

Because of this, we may not only have to revise completely all our ideas about the nature of Mind, but also our concept of just exactly what we mean by the word *weapon*.

If people such as George Adamski have anything to teach us, it is not that the gods are good, bad, or indifferent, but that they can manifest at all, that they can run riot like a cellular virus, sow their images in minds that become Malls, and vice versa. They show us also that we ourselves have power to create that sacred and utterly scandalous tomfoolery which is always at the heart of time, change, and product.

Afterword

The spring of 1965 had been hectic for Adamski. Although his reputation in Europe was on the wane, in America at least, he was still very much in demand for public appearances and lectures right up to the time of his death. On the 17th of March, 1965, he lectured at the First Unitarian Church in America. On the 18th of March WROC-TV recorded an interview for the Tom Decker Sunday Night Show. While in Rochester, Adamski was the guest of no less than the vice president of the Eastman Kodak Company, who had taken a great interest in the Silver Spring film shot on the 26th of February.

After yet more lectures and talks in Syracuse, Buffalo, Worcester, Lowell, and Rhode Island, an exhausted Adamski returned to the Rodeffer house in Rochester. He told Madeleine that he was having difficulty breathing.

It is 7:30 in the morning on Thursday the 22nd of April 1965 in Silver Spring, Maryland. An ambulance carrying Madeleine Rodeffer and the dying George Adamski leaves the Rodeffer home on its way to the Washington Sanatorium, in nearby Takoma Park, Maryland. With Madeleine Rodeffer's husband Nelson following behind in his car, the ambulance approaches a corner near the Rodeffer home where a car is parked. The car flashes its headlights on and off several times. Madeleine has a strange feeling about this vehicle. "I don't know if it was a space person," she said later, according to Timothy Good, "but it was like a sign."

The result of an electrocardiogram test at the Washington Sanatorium was not good. At midday the next day, Adamski complained about pains in his chest. After further tests, the doctors urged him to stay in hospital but he refused. Back in the Rodeffer house again, his breathing became even more difficult. By 7 pm his condition had become so bad that drastic treatment was necessary, and Madeleine took him on what was to be his last journey.

Adamski died sometime between 9:30 and 10 pm on the 23rd of April 1965. Dr. Beldon Reap, the deputy medical examiner for Montgomery County, confirmed the death as a heart attack. In a private service conducted by Chaplain Captain David F. Tate, and attended by Alice Wells, Adamski's ashes were interred at Arlington National Cemetery, Virginia.

It wasn't exactly the end he wished for. He told Madeleine that he would never admit himself to a hospital if he could help it, because at the very end of his life he was mortally afraid of being at the mercy of conspirators. Alice Wells said he wanted his ashes cast to the wind, but that was illegal.

We can rest assured, however, that he would have been proud that his last resting place was the great military shrine of his nation.

But in death, as in life, nothing about Adamski was certain. As a final act of defiance against the rules, he had the cheek to come back from the dead. To come back from the dead is the final ultimate achievement of the true Hero. Adamski died on 23rd April 1965. The day after that, Arthur Bryant, a groundsman at an old people's home in Britain claimed that he had seen a saucer land. One of the three humanoid occupants had "told" him that his name was "Yamski," adding that "With George—anything could happen and usually does!" The occupant then "spoke" to Bryant of a "Des or Les."

Ernest Arthur Bryant

Eileen Buckle in her 1967 book *The Scoriton Mystery,*[197] includes a clear full-plate photograph of Arthur Bryant. It is strange indeed that she does not comment (and neither do other investigators), on the craggy features of Devonshire countryman, Arthur Bryant. It's enough to raise the hairs on the back of your neck.

It looks like none other than George Adamski.

Notes

1   By T. Werner Laurie Ltd.
2   See this author's novel, *The Entertainment Bomb* (1996, New Futurist Books, Turnaround Publisher Services, London).
3   The names of Adamski's sisters are heavily erased in the FBI document, though the reasons for this are not known.
4   Quoted from Jerome Clerk's "Startling New Evidence in the Pascagoula and Adamski Abductions," *UFO Report*, vol. 6, no 2, August, 1978, p. 72
5   *George Adamski: The Untold Story* (Ceti Publications England 1953)
6   *Inside the Spaceships* p. 183 (Neville Spearman, 1956)
7   Ibid., p. 149
8   Ordo Templi Orientis in association with Falcon Press, Las Vegas, 1989.
9   Paperback Library Incorporated, New York, 1967, p 93. This was originally issued by Abelard-Schuman Limited 1961, with the title *Flying Saucers Farewell*.
10 *Gray Barker's Book of Adamski*, (Saucerian Books 1967), p. 8.
11 Harper and Row, 1975
12 *Inside the Space Ships*, pp. 197–198
13 Things do not change much in this respect. As late as February 2000, in a BBC "Any Questions" program, Lord Norman Tebbit, once a leading Minister in Margaret Thatcher's Cabinet, referred sneeringly to someone as a "supermarket manager," much to the amusement and approval of the entire team. Since he had been one himself when young, this is somewhat ironic because both Thatcher and Tebbit come from small trading families.
14 *Flying Saucers Have Landed*, p. 180
15 *Behind the Flying Saucer Mystery*, p. 60
16 See this author's article "Fort's Fat Monks" in *Fortean Studies* No 5, January, 1999, published by John Brown.
17 Macmillan London Ltd., 1981
18 *Flying Saucers Have Landed*, p.174
19 Ibid., p.175
20 Their Web address is http://www.gafintl-adamski.com.
21 The books of George Hunt Williamson, who was a well-educated and highly intelligent man, still stand today. His *Road in the Sky* (Neville Spearman 1959), for example, is as fresh as ever, and his scholarship and wide knowledge is quite astounding. Unfortunately, rather like Adamski, he had momentary flirtations with fascist groups, such as the American Nazi-inspired Silver Shirt movement, also known as the Christian American Patriots. Both Williamson and Adamski were much influenced by the writings of the proto-Nazi "channeler" William Dudley Pelley (1890–1965). Pelley was a rabid anti-Semite, and with his slogan for "Christ and Constitution," he ran for President in 1936. After a sentence of 15 years for sedition in 1942 (of which he served only seven years), he formed

the occult group "Soulcraft" and published the racist magazine *Valor*. For this information I am indebted to *Strange Creations* by Donna Kossy (Feral House, 2001, pp. 14–15).

22 This second book was published in 1955 by both Arco and Neville Spearman, Adamski's publishers in America and Britain respectively.

23 Curiously, this does not blow the tale apart. Rather than a crude "insertion" by Adamski (that *would* perhaps blow the tale apart), it could be that the phenomenon is feeding back his very best expectations of what he thought "contact" would be like. When we talk blithely about "advanced intelligence" we must be prepared to accept what "advanced" may mean in the fullest sense of the word.

24 The American contactee Laura Mundo claims to have met Orthon quite independently. She is the author of *Flying Saucer and the Father's Plan* and *Pied Piper from Outer Space*.

25 *Flying Saucers Have Landed*, p. 195

26 Fred Steckling was later to claim that the USAF filmed the whole event. If it was filmed, then it would in all likelihood have been from this B36.

27 Edwards Air Force Base was named after Glen Edwards as a salute to him and the entire crew who were lost on June 1948 when flying the Northrop prototype YB-49 flying wing. The base was named previously Muroc AFB.

28 *The Teachings of Don Juan: A Yaqui Way of Knowledge* by Carlos Castanada, (University of California Press, 1968)

29 Three of the photographs taken by Adamski on this date are reproduced in *Flying Saucers Have Landed* as plates 5, 6 and Frontispiece.

30 *Flying Saucers Have Landed*, p. 218

31 *Gray Barker's Book of Adamski*, p 29

32 Donald Keyhoe, in his book *Flying Saucers from Outer Space* (Wingate/Baker 1969), says that Scully himself started the "little men from Venus" story in an article in *Variety* and later expanded it for his book.

33 Gollancz, 1950

34 Dated January 31, 1954.

35 *Saucer News,* no 27. October, 1957

36 *Ibid.,* p.15

37 *George Adamsk: The Untold Story,* pp. 146–147. The letter Good refers to was published originally in Fred Steckling's *Why Are They Here?* (1969)

38 Ibid., p. 147

39 *Gray Barker's Book of Adamski*, p 10

40 Vantage Press, 1969. Purchasers of this book are advised to check the page numbering. This author's copy is distinguished by missing pages, and the remaining blocks of the remaining pages are bound out of sequence.

41 *Gray Barker's Book of Adamski,* p.10

42 Ibid., p.11

43 *Report from Europe,* Scandinavian UFO Information, Jylland, Denmark, 1964

44 See *The World of Ted Serios* by Jules Eisenbud, Jonathan Cape, 1967

45 *Gray Barker's Book of Adamski*, p.47

46 Ken Kesey is the author of the novel *One Flew Over the Cuckoo's Nest*.

47 *George Adamski: The Untold Story*, p.27

[48] One of his novels was *The Amazing Mr. Lutterworth,* (Allan Wingate Ltd, London, 1958)

[49] Sphere, 1974, Chapter 2, p.28

[50] Charles Hoy Fort (1874–1932) was an American writer who wrote four land-mark books: *The Book of the Damned, New Lands, Wild Talents* and *Lo!* Though he didn't do too well in his own lifetime, over the past thirty years his work has been revalued, and is now a considerable influence on culture and ideas. He has been called the first post-modern thinker.

[51] *Flying Saucers Have Landed,* pp. 37–38

[52] Neville Spearman, 1970

[53] Viking Penguin, 1998

[54] Timothy Good, in *Alien Base,* reproduces released FBI documents that show the fear of defense specialists at the many saucer sightings over sensitive establishments.

[55] It is interesting to note that the Bibliography recommends the Atlantis bookshop of Museum Street, London, which is still thriving and well after nearly one hundred years!

[56] The writer Christopher Allan is of the opinion that Allingham's book was a spoof, and that Allingham was himself part of the stage machinery. Allan, who thoroughly investigated this business at the time, says that in his opinion Patrick Moore, the amateur TV astronomer, was responsible for the whole thing. Allingham (if indeed that was his real name) made a single public appearance at a meeting in Tunbridge Wells presided over by Lord Dowding. Allan is of the opinion that this event was rigged to try and humiliate Lord Dowding and ridicule his opinions about extraterrestrial contact. Though Allan presents a most impressive case for all this, it still has to be explained why Moore would go against both his personality, his social background, and his politics to try and do such a thing to a very great Englishman as Dowding, to whom the nation owed everything. If Moore did indeed attempt such a thing, then he pulled the joke at the last minute, because Dowding remained unscathed. Moore did this knowing perhaps that such an action would not only see him kicked out of every house in middle England, but (more important to him certainly), would damage his burgeoning TV career.

[57] T. Werner Laurie Limited, 1954

[58] A photograph of this motor appeared in the September/October 1962 edition of *Flying Saucer Review.*

[59] See Berthold Schwarz's *UFO Dynamics,* (Rainbow Editions, 1988) pp 526ff.

[60] See this author's article in *The Anomalist* 7, "Intermediate States: Charles Fort's Degrees of Reality."

[61] For the detailed story of Silas Newton, see Karl Pflock's article "What's Really Behind the Flying Saucers? A New Twist on Aztec" in *The Anomalist* 8, pp.137–161.

[62] For a discussion on the Aztec incident, and Scully's book, and also Timothy Good, *Beyond Top Secret* pp.487–499. There have been many claims (such as that by William Moore) that the Aztec crashed saucer and recovered body incident was a hoax, but this has been refuted by William Steinman and

Wendelle Stevens in their book *UFO Crash at Aztec.*

63 See the excellent *Techgnosis: Myth, Magic, & Mysticism in the Age of Information* by Erik Davis (Serpent's Tail, 1999).

64 See *The Gulf War did not take place* (sic) by Jean Baudrillard (Power Publications Sydney, 1995). Translated by Paul Patton.

65 For more information on this fascinating subject, see *Cows, Pigs, Wars & Witches* by Marvin Harris (London: Hutchinson &Co Ltd 1975), and *The Trumpet Shall Sound* by Peter Worsley (London: MacGibbon and Kee Ltd 1957).

66 Amok, Los Angeles, 1995

67 Quoted from a discussion in *Amok Journal* of Edward Rice's book, *John Frum He Come.*

68 See Morehouse, *The Fatal Impact.*

69 *George Adamski: The Untold Story,* p. 164

70 Professor Hermann Oberth was a pre-war scientist who had the very highest reputation for his theory and practice of rocketry. In the early twenties he published a work entitled *The Rocket Into Interplanetary Space.* He would have joined von Braun's team like a shot, but Oberth's problem was that though he was a German, he was born in Rumania, and therefore not a German citizen. Because of this, he was not allowed to work at Peenemunde or other top rocket research centers. This did not deter him, however, because wartime Intelligence discovered that he was working independently at Szczecin in Poland on a thirty-ton rocket with a range of over 300 kilometres (see Joseph Garlinski *Hitler's Last Weapons,* Methuen Paperback, 1978). Fortunately for the world, due to lack of resources and the generally deteriorating situation in Poland, Oberth's work came to nothing, practically speaking.

71 For a modern view of Werner von Braun, see *Liquid Conspiracy* by George Piccard (Adventures Unlimited 1999). See also Norman Mailer's masterpiece *A Fire on The Moon* (Weidenfeld &Nicolson 1970). Von Braun joined the SS in 1940, and in 1945 personally ordered the public hanging of 12 slave workers at Nordhausen, where both V1 and V2 production was based. To understand just exactly what the term "V1 and V2 production" means, advancing American forces found at least 10,000 corpses at Nordhausen in 1945. See also this author's article on Jack Parsons in "Rocket in his Pocket" in *Fortean Times* 132, and *Sex and Rockets* by John Carter (Feral House, 2000).

72 Timothy Good quotes Oberth as saying, "We cannot take the credit for our record advancement in certain scientific fields alone; we have been helped." When asked by whom, he replied, "The people of other worlds." (*Beyond Top Secret,* Sidgwick &Jackson, 1996, p.40)

73 *Behind the Flying Saucer Mystery,* pp. 62–63. Published in 1961 by Paperback Library (Abelard-Schuman Limited), the original title was *Flying Saucers Farewell.*

74 Charles Fort (1874–1932). *The Complete Books of Charles Fort,* Dover Books, New York, 1974.

75 Fort, *op. cit.,* pp.142–143

76 Werner Laurie refused to publish this book. Arcos and Neville Spearman published the British edition a year later.

77 This author has had one UFO experience, and he does not want another.

78 Reproduced in Timothy Good's *Alien Base*, p. 113. This report is dated the 28th of January 1953.

79 Karl Pflock is a writer and ufologist and serves as Mutual UFO Network state section director for New Mexico.

80 Adamski's wife Mary is a bit of a mystery. We don't know when she left Palomar, or how long she and Adamski lived together on the property. Adamski mentions her twice in quite affectionate terms in his last book, *Behind the Flying Saucer Mystery*, which meant that she was still in his mind up to 1961.

81 Office of Special Investigations

82 Issue 112, page 54

83 See the brilliant *You Can't Tell the People* by Georgina Bruni (Sidgwick & Jackson 2000). This writer is from the Birdsall UFO magazine stable, a source that has produced the very best British books on UFOs by Timothy Good, Nicholas Redfern, and Nick Pope.

84 This is the date given by Lieutenant Colonel Philip Corso in *The Day After Roswell* (Simon and Schuster 1997).

85 *Inside the Spaceships*, p. 31

86 On the surface, it looks as if this remark is a straight look-back to 1953 from 1955. But what he is describing took place before *Flying Saucers Have Landed* was published. This is a good indication of Adamski's slight temporal dyslexia.

87 *Inside the Spaceships*, p. 34

88 *Ibid.*, p. 95

89 *Ibid.*, p. 96

90 Amherst Press, Wisconsin, 1957

91 See article in *The X Factor,* no 73, p. 2032–34

92 *Flying Saucers Have Landed,* p. 239 (Futura New Revised Edition, 1977, this being a reprint of the Neville Spearman Revised Edition of 1970).

93 See *UFO Magazine,* November/December 1999, pp 20–23.

94 *Inside the Space Ships,* p. 219

95 *Ibid.,* p. 178

96 It is interesting here to consider Lieutenant Colonel Philip Corso's claim that aliens provided human beings with such things as transistors. If they did, then originally they provided germanium PNP transistors, which were replaced within ten years by the much faster and cheaper silicon NPN transistors. In other words, if Corso is correct, the giving of this technology was equivalent to giving "primitive" tribes steam engines or covered wagons. Furthermore, if the alien material was found as *working* parts, say, in the Roswell wreckage, then the aliens were *using* technologies not much further ahead of existing earth technologies. It might also be useful to know whether the alleged cold-junction circuitry as discovered or "given" was arranged in an analogue or digital array. These inconsistencies and gaps in the information given in *The Day After Roswell* make Corso look rather like a fool and are more likely to be tomfoolery and decoys than anything else. In other words, they were (and are) cheap beads from even cheaper boxes. Very few, if any, investigators are prepared to consider joke-systems as alien manifestations. Their attempt to uncover high seriousness and their assumption that high seriousness must be a necessary condition of

what we call higher intelligence could well be a barrier to understanding. Even within strictly human terms, the greatest psychologists agree that the idea of play is an essential component of extremely high intelligence. Being a military man, of course, this is the one solution that Corso (and others like him) would be psychologically conditioned to reject. The phenomenon with which Adamski and many others like him were involved is likely to be what might be termed a non-cerebral system, and not one with linear directions. After all, this is the way our own society is "progressing." The Media-Entertainment Complex is an example of a non-cerebral system. It is not concerned with the "flow of factual information" in the old industrial sense at all. It is concerned with virtualism and images, and is based on the new paradigms of advertising, mass-suggestion, and play. The joke, of course, has no time vector, and any mouth, alien or otherwise, must have something like a most non-technological bucket to spew in on occasions.

97 See the books of Gerald Heard, Eileen Buckle, Gavin Gibbons, and Cedric Allingham.

98 *Inside the Spaceships,* p. 98

99 It is important to realize here that for many non-Western cultures, "imagination" has no meaning near to that meant by imposture or lying. To imagine in this finer sense is to achieve the highest and most profound personal integration and communal belonging.

100 At this time, digital telemetry and stored memories did not exist outside the most advanced research laboratories.

101 See account in *The UFO Encyclopedia* by Margaret Sachs (Corgi, 1981, p.125).

102 *Simulations,* translated by Nicola Dufresne (New York: Semiotext 1983).

103 See this author's article in *Fortean Times* 148 on Candy Jones.

104 For an excellent discussion and analysis of Ruppelt's life and work, see *Captain Edward J. Ruppelt: Summer of the Saucers—1952* by Michael David Hall and Wendy Anne Connors (Rose Press International, Albuquerque, NM U.S.A.) email: ProjectSign@msn.com.

105 Karl Pflock is the author of *Roswell: Inconvenient Facts and the Will to Believe.* (Prometheus Books, 2001). He is also a contributing editor to the newsletter *Saucer Smear.*

106 Essay "What's Really Behind the Flying Saucers? A New Twist on Aztec" in *The Anomalist* 8, p.137.

107 (Holt and Co., New York, 1950) This book was one of the very first on flying saucers.

108 See this author's article "Fort's Fat Monks" in *Fortean Studies* 5 on the physicist Barkla.

109 An internationally infamous financial fraudster once said to this author that the really frightening thing about her work was not the prospect of spending long years in jail, or being murdered or injured. She said that it was seeing the criminal practice create a world of its own. This was not so much a "false" world as a partial one intermingled with the interstices of the "real" one. This partial world consisted of coincidences that she likened to the smiling monster's hand first reaching out to Dr. Frankenstein. To refuse the hand (as did Dr. Frankenstein) was to court disaster. She added that the coincidences were what she called an old "forest floor" language. If she ignored them, danger came near. If she

"listened," danger went away. Needless to say, she was never caught, though there is time yet.

110 Pope is the author of *Open Skies, Closed Minds* (Simon and Schuster, 1996)

111 See *UFO Magazine,* May/June 1999

112 British skeptics in particular are the very last true Victorians. Most have not reached the New Age period, never mind the Chaos Theory and Media ages. Young or old, almost all are straight out of the novels of Erskine Childers and John Buchan. Of an anorak disposition, most are preoccupied with timetables and dates, and the compiling of fully-referenced notes and queries. They appear to belong to an era of wigs, false moustaches, and the hampers and japes of Billy Bunter. Today, one imagines them as train-spotters and collectors of old watch parts. Others pursue contactees and UFO witnesses as foxhunting squires once pursued imposters, tricksters, bounders, and the seducers of daughters. The great Holmes himself would have lectured them all most severely on their intimations of certainty.

113 Vol. 5 No.2

114 This was a trading standards organization and part of the Los Angeles civic authority.

115 This description is based on an FBI report dated the 10th of December 1953, and released in 1982.

116 *George Adamsk: The Untold Story,* p. 164

117 It is comforting to know that this dog was humanely poisoned by the last mouthfuls of its food-supply.

118 *Legend* by Edward J. Epstein (Hutchinson, 1978, p. 106)

119 *Project Seek* (Onassis, Kennedy, and the Gemstone Thesis) by Gerald A. Carrol, Bridger House Publishers Incorporated, 1994.

120 *Goddess* by Anthony Summers (Gollancz, 1985, p.244)

121 See *Inside the Gemstone File* by Kenn Thomas & David Hatcher Childress (Adventures Unlimited, 1999) p.145, and *Mind Control, World Control* by Jim Keith (Adventures Unlimited, 1997)

122 *Liquid Conspiracy* by George Piccard (Adventures Unlimited, 1999) p. 55.

123 Eight years later, in 1966, Charles Wilhelm heard a story from a friend in the Army Reserve whose father worked with Project Blue Book at Wright-Patterson Field and held high security clearance. On his death bed, he related to his son that he had seen two disc-shaped craft, *one intact and one damaged,* and four preserved alien bodies "packed in chemicals." I am indebted to Leonard Stringfield's book *Situation Red* (Sphere Books Ltd., 1978) for this information.

124 *Behind the Flying Saucer Mystery,* p.109

125 *Ibid.,* p. 111

126 *Ibid.,* p. 111

127 *Ibid.,* p. 295

128 *Ibid.,* p. 115

129 *Ibid.,* p. 116

130 Later published by Fontana in 1973 as *Temple of the Stars.*

131 The full Hansard text of this debate was published by Open Head Press, 2, Blenheim Crescent London W11.

132 Simon and Schuster, 1997, p.293

133 Public Record Office file: AIR 2/16918

134 Routledge & Kegan Paul Ltd., London, 1959

135 *Rumor, Fear, and the Madness of Crowds* (Ballantine)

136 Ibid., pp. 133–134

138 Most historians agree that Lindemann was a bit of a disaster as a scientist. He was a gadget man, not a theoretician, and by 1940 he was hopelessly out of date. He kept his position because Churchill loved his pompous and bombastic style. Lindemann certainly placed obstacles in the paths of very brilliant men such as Professor Tizzard, Watson-Watt, and in particular R. V. Jones, Chief Scientific Officer, Air Ministry Directorate of Intelligence, 1939–1945. He wrote the major historical work, *Most Secret War.*

139 The British skeptical magazine, *Magonia* (Issue 75 July 2001) published a so-called "exposure" of the Darbishire pictures. The problem with this journal is that it sees all and everything as impostures. The issues are almost identical in this respect, and *Magonia* has been playing its very English one-note Samba for many years. Skepticism in Britain is, of course, a national malaise. It nearly killed the tank, the airplane, and the nation itself in the Somme and on the beaches of Dunkirk. Its corrosive effect on enterprise, cultural initiatives, and technological innovation has thus brought the nation near to disaster twice in the 20th century. While this fundamental problem with the lack of a concept of the mysterious cannot be described as a mental illness exactly, chronic skepticism certainly has pathological characteristics. Its fantasies of certainty, "solidity," and input=output indicate a deeply depressing and paranoid view of the mundane nature of things that restricts and curtails all and every inspiration. Skepticism is, of course, truly "psycho-social" in that historically it is the singular view of a very narrow trading group within Western society.

As far as *Magonia* magazine and its American equivalent *The Skeptical Enquirer* are concerned, it must be said, however, that the idea of a universe consisting of nothing but imposters is a very interesting idea, and skeptics despite themselves, create a world somewhere between Borges and Castanada, which is not all that far away from the world of the contactees. The inhabitants of such a world, being imposters, will, of course, all be hoaxing one another. This surely makes the first skeptical work of art, for which the phrase *skeptical mysticism* might be suitable. As par for the course, the Darbishire "exposure" article is so full of mistakes, misidentifications, plain disinformation, and typical juvenile silliness, it is a beautifully-faceted hoax in itself, though probably unconscious. The idea of an unconscious hoax is, of course, as good a piece of deviousness as anything in the works of George Adamski. James Easton's "Flight of Fancy" in *Fortean Times* 137 was a similar (though conscious) hoax intended to draw the fire of UFO "believers" and was organized by a group of skeptics apparently with the ominous and full co-operation of *Fortean Times.* Easton's idea was that Kenneth Arnold had seen a flight of Pelicans! Such anarcho-mystical skepticism is worthy of being put on alongside the half and partial forms exhibited in David Wilson's Museum of Jurassic Technology in Los Angeles, whose motto should be "some people will disbelieve anything". None of this, of course, is anything to do with truth or falsehood, but is a perfect example of the postmodern view of believers versus unbelievers as different actors in different theatres, as expressed by my own article "Recipe for a Universe" in *Fortean Times* 140, p.49.

[140] *Alien Base*, p. 210

[141] Commander of Allied First Airborne Corps in 1944

[142] Vol. 26, No. 5, 1980, pp. 2–4

[143] Collins, London, 1985

[144] W.H. Allen & Co., 1987

[145] Ibid., pp.113–114

[146] This almost certainly refers to an incident in 1946 at White Sands test grounds described by Gerald Heard in his 1950 book, *The Riddle of the Flying Saucers.*

[147] This might well be contrasted with the statement by President Gorbachev, when he met President Reagan at the Geneva summit in 1985: "The US President said that if the Earth faced an invasion by extraterrestrials, the United States and the Soviet Union would join forces to repel such an invasion."

[148] This was the kind of project that the young Stanton Friedman worked on.

[149] UPI, Washington, DC, 14th April, 1962

[150] Neville Spearman, 1959, translated from the original Spanish text.

[151] March/April 1959, p.8

[152] Timothy Good, *Beyond Top Secret* (Pan, 1997) p.360.

[153] *Behind the Flying Saucer Mystery*, p. 122

[154] This situation has changed hardly. In a recent article (January 27, 1999, p. 10) in the *Daily Express* Michael Hanlon comments: "Science does not sell in Britain. Our chattering classes, governed by the latest arts mafia, choose to chatter away not about the latest Pentium chips or the developments in gene therapies or space exploration but about the comings and goings of political press secretaries and artistic gentilities."

[155] *Behind the Flying Saucer Mystery,* p. 123

[156] Ibid., p. 124

[157] Sphere Books, London, 1978

[158] I am most grateful to Christopher Allan for letting me have numerous newspaper clippings from this period.

[159] Somerton Publishing Company (Isle of Wight), 1966

[160] A new book by Cramp, *Cosmic Matrix* has recently been published by Steamshovel Press.

[161] *Behind the Flying Saucer Mystery,* p. 125

[162] Twenty years later, Prince Bernhardt was involved in corruption charges with regard to Dutch contracts with Boeing.

[163] This is always one of the most annoying arguments of skeptics. It is always as if they expect any aliens to enter a studio and hence get good footage. If this ever happened, no doubt this would give them good grounds for rejection of validity on the grounds that such footage was "too clear." This is the same argument as rejecting the claims of a UFO witness because he or she had seen "too many" UFOs, or that wonderfully Orwellian Catch-22, that is a "tendency to believe."

[164] According to David Guyatt, writing in *Nexus* Vol. 7, No. 5, "Holy Smoke and Mirrors," Prince Bernhardt founded the mysterious Bilderberg organisation in 1954.

[165] *Behind the Flying Saucer Mystery*, p.130

[166] *Fortean Times* 119, p. 23

[167] *George Adamski: The Untold Story*, p. 40

[168] *Behind the Flying Saucer Mystery*, p. 136

[169] This phrase occurs often in describing the speech of aliens. Since the English language is a mass of deeply historical imperfections, it is difficult to know what is meant by "perfect" English. A native-born English speaker, educated or otherwise, will, when speaking, show inevitably a wide variety of such imperfections. When English is spoken, a line is necessarily revealed back to Chaucer's expression and indeed Early Middle English usage, and beyond that, to the Anglo-Saxon language and many other languages, including Norman French. This situation will be reflected in grammar and semantics, in pronunciation, regional accent, emphasis and sentence-structure. Thus both English speech and language are almost immediately locatable, culturally, socially, historically, and educationally. In this sense grammar and syntax are pure literary DNA. In this respect, one would love to hear a tape of an alien voice. Perhaps it would confirm (what a few believe) that some aliens live in Yorkshire! Given the ideas of Relativity, it would be fascinating also to know whether a being from another planet speaks of his homeland in the present or past tense, and how he or she uses, say, the subjunctive and passive voice, since these relate to the sociology and culture of planet Earth. Such a tape would be equivalent to providing the name and address of either the person or institution who or which provided originally the teaching and the basic information. Even digital translation, of course, announces itself immediately in such a manner, and avoids none of these identifications. Digital *enciphering* again inherits all of these characteristics, which can be readily detected using modern computer techniques.

[170] It will appreciated that it is extremely difficult if not impossible to produce strings of random configurations, particularly by hand-crafted means. Even our mightiest computers have difficulty producing patterns that do not repeat. Degrees of "randomness" are, of course, a measure of our lack of knowledge, and not a state of nature.

[171] See *The Man Who Broke Purple* by Ronald W. Clark (Weidenfeld and Nicholson, 1977). Sections of the Voynich manuscript are reproduced in *The Unexplained* 70, pp. 1381–1385. It is interesting to compare the Voynich sections with Plate 42.

[172] In 1949 William Friedman (1891–1969) became Special Assistant to the National Security Agency's Director, General Canine.

[173] *Behind The Flying Saucer Mystery*, p. 141

[174] For strange examples of the psychology of racism, see *Kooks* by Donna Kossy (Feral House, 2001). Her book is also a wonderful illustrated discussion and analysis of way-out theories, and includes much material seeing the light of day for the first time.

[175] *Behind The Flying Saucer Mystery*, p. 141

[176] In a conversation with this author, Timothy Good said that he was almost certain that Adamski had Romany blood.

[177] *George Adamski: The Untold Story*, p. 68

178 For a blow-by-blow detailed account of this conflict, see *George Adamski: The Untold Story.*

179 See *To Whom It May Concern,* an open letter by George Adamski to readers of his "Get Acquainted" Newsletter, circa 1963.

180 A quite similar set of confusions is depicted in the book *Briefing For A Landing on Planet Earth* by Stuart Holroyd (W.H. Allen London 1977). In this work, Uri Geller and Andrija Puharich are the direct equivalents of Adamski and Honey.

181 *George Adamski: The Untold Story,* p. 6

182 Fort, *op.cit.,* p. 736

183 Fort, *op.cit.,* p. 578

184 Fort, *op.cit.,* p. 580

185 See article "Keen on Crop Circles" in *The Anomalist* 4, (Autumn 1996), by Montague Keen, and my own article "Recipe for a Universe" in *Fortean Times* 140, p.49.

186 *The Day After Roswell* by Colonel Philip J. Corso (Simon and Schuster 1997)

187 G. N. M. Tyrell, in *The Personality of Man* (Pelican, 1946 p. 260). also speaks of two similar incidents.

188 See this author's article "Intermediate States" in *The Anomalist* 7.

189 See article "On the Role of Stage Magicians in Biological Research" by Jacques Benveniste and Peter Jurgens in *The Anomalist* 6 (Spring 1998).

190 If Adamski's flying saucer pictures were made by the fraudulent use of models, then whoever made such things faced quite a task. It must be emphasized that Adamski was anything but a loner. He was socially gregarious, always with groups of friends, living for most of his life in fairly primitive semi-religious communities in remote areas where the facilities and time for organizing complex electromechanical photographic frauds were practically non-existent. Adamski had neither the money, the training, nor indeed the brains (bless him), to organize techniques unavailable in either Hollywood studios or government or corporate research laboratories of the time. Though in 1965, very crude transistorized logic (executed mainly by the now obsolete PNP transistor), was available for the guidance of model airplanes and boats, component boards of average size at that time contained, at the most, a few score transistors. The "integrated circuit" (which later became the "chip") had not arrived, and flexibility of control (particularly of airborne structures) was extremely limited. Another important factor was the low amount of memory available. In 1965, a designer was lucky if he got more than a few hundred bytes to play with, particularly on the home-construction front, or the domestic area, where very primitive logic was first beginning to appear in American washing machines and the electrical systems of cars and trucks. Designing within such parameters meant that only very crude commands could be executed, and not with any great reliability. Even when transistorized, the logic commands were still physically executed by the same heavy solenoids and relays used by the previous vacuum-tube equipment, and hardly changed through four decades of history.

The synchronized automatic management involving the complex motion and shape-changing seen in the Silver Spring film, would in 1965, have been extremely difficult to execute. It must be remembered that most by far of the state-of-the art military guided missiles of this time still had vacuum-tube technology. Also, most were somewhat unreliable, and despite many millions of dollars being spent, a good number were complete failures, including those in the unit Lieutenant-Colonel Corso commanded in Europe. In the 1950s, there were available no user-friendly "programs" in the modern sense, and hence the integrated shape-change and movement-management shown by Adamski's UFO is extraordinary. Of films Adamski took before 1965, say in the early mid-to-late 1950s, then transistors would hardly been available to anyone outside a R&D laboratory. We can exclude common vacuum-tube technology because of size, weight, high bias voltages, and heavy current demand of heater filaments.

No control surfaces can be seen, and the object does not appear to have any visible form of propulsion other than being projected into the air by mechanical means, or compressed air. Available at this time were small "jet-engines" for model aircraft that worked on combustible solid-fuel pellets, but they were little more than fireworks. Such a model would need constant repair, maintenance, and replacement of parts before the right shots were achieved. It must be realized also that the object has no aerials visible, and VHF radio-control techniques of those days certainly required them, since modern flat dielectrics did not exist. Simple physical suspension can be ruled out, because contemporary enhancement techniques can resolve almost down to molecular dimensions, and any strings would likely show up as volcanic disturbances within the film emulsion. Such evidence would lay the Adamski ghost to rest, but modern opinion is coming to the conclusion that the films captured what Adamski saw at the time, whatever that was.

Changing the envelope of the structure while in flight, of course, was quite an achievement. Such a change *should* have introduced dangerous axial instability with the airborne structure, together with spin and various oscillations. But it obviously did not. Here is yet another magnificent "fraud" by Adamski—he solved the problems of variable-geometry airframes, problems that took the world's aircraft designers another ten years to solve after 1965. We can be sure that Ed Heinemann of Douglas Aircraft (the greatest airplane designer of his time—he designed the *Dauntless* dive bomber which Admiral Halsey said "saved us at Midway") would have loved to have seen the film.

[191] pp. 444–445
[192] *George Adamski: The Untold Story*, p. 166
[193] W.H.Allen, 1977
[194] *George Adamski: The Untold Story*, p. 167
[195] *Ibid.*, p. 169
[196] Charles Fort, *op.cit.*, p. 3
[197] Neville Spearman, 1967

Acknowledgments

I would like to thank the following people, who have given me much advice, help, and material for this book: John Michell, Timothy Good, Karl Pflock, Christopher Allen, John Chambers, Jim Moseley, and my patient and long-suffering editor, Patrick Huyghe, without whose encouragement and initiative the book would probably not have seen the light of day.

Printed in the United Kingdom
by Lightning Source UK Ltd.
1163